AMERICA

History Examined

Alan Axelrod, PhD

ALPHA

A member of Penguin Random House LLC

Publisher: Mike Sanders
Senior Acquisitions Editor: Janette Lynn
Cover Designer: Rebecca Batchelor
Book Designer/Layout: Ayanna Lacey
Copy Editor/Proofreader: Laura Caddell
Indexer: Brad Herriman

Published by Penguin Random House LLC
001-312950-JANUARY2019
Copyright © 2018 by Alan Axelrod, PhD

International Standard Book Number: 978-1-46548-072-9
Library of Congress Catalog Card Number: Available upon request

20 19 18   10 9 8 7 6 5 4 3 2 1

Interpretation of the printing code: The rightmost number of the first series of numbers is the year of the book's printing; the rightmost number of the second series of numbers is the number of the book's printing. For example, a printing code of 18-1 shows that the first printing occurred in 2018.

Printed in the United States of America

Note: This publication contains the opinions and ideas of its author. It is intended to provide helpful and informative material on the subject matter covered. It is sold with the understanding that the author and publisher are not engaged in rendering professional services in the book. If the reader requires personal assistance or advice, a competent professional should be consulted. The author and publisher specifically disclaim any responsibility for any liability, loss, or risk, personal or otherwise, which is incurred as a consequence, directly or indirectly, of the use and application of any of the contents of this book.

Most Alpha books are available at special quantity discounts for bulk purchases for sales promotions, premiums, fund-raising, or educational use. Special books, or book excerpts, can also be created to fit specific needs. For details, write: Special Markets, Alpha Books, 345 Hudson Street, New York, NY 10014.

Reprinted from *The Complete Idiot's Guide to American History, Fifth Edition*

AMERICA

History Examined

As ever, for Anita.

Contents

CONTENTS XV

Introduction

Most of the world's nations are *places*—places with a past, certainly, and with traditions and a heritage, but places nevertheless. The United States is different. It's a place, but it's also an *idea*. Sure, democracy was not exactly a new idea in 1776—the word *democracy*, meaning "government by the people," was coined in ancient Greece—but no one had really tried it before. Few people thought it would work.

The story of gambling on an untried notion is bound to be fascinating. When you have a stake in that gamble, the story can be downright riveting. My purpose is to give you a rapid but comprehensive overview of American history. Obviously, a book of this length is also grossly incomplete. Search online for books on American history, and you will be swept away in a tsunami of titles. The great thing is that so many of them are worth reading. Like a roadmap, this book doesn't show you everything and everyone. But it's a great way to start your journey through the American story.

Part 1, The New World, takes us back maybe forty some thousand years (nobody is sure how far back to go) to the epoch of the first immigrants, the people who crossed the long-vanished Bering "land bridge" from Asia to North America. The discussion then shifts to the collision of Old World and New as Europe invaded the Native American realm beginning in the fifteenth century, transforming the continent into a battlefield on which a nation was forged.

Part 2, The World Turned Upside Down, covers the American Revolution, from origins to outcome, including issues of economic, political, and spiritual independence.

Part 3, Building the House, discusses the creation of the Constitution, the War of 1812, the rise of Andrew Jackson, and the era of the common man, as well as the forced removal of the Indians from the East to the West.

Part 4, The House Divided, analyzes the causes of the Civil War, the early steps toward western expansion—including the U.S.-Mexican War, by which much of the present U.S. Southwest was acquired—the Civil War itself, and the Reconstruction era following it.

Part 5, Rebuilding the House, covers the major period of western expansion, including the homestead movement, the building of the transcontinental railroad, the Indian Wars, the growth of the western cattle empire, and the economic and technological boom of the later nineteenth century. This part also discusses the immigrant experience, the labor movement, and the rise of urban political machines.

Part 6, World Power, charts the nation's evolution as a world power (beginning with the Spanish-American War and World War I), the isolationist reaction against that evolution, the culture of the Roaring Twenties (including the heyday of Prohibition Era gangsters), the stock market crash, and the Great Depression. This part also outlines the origins of World War II and the nation's fight to victory in that war, from which it emerged as a nuclear superpower.

Part 7, Superpower, covers the Cold War years, the Korean War, the Civil Rights movement, and the social revolution wrought during the administrations of John F. Kennedy and Lyndon Johnson. This part concludes with the Vietnam War.

Part 8, Identity Crisis, surveys the turbulent home front during the Vietnam era, including such highs as the *Apollo 11* moon landing and such lows as the Watergate scandal. The women's liberation movement is also discussed, as are the energy crisis and the economic crises of American cities and industry, which created fertile ground for the growth of Reaganomics.

Part 9, America, Disrupted, begins with the Reagan years and covers the end of the Cold War, including the experience of the first Gulf War. The final three chapters in this part look at recent events, including: the terrorist attacks on the United States; the wars in Iraq and Afghanistan; the financial and ethical collapse of some major corporations; challenges to the economy and the environment; the division of the nation into "red states" and "blue states"; the troubled presidency of George W. Bush; the election of 2008, which brought the United States its first African-American president; and the open question that is the election and presidency of Donald J. Trump.

Extras

In addition to the main narrative of *America: History Examined,* you'll find other types of useful information, including capsule histories of major events, brief biographies of key people in American history, digests of important statistics, and quick definitions of historical buzzwords. Look for these features:

AMERICAN ECHO

These are memorable statements from historically significant figures and documents.

AMERICAN LIFE

This feature provides biographical sketches of an era's most significant and representative figures.

WHAT'S THE WORD?

This feature defines the buzzwords that defined a time and place.

VITAL STATISTICS

Here you'll find key numbers relating to an era or event, including such items as population statistics, war casualties, costs, and so on.

REMEMBER THIS

Here you'll read about the most significant or representative single event of an era, ranging from historical milestones to pop culture landmarks.

Trademarks

All terms mentioned in this book that are known to be or are suspected of being trademarks or service marks have been appropriately capitalized. Alpha Books and Penguin Random House LLC cannot attest to the accuracy of this information. Use of a term in this book should not be regarded as affecting the validity of any trademark or service mark.

PART 1

The New World

The "New World" was new only to Old World eyes. North America has been populated for perhaps more than 40,000 years, and the people Christopher Columbus misnamed "Indians" might well be members of the oldest identifiable human race on the planet. Except for a brief visit from Vikings about 1000 c.e., the New World and the Old remained unknown to one another until October 12, 1492, when Columbus, the prodigal son of a Genoese weaver, claimed a Caribbean island for Spain. For the next 150 years, Europeans carved up the land of the Indians. For the next 400, the colonists, settlers, and citizens of Euro-America fought the Indians, fought one another, and eventually managed to forge a new nation. This part of the book tells the story of that long, exciting, and sometimes tragic process.

The First People (40000-19000 B.C.E. to 1500s C.E.)

Look at a map that shows the northern Pacific Ocean. You'll find the Bering Sea, an arm of the Pacific bounded on the east by Alaska, on the south by the Aleutian Islands, and on the west by Siberia and the Kamchatka Peninsula. Near the north end of the Bering Sea is the Bering Strait, which, lying between Alaska and Siberia, connects the Bering Sea with the Arctic Ocean's Chukchi Sea. At its narrowest, the strait is only 55 miles across, the shortest distance between the North American and Asian continents.

Neolithic Journey

About 25,000 years ago, Beringia, a geographic feature popularly known as a "land bridge," emerged in the Bering and Chukchi Seas as the sea level dropped due to the expansion of the ice cap surrounding the North Pole. What's a bridge for? Moving.

Where'd Everybody Come From?

Indians—Native Americans—share many racial characteristics with the peoples of Asia. This suggests that they share a common geographical origin with the Asians. In the twenty-first century, two theories have emerged. The "short chronology" says that some Asian peoples began a gradual migration to the Americas via Beringia about 19,000 years ago. The "long chronology" puts this migratory period somewhere between 21,000 and 40,000 years ago. It is believed that rising ocean levels covered the land bridge some 11,000 years ago, thereby cutting off this migratory route between Asia and the Americas. By 1491, the year before the arrival of Columbus, perhaps 50 million people lived in the Americas.

What Happened to Everybody?

Today, about 2.5 million Indians live in the United States. What happened to everybody?

History suggests that Indians died in horrific numbers from diseases brought by the Europeans. Native Americans had never been exposed to these and thus no natural immunity to ailments common among whites.

Western Civilizations

The trek across Beringia must have consumed thousands of years. By 9000 B.C.E., it's likely that the former Asians reached Patagonia, at South America's southern tip, and populated much of the territory between this region and the Arctic Circle.

The Anasazi

In what is now the U.S. Southwest, archaeologists have identified a people they call either the Ancestral Puebloans or, more colloquially, the Anasazi (from a Navajo word meaning "the ancient ones"). There's much debate on when a definable Anasazi culture emerged, but the theory currently prevailing puts the emergence in twelfth century B.C.E. During the period of 700 to 1100 C.E., the Anasazi began building what Spanish invaders would later call *pueblos* (Spanish for "town," "village," or "people"). These were fantastic groupings of stone and adobe "apartment buildings," cliff dwellings seemingly hewn out of lofty ledges, the most spectacular of which survive at Mesa Verde National Park in southwest Colorado.

The Mound Builders

In the meantime, to the East, in a vast area stretching from the Appalachian Mountains to the eastern edge of the prairies, and from the Great Lakes to the Gulf of Mexico, other Native Americans were building cultural monuments of a different kind. Beginning about 3500 B.C.E. to after 1500 C.E., many different Indian societies constructed earthworks that modern archaeologists call burial mounds.

The Cahokia Tragedy

Cahokia, near present-day Collinsville, Illinois, is a 2,200-acre site that includes many mounds, evidence of the "Mississippian culture," an Indian civilization that developed advanced societies centuries around 600 C.E.

Based on pottery and stone tool remains, it is believed that Cahokia traded with communities as far away as the Great Lakes and the Gulf Coast.

No one knows why Cahokia, a city of 40,000, was abandoned by the end of the fourteenth century. Some believe that the European conquest precipitated a rapid political collapse.

Long Before Columbus

Historians commonly use the term "pre-Columbian" to refer to Indian life and culture as it existed before the arrival of Christopher Columbus in the so-called "New World" in 1492 C.E. In truth, the first European contact was made by Vikings some 500 years before Columbus sailed. The very first Old-World dweller to set eyes on the continent of North America was likely a Norseman named Bjarni Herjulfsson in 986 C.E., but it was not until the next decade, about 1000 C.E., that the Norse captain Leif Eriksson led an expedition that touched a place called Helluland (probably Baffin Island) and Markland (most likely Labrador). Most historians believe that Leif and his men spent a winter in crude Viking huts hastily erected on a spot called Vinland on account of its abundance of berries and grapes. After Leif the Lucky left Vinland, his brother Thorvald Eriksson paid a visit to the tenuous settlement in about 1004 C.E. In 1010 C.E., another Icelandic explorer named Thorfinn Karlsefni attempted to establish a more permanent settlement at Vinland.

After three lethal winters, Karlsefni and the others abandoned Vinland. There is good evidence that Christopher Columbus heard of the Vinland tradition when he was a young man. Many believe it inspired his dream of sailing there himself.

The Least You Need to Know

- ✪ Native Americans—"Indians"—probably immigrated to the Americas from Asia across an Ice Age "land bridge" where the Bering Strait is today.

- ✪ The Indian population's rapid decline was largely the result of epidemic and pandemic diseases.

- ✪ The European discoverer of America was (most likely) Leif Eriksson in about 1000 C.E.

West to East (1451–1507)

Everyone's heard the Columbus story so many times and in so many bits and pieces that most of us just stop listening, and we fail to imagine the creativity, the capacity for wonder, the courage, and the sheer madness that sent a Genoese seafarer and crew in three small ships across an unknown expanse of ocean to (it turns out) they knew not where.

The Weaver's Son

Cristoforo Colombo—to use the native Italian form of his name—was born in Genoa in 1451 to a weaver and did not learn to read and write until he reached adulthood. As a youth, he took not to books, but to the sea and claimed to have sailed as far as Iceland. Likely, he heard there the old Viking tales of Vinland.

Columbus returned to Genoa in 1479 and went to Portugal, where he married and learned to read, devouring shadowy accounts of westward voyages. He swallowed whole Marco Polo's calculations concerning Japan's location—1,500 miles east of China and was also misguided by the work of the Greek astronomer Ptolemy (ca. 100–70 C.E.), who seriously underestimated Earth's circumference. Confirmed in these errors by reading the miscalculations of the Florentine cosmographer Paolo dal Pozzo Toscanelli, Columbus decided that Japan—he knew it as Cipangu—was a mere 5,000-mile voyage *west* of Portugal, over an ocean covering a round Earth.

VITAL STATISTICS

Earth's actual circumference at the equator is 24,902 miles. The distance from the Spanish coast to the Bahamas, via the route Columbus took, is about 3,900 miles.

In 1484, Columbus tried to persuade King John II of Portugal to fund a 5,000-mile voyage to Japan. When King John II turned him down, Columbus approached Don Enrique de Guzmán, Duke of Medina Sidonia, only to be rebuffed. He appealed next to Don Luis de la Cerda, Count of Medina Celi, who was sufficiently intrigued to arrange an audience, on or about May 1, 1486, with Queen Isabella I of Castile.

It was not until early in 1492 that a courtier named Luis de Santangel succeeded in persuading Isabella and her husband, Ferdinand II, to fund Columbus's voyage. He set sail from Palos on August 3, 1492, commanding three small ships, the *Niña* (skippered by Vincente Yáñez Pinzón), the *Pinta* (under Vincente's brother, Martin Alonso Pinzón), and his own flagship, the *Santa Maria*.

Trouble on the Horizon

During its first month and a half the vessels were propelled by highly favorable winds, but, between September 20 and 30, the winds yielded to doldrums. The cowering crews began to grumble their doubts concerning the Admiral. Columbus responded by keeping two logbooks—one, for the benefit of the crew, containing fictitious computations of distances, and another, for his own records, consisting of accurate figures. The deception worked for a time, but, by the second week in October, the crews of all three ships verged on mutiny.

Columbus Day, 1492

With his sailors ready to revolt, land—as if cued by a hack playwright—suddenly materialized at the horizon on October 12, 1492. What the *Santa Maria*'s lookout sighted was a place the natives called Guanahani and Columbus christened San Salvador. Most modern historians believe the ships put in at present-day Watling Island, although some have suggested it was Samana Cay, 65 miles south of Watling.

Friendly Arawaks greeted the seafarers. Believing that he had reached Asia—generically referred to as the "Indies"—Columbus called these people Indians. He sailed on to Cuba, searching for the great Khan, Mongol emperor of China. Failing him, Columbus set off for an island he called Hispaniola (today divided between Haiti and the Dominican Republic), where the *Santa Maria* was wrecked during a Christmas Day storm. The Admiral ushered his crew safely onto shore and, seeing that the Indians were docile, left a garrison of 39 at the place he named La Navidad. On January 16, 1493, Columbus returned to Spain on the *Niña*.

At the Canary Islands, Columbus paused on February 15, 1493, to replenish supplies and to dash off a letter to Luis de Santangel. Columbus's proud patron had the letter printed, publishing to the Old World the discovery of the New. Columbus wrote of "many spices and vast mines of gold" and pronounced the "Indians … extraordinarily timid."

Paradise Killed

No sooner had Columbus departed La Navidad than the 39-man garrison he left behind set about despoiling Native goods and Native women. The "timid" Indians retaliated. When Columbus returned in November 1493, not a single Spaniard was left alive.

Three More Voyages

Ferdinand and Isabella sent Columbus on a second voyage (from Cadiz, on September 25, 1493). After discovering the grim fate of the La Navidad garrison, Columbus planted a new colony, Isabella, about 70 miles east of that bloody site. He explored the Caribbean for some five months and then tried to govern the fledgling colony he had planted, only to prove that a great sailor can be a disastrously inept administrator.

Columbus returned to Spain in 1496, leaving his brother Bartolomé in charge with instructions to move the settlement to the south coast of Hispaniola. Renamed Santo Domingo, this became the first permanent European settlement in the New World.

In June 1496, Columbus landed at Cadiz. Although he continued to claim that he had found a shortcut to Asia, he had not located the mainland, where, presumably, the gold and spices were kept. Discouraged colonists trickled back to Spain with complaints about the Admiral's cruel incompetence. Nevertheless, Isabella and Ferdinand funded a third voyage. Six ships departed Spain in May 1498, reaching Trinidad on July 31, 1498. On August 1, they landed on the mainland, and Columbus thereby became the discoverer of South America.

Sailing across the Caribbean to Hispaniola, Columbus found the colonists in a full revolt. The disgruntled Spanish sovereigns dispatched a royal commissioner, Francisco de Bobadilla, who arrived from Spain in 1500 and stripped the Columbus brothers of governing authority, sending them back to Spain—in chains.

AMERICAN ECHO

"Now that these regions are truly and amply explored and another fourth part has been discovered by Amerigo Vespucci I do not see why anyone can prohibit its being given the name of its discoverer, Amerigo, wise man of genius."

—Martin Waldseemüller, *Cosmographiae Introductio,* 1507

The captain of the returning vessel thought Columbus had gotten a raw deal and removed the shackles, but Columbus insisted that he appear before Isabella and Ferdinand in his chains. Stricken by this spectacle, the royal pair ordered him freed and, in May 1502, sent him on a fourth and final voyage.

Landing briefly at Martinique, Columbus sailed on to Hispaniola, only to be refused permission to land. He explored the Central American coast before returning to Spain in November 1504, where he died two years later, still claiming he had reached Asia.

Why We're Not Called Columbia

In the end, Columbus was cheated even of the honor of having his major discovery named for him. The Florentine explorer Amerigo Vespucci (1454–1512) claimed to have made four Atlantic voyages between 1497 and 1504. Following his 1501 voyage, Vespucci coined the phrase *Mundus Novus*—New World—to describe the region. The name stuck, and in 1507, the German cartographer Martin Waldseemüller published an account of Vespucci's voyages, along with a map titled *Cosmographiae Introductio* (*Introduction to Cosmography*). Waldseemüller used a Latinized form of Vespucci's first name—America—to label the New World.

The Least You Need to Know

- Columbus thought he was sailing to spice-rich Asia; he had no intention of finding a "New World."

- Despite the Indians' friendly overtures, the Spanish attacked them and then suffered terrible retaliation. This inaugurated 400 years of white-Indian warfare in the Americas.

- Columbus derived little benefit from his four voyages; even the land mass he discovered—America—was named for a later explorer, *Amerigo* Vespucci.

New Blood for Old Spain (1400–1600s)

In Columbus's wake, the Portuguese scrambled to launch a series of expeditions, as did Spain. These were undertaken not in the spirit of selfless exploration, but to conquer and colonize, while, in the bargain, also converting "heathens" to Christianity. Accordingly, two classes of professionals were represented among the early Spanish explorers: *conquistadors* ("conquerors") and priests, bearing swords and Bibles.

The Conquistador's Sword

The conquistadors followed in Columbus's footsteps. From 1508 to 1509, Juan Ponce de León (ca. 1460–1521) subjugated Puerto Rico. According to partially credible legend, León had come to the New World in search of the fabled Fountain of Youth. Next, Jamaica and Cuba fell easily to the Spaniards in 1510 and 1511.

Far more spectacular was the brief, bloody war by which Hernán Cortés conquered the Aztec empire of Mexico by August 13, 1521.

Borderlands

Cortés achieved what every conquistador sought: wealth beyond imagining. His success was the golden carrot that lured a legion of conquistadors after him. After Cortés, numerous conquistadors traipsed across America, looking for the Seven Cities of Cibola (the Seven Cities of Gold).

Estevanico, a Berber slave who had survived a typically calamitous 1520 expedition of Panfilo Narváez, joined an expedition led by Marcos de Niza in 1539, in search of Cibola. Zuni Indians killed Estevanico in a battle outside the Hawikuh pueblo in New Mexico, but de Niza returned to the Spanish colonial capital of Mexico City. There he delivered a dazzling account of the pueblo and its treasures. True, he himself had failed to gain entry into Hawikuh, but he had heard all about the gold from others.

Hearsay was quite enough for Francisco Vázquez de Coronado. From 1540 to 1542, he traveled throughout the Southwest, as far as present-day Kansas. Early in the expedition, in July 1540, he and his troops rode into Hawikuh, imperiously demanding the surrender of the pueblo. In response, the Zuni showered stones upon the conquistadors, knocking Coronado unconscious. Within an hour, however, Hawikuh fell and Coronado and his men entered it—finding nothing of value to them.

Dreams die hard. Coronado pressed on in fruitless search of Cibola. Traveling through the Pueblo region along the Rio Grande, he captured one Zuni or Hopi town after another, forcing the inhabitants into slavery and taking from them whatever food and shelter he required. In the wake of his invasion, during the summer of 1541, the Pueblos rebelled but were crushed by the forces of Niño de Guzmán, governor of New Spain.

Oñate the Terrible

With Coronado's repeated disappointments, the legend of the Seven Cities of Cibola finally dimmed, as did Spain's interest in the American Southwest. But in 1579, the English sea dog Sir Francis Drake landed on the central California coast and claimed a swath of territory he christened "New Albion," using an archaic name for England. Alarmed, the Spanish viceroy in Mexico City alerted Madrid that Spain's New World monopoly was imperiled. Busy with European wars, the Spanish crown did nothing to defend the northern frontier of its colonies for another 20 years. At last, in 1598, the ambitious Don Juan de Oñate led an expedition northward from Mexico. At the site of present-day El Paso, Texas, Oñate claimed for Spain all of "New Mexico," by which he meant a region extending from Texas to California.

With 400 men, women, and children—plus 7,000 head of cattle—Oñate colonized deep into Pueblo country, depositing clutches of settlers at various sites. In no place in western Mexico did he meet resistance, except at the Acoma pueblo. There, Indians killed 13 members of his advance guard. Perched atop a high-walled mesa, the Pueblo's defenders believed their position impregnable. But in January 1599, the main body of Oñate's troops fought their way to the top of the mesa, killed most of the Pueblo warriors, taking captive 500 women, children, and noncombatant men.

The "Black Legend"

The conquistadors came to the Americas steeped in a bloody eight-century tradition of racial warfare against the Moors (North African Muslims who contended for control of Spain). Moreover, Spanish colonizers staked their fortunes on profiting from conquest. When Oñate and others failed to find gold, they worked the Natives ruthlessly, aiming to wring profit from agricultural enterprise. In the end, the subjugated people failed to produce sufficient food even to sustain the colonists, let alone sell.

The Black Legend was further fostered by the *encomienda system,* which dominated Spanish colonial government from the sixteenth to the eighteenth century. By 1503, the crown began granting loyal colonists deeds called *encomendaros,* granting them land *plus* the labor of Indians living on it, at least for a specified number of days per year. They weren't called slaves, but they were typically worked to death.

WHAT'S THE WORD?

The **encomienda system** was the Spanish method of colonization, whereby certain settlers were granted a type of deed (called an **encomendar**) to specific tracts of land, which also entitled them to the labor of the Indians living on the land.

Some of the cruelty of the encomienda system was balanced by the ministry of the Spanish missionaries. While the Indians were given no choice in deciding whether they wanted to be "saved" by conversion to Christianity, the best of the missionaries did have an abiding concern for their spiritual and physical welfare. Tragically, such concern also served to perpetuate the horrors that Oñate and others visited upon the Indians. For, it is not likely that Spain would have continued to support its colonial outposts north of the Rio Grande on the basis of return on investment. Gold was not forthcoming, and agricultural enterprises produced more loses than profits. Yet the friars were creating a population of new Christians. This was to the glory of the Spanish sovereigns, who could not countenance the abandonment of their now-sanctified souls.

Native American Revolutions

By the middle of the seventeenth century, after 50 years of tyranny, some of the Pueblo Indian groups forged a desperate alliance with their hereditary foes, the Apaches, whose very name comes from a Zuni word meaning "enemy." The Apaches terrorized the Spanish Southwest during the 1670s and, with the Pueblos, waged a long guerrilla war against their common foe. This led to the rise of an Indian leader from the Tewa pueblo named Popé, who coordinated a mass uprising among the Pueblos, which was launched on August 10.

"Popé's Rebellion" was devastating. Missions at Taos, Pecos, and Acoma were burned, and the priests murdered, their bodies heaped on the altars of their despised religion.

On August 15, Popé led a 500-man army into Santa Fe, having already killed 400 settlers and 21 of 33 missionaries. The Santa Fe garrison consisted of just 50 men, who, however, had a brass cannon. They used it to resist the invasion for four days before evacuating, along with Governor Oterrmín, on August 21. Some 2,500 survivors of the onslaught fled as far as present-day El Paso, Texas, abandoning all their possessions to Indian looters.

Sadly, for the Natives, Popé capped his triumph by installing himself as an absolute dictator who ruled as oppressively as any Spaniard. By the time of Popé's death (from natural causes) in 1688, the Pueblo region was in a chronic state of civil war. Their former unity shattered, the Pueblos fell easy prey to Spanish reconquest a year after Popé's death.

The Spanish frontier did not long remain at peace after the reconquest of the Pueblos. In 1695, the Pimas of lower Pimeria Alta—the region of present-day Sonora, Mexico, and southern Arizona—rose up, only to be quickly suppressed. More than 50 years passed before the Pimas of upper Pimeria Alta, many descended from earlier rebels who had fled north, staged another revolt, which became a century and a half of guerrilla fighting, first against the Spanish, then the Mexicans, and finally the Americans.

The Black Robes

Enslavement and warfare were not the sole legacies of the Spanish in the American Southwest. The priests—whom the Indians called "black robes"—not only brought their religion to the Americas but created a Euro-Indian culture centered on the many missions they established. By 1680, missions had been built among most of the Indians in New Mexico as well. As Englishman Sir Francis Drake's presence in California had stirred Spanish concerns in 1579, a French landing on the Texas coast in 1684 led by Robert Cavelier, Sieur de La Salle, prompted the Spanish to build missions in that area.

Between 1687 and 1711, Father Eusebio Kino established many missions in northern Mexico and Baja, California, as well as some in southern Arizona, the most famous of which was Mission San Xavier del Bac. But the Spanish missionaries are best known for the chain of 21 Franciscan missions, linked together by El Camino Real ("The Royal Road") and extending along the California coast from San Diego in the south to Sonoma in the north. The first, Mission San Diego de Alcala (at San Diego) was founded by Father Junipero Serra in 1769. Serra would go on to found nine more.

Whereas the conquistadors treated the Indians as bestial enemies to be subdued and enslaved, the padres regarded them as miscreant children to be supervised and regulated. Neither extreme admitted their humanity, and both traditions fostered implacable enmities between white and red, leaving scars on the region's history so deep that they would not begin to fade until the end of the nineteenth century.

The Least You Need to Know

- The sensational exploits of Cortés in Mexico and Pizarro in Peru inspired exploration of the "borderlands" (the area of the present American Southwest).
- Don Juan de Oñate was all too typical of the oppressive colonial authorities who ruled the borderlands.
- In addition to a hunger for wealth and power, the Spanish colonizers were driven by a desire to convert the Indians of the New World to Christianity.
- The encomienda system, at the heart of Spanish colonial policy, made virtual slaves of many Indians in Spanish-controlled territory.

Errand into the Wilderness (1497–1608)

According to recent U.S. Census Bureau projections, people of Hispanic heritage will comprise slightly more than a quarter of the U.S. population by 2044. Up to the present, most American history has been told from a distinctly Anglo point of view. All too often, Anglo-American historians have portrayed the Spanish colonial experience as exclusively driven by greed for gold and absolute power; in contrast, they portrayed the English experience as motivated by a quest for religious freedom. As more of history is told from the Hispanic perspective, the imbalances will doubtless be corrected. In any case, the motives for American conquest and colonization were never so simple.

England Joins the Age of Discovery

In 1497, Henry VII (1457–1509) sponsored England's first voyage to the New World. To a Genoese immigrant, Giovanni Caboto, whom the English called John Cabot, Henry VII granted letters of patent, empowering him to claim hitherto unspoken-for territories for the crown.

Sailing from Ireland, in May 1497 with a crew of just 20, Cabot landed in Newfoundland on June 24 and likely probed as far south as Maine. After looking around for just three weeks—long enough to come to the confident and erroneous conclusion that he had reached the northeast corner of Asia—Cabot returned to England with the exciting news. Eager to believe him, Henry VII granted Cabot an annual pension of £20 and rushed him off on a second voyage, bound for what Cabot thought was Japan. Setting out in May 1498, this time with 200 men in 5 ships, he and his crews were lost at sea.

Passage to India? No Way

Undaunted by the loss of John Cabot, Henry VII commissioned his son Sebastian (ca. 1482–1557) in 1508 to make another voyage, which probably took him to what would later be called Hudson (or Hudson's) Bay.

Despite the claims of Columbus and John and Sebastian Cabot that they had reached Asia, explorers began to realize that the New World really was a *new* world, a continental land mass separating the Atlantic and Pacific oceans, and therefore separating Europe from Asia, at least as far as any *western* shortcut was concerned. The early explorations had revealed many bays and rivers along the northern coast of the new continent, which suggested the possibility of a water passage clear through the land mass, maybe all the way to the Pacific.

The quest for a "Northwest Passage" began in 1534, when the French navigator Jacques Cartier explored the St. Lawrence River, hoping for a passage to China. The English weighed in when 29-year-old Sir Humphrey Gilbert (ca. 1539–1583) published *A Discourse to Prove a Passage by the Northwest to Cathia* ("Cathia" = Cathay = China) in 1566. Eleven years later, this work indirectly led Sir Francis Drake to sail his famed vessel, the *Golden Hind,* down the Atlantic coast of South America, around Cape Horn, and northward, just beyond San Francisco, California.

But Martin Frobisher (ca. 1539–1594) was the first Englishman to search for the Northwest Passage on purpose. He made three attempts. The first, in 1576, yielded the discovery of an inlet in Baffin Island, now known as Frobisher Bay, which Frobisher believed was the Northwest Passage's opening. He also became excited by the presence of an ore that looked a lot like gold. It attracted investors, who created the Company of Cathay, which backed a second voyage in 1577 and a third in 1578.

Neither subsequent expedition found gold, and in July 1578, when Frobisher sailed up what was later named Hudson Strait, he realized it was not the Northwest Passage. Naming his discovery "Mistaken Strait," he gave up the search. Another Englishman, John Davis (ca. 1550–1605), made three voyages between 1585 and 1587, exploring the western shores of Greenland, before giving up.

Henry Hudson, the next seeker of the "passage to India," became the victim of his own crew. In 1610 and 1611, after fruitlessly exploring Hudson Bay—an inland body of water so vast that it seemed certain to be the fabled passage—his sailors mutinied, casting adrift and to their deaths Hudson and a few loyal men.

Still, the search continued. Between 1612 and 1615, Englishmen Thomas Button, Robert Bylot, and William Baffin made additional voyages to Hudson Bay, looking for both the Northwest Passage and any sign of the missing Henry Hudson. Although these expeditions failed to achieve either of their objectives, they stirred interest in the region and led, in 1670, to the creation of the Hudson's Bay Company, which became one of the most powerful forces for trade and settlement in North America.

A Colony Vanishes, Another Appears

A passage to the East was not the only reason for English interest in the New World. Sir Humphrey Gilbert, author of the provocative tract on the Northwest Passage, earned renown as a soldier in the service of Queen Elizabeth I. She knighted him in 1570 and, eight years later, granted him a charter to settle any lands not already claimed by a Christian nation. The ambitious Elizabeth wanted her island realm to become the center of a new world, the locus of a great trading empire—and she wanted to do this before Spain and Portugal succeeded in grabbing all that new world for themselves. With her blessing, Gilbert sailed in 1579 but was compelled to return when his fleet broke up. He set sail again in June 1583 and reached St. John's Bay, Newfoundland, in August, claiming that territory for the queen. On his way back to England, Gilbert's badly overloaded ship foundered with the loss of all hands. The charter was inherited by Gilbert's half-brother, Sir Walter Raleigh, the 31-year-old favorite of the queen.

The Continent Swallows a Colony

In 1584, Raleigh sent a small fleet to what would become Croatan Sound in North Carolina's Outer Banks. They returned with glowing reports of a land inhabited by "most gentle, loving and faithful" Indians who lived "after the manner of the Golden Age." Knighted by his "Virgin Queen," Raleigh named the new land after her: Virginia. In 1585 and 1586, he dispatched Sir Richard Grenville with a small group of would-be settlers. Sir Francis Drake encountered them a year later, starving and wanting nothing so much as passage back to England. Undaunted, in 1587, Raleigh launched three ships and 117 people (men, women, and children) to what is now called Roanoke Island, off the coast of North Carolina. After establishing them on the swampy island, their leader, John White, sailed back to England to fetch supplies.

When White returned to the colony in 1590, he found no settlers and only the barest trace of a settlement—a few rusted hardware items and what was apparently the name of a neighboring island carved into a tree: CROATOAN.

Had the colonists fallen prey to disease? Starvation? Hostile Indians—who took them captive to a place called "Croatoan"?

To this day, no one knows, but the most important recent theory claims that the settlers were absorbed into local Native American tribes.

Starving in Jamestown

Raleigh's disaster did not shatter English dreams of colonial expansion. In 1605, two merchant groups, the Virginia Company of London (usually abbreviated as the London Company) and the Plymouth Company, joined in a petition to James I for a charter to establish a colony on Raleigh's patent. As far as anyone knew, the patent territory was vast, encompassing whatever portion of North America had not been claimed by Spain. The

Virginia Company was granted a charter to colonize southern Virginia, and the Plymouth Company was given rights to northern Virginia.

The Virginia Company recruited 144 settlers, including the families of moneyed gentlemen, as well as poor people. The latter purchased their passage to America and the right of residence in the colony by binding themselves to serve the Virginia Company for a period of seven years, working the land and creating a settlement. In December 1606, the hopeful band of men, women, and children boarded the *Susan Constant,* the *Discovery,* and the *Goodspeed.* Thirty-nine perished during the voyage. The remaining 105 arrived at the mouth of a river—they called it the James—on May 24, 1607. Where river joined sea, they scratched out the Jamestown settlement.

Jamestown was established in a malarial swamp well past the time of year favorable for planting crops. The "gentlemen" of the venture—those who were not *indentured servants*—were unaccustomed to manual labor. Hacking a colony out of the wilderness required the hard work of all hands. Within months, half the colony was either dead or had fled to the mercies of the local Indians. Things only got worse from there.

WHAT'S THE WORD?

Most of the colonists obtained passage to the New World by signing a contract called an **indenture**, thereby becoming **indentured servants**—in effect, slaves for the seven-year term of the agreement. This would prove a very popular method of bringing settlers to the fledgling English colonies.

John Smith and Pocahontas

In 1609 came what the colonists called "the starving time." Desperate, the survivors resorted to acts of cannibalism and even looted the fresh graves of their own number, as well as those of local Indians.

Jamestown would certainly have joined the Roanoke colony in a common oblivion had it not been for the soldier of fortune the Virginia Company had hired to look after the colony's military defense. The intrepid Captain John Smith (ca. 1579–1631) managed to get himself adopted by the local Indians, who were led by the powerful old chief

Wahunsonacock (called Powhatan by the English). Captain Smith obtained enough corn and yams from them to keep the surviving colonists from starving. He also instituted martial law in the colony, sternly declaring that only those who worked would eat. Enforcing this iron discipline, Smith saved the fledgling colony.

Relations were always strained between the colonists and the "Powhatans" (the English used the same name for the chief and the numerous Algonquin villages he controlled). Simply by refusing to share their food, the Powhatans could have wiped out the struggling colony at will. Yet they did not do so, probably because they wanted an alliance with the English against the powerful Narragansett tribe. Nevertheless, the Powhatans repeatedly threatened war. Hoping to intimidate Chief Powhatan and his people into maintaining peaceful relations, in 1613, Captain Samuel Argall kidnapped the chief's seventeen-year-old daughter Pocahontas and took her to Jamestown (and, later, to Henrico). Fascinated by the English, the "Indian princess" quickly learned their language and customs. She rapidly evolved from hostage to ambassador. In 1614, with the blessing of her father, she married John Rolfe, a tobacco planter. The union brought eight years of peace between the Indians and the settlers, a period crucial to the colony's survival and development. (Rolfe took his bride on a voyage back to England, where she was a favorite with London society and the royal court. Sadly, this remarkable young woman succumbed to an illness and died in England on March 21, 1617, at the age of 22.)

Tobacco Empire

To what must have been the great surprise of anyone who had witnessed the first terrible year at Jamestown, the colony survived and even prospered. Having fulfilled their obligations, the indentured colonists took control of their own land, on which they planted tobacco as the Indians had taught them. A great fondness for the weed developed in Europe, and America found its first significant export. The prospect of growing rich from tobacco cultivation attracted more settlers, who had visions of ruling a tobacco empire. That never quite came to pass, but the Virginia enterprise was successfully launched, and the world, New and Old, would never be the same.

The Least You Need to Know

- ✪ England's first foray into the New World, the Roanoke Colony, vanished virtually without a trace.

- ✪ In 1607, Jamestown became the first permanent—albeit precarious—English settlement in America.

- ✪ The Jamestown experience occasioned the emergence of the first American hero-heroine pair, John Smith and Pocahontas.

- ✪ Tobacco, the cultivation of which the colonists learned from the Indians, became the first reliably profitable export from the Americas.

A Rock and a Hard Place (1608–1733)

The settlement of Virginia was motivated by a combination of commercial enthusiasm and the intense social and economic pressures of an England that had outgrown its ancient feudal system. Farther north in America, in the area still known today as New England, settlement was motivated more immediately by religious zeal.

As early as the reign of Elizabeth I, certain members of the Church of England (which the queen's father, Henry VIII, had severed from the Roman Catholic Church between 1534 to 1540) had become intensely critical of what they deemed compromises made with Catholic practice. A group of Anglican priests, most of them graduates of Cambridge University, advocated a direct personal spiritual experience, rigorously upright moral conduct, and radically simple worship services. They held that the mainstream Anglican Church had not gone far enough in reforming worship and purging itself of Catholic influence. When James I ascended the throne in 1603, Puritan leaders clamored for reform, including the abolition of bishops. James refused, but Puritanism gained a substantial and popular following by the early seventeenth century.

The government and the mainstream Anglican Church reacted with repressive measures amounting to a campaign of persecution. Some Puritans left the country, settling in religiously tolerant Holland. Others remained in England and formed a powerful bloc within the Parliamentarian party that, under the leadership of Oliver Cromwell, ultimately defeated (and beheaded!) Charles I in the English Civil War (1642–1646).

Promised Land

The Puritans who left England were, logically enough, called Separatists. One group that settled in Holland found religious freedom there but were concerned that their children were growing up Dutch rather than English. In 1617, they voted to emigrate to America.

Their leader, William Brewster, knew Sir Edwin Sandys, treasurer of the Virginia Company of London, and, through him, obtained patents authorizing them to settle in the northern part of the company's American territory. Neither rich nor powerful, Brewster's group struck a deal with the Virginia Company to split the cost of a voyage by taking with them a number of ordinary Anglicans. They called these fellow travelers "Strangers." They were people who already enjoyed religious freedom and wanted nothing more than economic opportunity in America. Ultimately, 102 souls (fewer than half of whom were Puritan Separatists), piled into the ship *Mayflower,* and set sail on September 16, 1620.

After a grueling 65-day voyage, the Pilgrims (as their first historian and early governor, William Bradford, would later denominate them) sighted land on November 19. Rough seas off Nantucket may have forced the *Mayflower*'s skipper, Captain Christopher Jones, to steer away from the mouth of the Hudson River, where the Pilgrims were supposed to establish their "plantation" on lands controlled by the Virginia Company. Jones headed instead for Cape Cod, outside of the Virginia Company patent. Some historians believe that the Pilgrims bribed Jones to alter course to ensure the group's independence from external authority. Either way, the *Mayflower* dropped anchor off present-day Provincetown, Massachusetts, on November 21.

"A Civil Body Politick"

The settlers consisted of the Separatists, united by their religious beliefs, and the Strangers, united by nothing other than a desire for commercial success. While riding at anchor, the two groups drew up the first constitution written in North America. In this "Mayflower

Compact", all agreed to create a "Civil Body Politick" and abide by laws created for "the general good" of the colony.

The settlers searched for a place to land and soon discovered Plymouth Harbor on the western side of Cape Cod Bay. On December 12, an advance party set foot on shore— supposedly (but probably not really) on a rock now carved with the year 1620. The main body of settlers disembarked on December 26.

They could hardly have picked a less favorable time and place for their landing. A bitter New England winter was blowing, and the site boasted neither good harbors nor, given its flinty soil, extensive tracts of fertile land. As at Jamestown, people began to die, more than half during the first winter.

Indian Diplomacy

The colony would have been wiped out without the succor of the neighboring Wampanoag Indians. Two in particular, Squanto (a Pawtuxet living among the Wampanoags) and Samoset (an Abenaki), gave the Pilgrims hands-on help in planting crops and building shelters.

The "friendliness" of the local Indians was not an instance of selfless humanity, but a savvy stroke of diplomacy. Recently devastated by epidemic disease, the Wampanoags wanted to build up alliances against rival tribes and also establish profitable trading relationships.

New Traditions of Liberty and Worship

Inspired by the Plymouth settlement's success (but ignoring the hardships involved in it), another group of Puritans landed at Massachusetts Bay in five ships in 1630. Eleven more ships arrived the next year. Under the auspices of the Massachusetts Bay Company (a joint stock trading organization chartered by the English crown in 1629), 20,000 immigrants, mostly Puritans, arrived by 1642, authorized to colonize a vast area extending from 3 miles north of the Merrimack River to 3 miles south of the Charles River. Led by John Winthrop, the new Massachusetts Bay Colony was centered in a city called Boston, and it soon prospered.

The Puritans wanted to create in the New World a new center of right religion and to build what their sermons (with reference to the Old Testament) frequently called "the city on a hill," a place of holiness that would be a shining example for all humankind. They saw themselves as living out a kind of Biblical allegory and prophecy in which they were on an "errand into the wilderness," chosen by God to build the "New Jerusalem." The most immediate practical effects of these beliefs were the creation of Boston's High and Latin Schools as early as 1635 and Harvard College the very next year.

Rhode Island: Haven for the Heterodox

One of the most brilliant masters of religious debate was the Reverend Roger Williams (ca. 1603–1683), who emigrated from England to Boston in 1631. He declined an offer to become minister of the first Boston congregation because it had not formally separated from the Anglican Church. Instead, Williams moved first to Salem, then to Plymouth, and then back to Salem. In each place, he was criticized for his "strange opinions," which included a conviction that the lands chartered to Massachusetts and Plymouth rightfully belonged to the Indians, that a civil government had no right to enforce religious laws ("Coerced religion stinks in God's nostrils," he said), and that religion itself ultimately rested on profoundly individual conscience and perception. When he refused to obey the Puritan clergy, Williams was banished from the Bay Colony. In January 1636, he and a handful of followers found refuge among the Indians on Narragansett Bay. At the head of that bay, Williams purchased from his protectors a small tract and founded a town he called Providence, the first settlement in Rhode Island.

During the next four decades, Williams welcomed to Rhode Island those of all Protestant persuasions. In 1644, during the English Civil War, he secured a patent for the colony from the Puritan-controlled Parliament and established a genuinely representative government founded on the principle of religious freedom.

Maryland: Catholics Welcome

The founding and survival of heterodox Rhode Island made it clear to the Puritans that their "city on a hill" would not stand alone in America. In yet another colony, the interests of a group even more repugnant to the Puritans were taking root.

In 1632, King Charles I of England, under siege from the Puritan faction that would soon overthrow him, granted the Roman Catholic George Calvert, First Baron Baltimore, a charter to settle North American lands between the 40th parallel and the south bank of the Potomac. The First Baron Baltimore died before the papers were executed, and the charter passed to his son Cecil Calvert, Second Baron Baltimore. In November 1633, 200 Catholic colonists set sail from England in the *Ark and the Dove,* which landed on March 24, 1634, on an island at the mouth of the Potomac they named Saint Clement (now called Blakistone Island). The colonists purchased the Indian village of Yaocomico and called it St. Mary's (it is present-day St. Mary's City), which served for the next 60 years as the colony's capital. Under Lord Baltimore's direction, in 1649, the Colonial Assembly passed the Act Concerning Religion, the first law in the American colonies that explicitly provided for freedom of worship, although it applied only to Christians.

Pennsylvania: Quaker Colony

Freedom of worship was the theme for the creation of yet another non-Puritan colony. The Society of Friends—commonly called Quakers—was founded in seventeenth-century England by a visionary leader named George Fox. He believed that divine guidance was not "mediated" by Scripture, ceremony, ritual, or clergy, but came directly to each individual from an "inward light." Quakerism was thus subversive of authority imposed from the outside, and the religion was quickly perceived as a threat to the dominant order. Persecuted, some Quakers immigrated to America, settling in the Middle Atlantic region and North Carolina. An early enclave was established in Rhode Island.

The Quakers had a number of powerful adherents, one of whom was William Penn, the brilliant young son of a prominent British admiral. On March 14, 1681, Penn obtained from King Charles II a charter granting him proprietorship of the area now known as *Pennsylvania.* In 1682, Delaware was added to the charter. In 1682, Penn founded Philadelphia, a name he formed from two Greek words together meaning "brotherly love." The name expressed the intent of what Penn planned as a "holy experiment" in harmonious living.

Under Penn, "The Great Law of Pennsylvania" extended male suffrage to those who professed a belief in God and met modest property requirements. This law all but eliminated imprisonment for debt and restricted the death penalty to treason and murder cases. Dramatically foreshadowing the U.S. Bill of Rights, the Great Law specified that no person could be deprived of life, liberty, or "estate" (property) except by due, fair, and impartial trial before a jury of 12.

Dreams and Shackles

Founded on firm—although diverse—religious principles, Plymouth, the Massachusetts Bay Colony, Rhode Island, Maryland, and Pennsylvania were all expressions of hope and variations on a theme of desire for a better life. The origin of Georgia was even more explicitly utopian.

In 1732, James Edward Oglethorpe organized a group of 19 wealthy and progressive men into a corporation that secured a royal charter to colonize Georgia as a haven for various Protestant dissenters. Oglethorpe also intended Georgia to accommodate the ever-growing class of insolvent debtors who languished in British prisons and persons convicted of certain minor criminal offenses.

Selflessly, Oglethorpe and the other philanthropists agreed to act as the colony's trustees without taking profits for a period of 21 years. To promote a utopian way of life, Oglethorpe prohibited the sale of rum and outlawed slavery in the colony. He also set regulations limiting the size of individual land holdings in an effort to create equality. But this arrangement, key to the utopian tenor of the project, was quickly abandoned. To begin with, few of the original 100 colonists were debtors, victims of religious persecution, or criminals ripe for rehabilitation. They were speculators looking for opportunity. They soon found ways of circumventing all limits and, after large plantations were established, slavery followed. Georgia became no different from England's other southern colonies.

Slave Country

Just as Georgia was a latecomer into the British colonial fold, so it had adopted slavery late in the scheme of things. In 1619, just 12 years after Jamestown got its shaky start, Dutch traders imported African slaves at the behest of the Virginia tobacco farmers. The first 20 or so landed at Jamestown and were not racially discriminated against but were classed with white indentured servants brought from England under work contracts. Indeed, many years passed before African slaves were brought to the colonies in large numbers. At first, they were purchased primarily to replace indentured servants who had either escaped or had served out the term of their indentures.

As the plantations of the southern colonies (Virginia, the Carolinas, and Georgia) expanded, demand for slavery and commerce in slaves grew. The so-called "triangle trade" developed: Ships leaving England with trade goods landed on the African west coast, traded the merchandise for African slaves, transported this "cargo" via the "Middle Passage" to the West Indies or the mainland English colonies, where the slaves were exchanged for the very agricultural products—sugar, tobacco, and rice—slave labor produced. The final leg of the triangle was back to England, laden with New World produce.

The Least You Need to Know

- ✪ The Pilgrims were Puritans who left England, settling first in Holland and then in New England (at Plymouth) in 1620. Separatists were somewhat less radical Puritans who settled in New England (at Massachusetts Bay) beginning in 1630.

- ✪ The other major English colonies were also established as havens for freedom of worship; Georgia was meant to be a utopia.

- ✪ Intolerance among the Separatists and slavery in the South marred the colonies' ideal of liberty.

Colonial Contenders (1608–1680s)

Compared to the Spanish, the English got off to a slow start in the New World, but they soon became one of the three principal colonial powers in the Americas. Besides Spain, the other was France, which directed its main efforts at settlement along the St. Lawrence River in present-day Canada and in the West Indies. Although "black robes," Catholic priests, followed in the wake of French exploration and set up missions among the Indians, religion was never as strong a component of French settlement as it was for the Spanish, nor so compelling a motive for settlement as it was for the English. The fact was that the ambitious Cardinal Richelieu (1585–1642), who, in effect, ruled France as prime minister under the weak-willed Louis XIII, needed money to finance his campaign to make France the dominant power in Europe. The New World, he believed, offered opportunity for profit.

Champlain Sails In

Samuel de Champlain (ca. 1570–1635) was commissioned by the French government no fewer than a dozen times between 1603 and 1633 to explore the waters of North America and to probe inland. As with so many other explorers of the time, Champlain's primary objective was to find the Northwest Passage to Asia, but he also worked to promote trade in furs and other commodities. Richelieu also authorized Champlain to establish colonies and to promote Christianity (Richelieu was a cardinal of the Roman Catholic Church).

Champlain thoroughly mapped the continent's northern reaches, established settlements, got the French fur trade off to a most promising start, and struck alliances with the *Algonquin* tribes and Hurons against the tribes of the powerful Iroquois League. These alliances strengthened the French position in the New World at the expense—often paid in blood—of their archrivals, the British. Beginning with Champlain, the lines of alliance and enmity among Frenchman, Englishman, and Indian were sharply drawn.

The Sun King Beams

Unlike his father, Louis XIII, and Cardinal Richelieu, Louis XIV wanted New France to be more than a source of quick trade profit. He understood that, to build an enduring colony, it had to be peopled not just by *coureurs de bois* but by stable yeoman farmers.

WHAT'S THE WORD?

Coureurs de bois, runners of the woods, was a name applied to a class of men who made their living by trapping fur-bearing animals, chiefly beaver. Their profession required them to combine the roles of explorer, woodsman, diplomat, trader, hunter, and trapper. The coureurs, although often barely civilized themselves, were the pioneers of civilization in the upper Northeast.

In 1671, Pierre-Spirit Radisson and Médart Chouart, two coureurs, proposed to the king creating a company that would effectively monopolize the northern fur trade. They promised also to find the Northwest Passage, which (they said) would become an exclusively French route for the transportation of fur directly to Asia. In response to the proposal, Louis XIV sent women to New France, hoping to entice trappers like Radisson and Chouart to settle down. He offered a cash bounty to those who sired large families in New France. Finally, he urged the Church to excommunicate men who abandoned their farms without the government's permission. Radisson and Chouart defied the king by going to the English and securing backing to create the Hudson's Bay Company, destined for years to be the single most powerful mercantile force in North America.

Two years later, the French *intendant* (chief administrator) in Canada, Jean Baptiste Talon, stuck his neck out, defying royal policy by hiring a fur trader named Louis Jolliet to follow up on an Indian tale concerning a "father of all the rivers." Perhaps this would prove to be the passage to the Pacific. The Indians called it the "Mesippi."

Accompanied by a Jesuit priest named Jacques Marquette, Jolliet did not find a shortcut to the western ocean, but he did find the Mississippi River, thereby establishing France's claim to a vast portion of what one day would be the United States. In honor of their monarch, they called the territory Louisiana, and it encompassed (as the French saw it) the expanse of land between the Appalachian and Rocky Mountains.

Not that the French really knew what to do with all they had claimed. By the end of Louis XIV's long reign and life, New France consisted of nothing more than a scattering of precarious settlements in Nova Scotia, along the St. Lawrence, and one or two isolated outposts in Louisiana.

A Small Investment

In 1609, Henry Hudson, an Englishman sailing in the Dutch service, reached the site of present-day Albany. Like everybody and his brother, he was looking for the Northwest Passage. Like everyone else who looked for it, he failed. His search, however, did give the Netherlands a claim on the richest fur-bearing region of North America south of the St. Lawrence. When the Dutch West India Company was founded in 1621, a full-scale Dutch colonial movement began.

In 1623, the territory staked out by Henry Hudson was christened New Netherland. The following year, the Dutch West India Company established a trading post at Fort Orange (present-day Albany) and, in 1626, dispatched Peter Minuit (ca. 1580–1638) to serve as the colony's first director-general.

Minuit's first step was to legitimize Dutch claims to New Netherland by purchasing Manhattan Island from the Metoac Indians for trade goods valued in 1626 at 60 guilders. That figure was computed by a nineteenth-century historian as being the equivalent of $24. Generations have chuckled over what has been called the greatest real estate bargain in history, but the joke was not on the Indians, who never claimed to own Manhattan Island. As they saw it, land was part of the natural world, and you could no more own the land you walked on than the air you breathed. If Minuit wanted to pay them for breathing, the Manhattan Indians agreed happily.

Minuit built a fort at the tip of the island and called it New Amsterdam. The Dutch established a profitable trade with the local Indians during the 1620s and 1630s, a period (as you will see in the next chapter) during which New England settlers were locked in bloody war with their Native American neighbors. When the local supply of beavers (whose pelts were the principal trade commodity) became depleted with over-trapping, the Dutch started to stake out farms, displacing Indians and creating a cause for war.

Kieft the Killer

By 1638, when Willem Kieft (1597–1647) arrived in New Netherland as the colony's fifth governor, two related truths were operative: violence between the Dutch and Indians had become frequent, and aggressive territorial expansion had become a prime Dutch objective. Kieft assumed dictatorial powers, imposing a heavy tax on the local Indians in return for defending them against "hostiles," mainly the Mohawks. In truth, the Mohawks had become important trading partners with the Dutch and were now allies—henchmen, really—whom Kieft deliberately used to terrorize other tribes. The "defense" tax was a shakedown, and Kieft was behaving no better than a modern gangster.

When the Raritan Indians, living near New Amsterdam, refused to pay the protection money in 1641, Kieft waged war. Two years later, he put the squeeze on the Wappinger Indians, who lived along the Hudson River above Manhattan. To persuade them of the wisdom of paying tribute, he unleashed the Mohawks on them. The Wappingers fled down to Pavonia (present-day Jersey City, New Jersey), just across the Hudson from Manhattan. Failing to understand the situation, they appealed to Kieft for aid. In response, he dispatched the Mohawks to wreak havoc on Pavonia, and then he sent Dutch troops in to finish off those refugees the Mohawks had spared. During the nights of February 25–26, 1643, Dutch soldiers killed men, women, and children in what was later called the "Slaughter of the Innocents." The heads of 80 Indians were brought back to the dusty streets of New Amsterdam, where soldiers and citizens used them as footballs. Thirty live prisoners were publicly tortured to death.

Following the atrocity, 11 local tribes united in war against the settlers of New Netherland. His panic-stricken colony threatened rebellion, and in 1645, the Dutch West India Company replaced Kieft with a crotchety one-legged son of a Calvinist minister, Peter Stuyvesant.

Stuyvesant Takes Charge

The autocratic Stuyvesant immediately set about whipping the colony into shape, among other things building a defensive wall on the northern edge of New Amsterdam along a "cross-town" pathway that would eventually be named for it: Wall Street.

As to the Indians, Stuyvesant strove to re-establish peaceful trading relationships but continued Kieft's policy of brutality, especially against the Esopus, whose children he captured and sold into the West Indian slave trade.

Stuyvesant's despotism led to the decay of his power as the burghers of New Amsterdam clamored for increased self-government, which the West India Company finally granted them.

New Netherland Becomes New York

Relations between New Netherland and New England became increasingly strained as the colonies competed for Indian loyalty and trade. The Dutch were at a disadvantage not only militarily, but also as victims of the settlement scheme established by the Dutch West India Company. Whereas the English settled New England and the southern colonies rather quickly, putting in place a combination of wealthy planters and yeoman farmers, the Dutch settlement was hampered by the patroon system, whereby land grants approximately 16 miles along one side of the Hudson (and other navigable rivers) or about 8 miles on both banks (and extending for unspecified distances away from the river) were made to absentee landlords who installed tenant farmers. Thus, New Netherland was mostly a colony of mere tenants, and this state of affairs retarded settlement and made patriotism among the New Netherlanders a scarce commodity. Who wanted to fight, let alone die, for a rented country?

By the 1660s, New Netherland was torn by dissension. Stuyvesant stumped about on his peg leg, rattling his saber, but he could not rally his countrymen. On September 8, 1664, a fleet of British warships sailed up the Hudson. Defying Stuyvesant, the Dutch surrendered. The British promptly renamed both the colony and its chief town after the Duke of York (the future King James II), and Stuyvesant retired peacefully to his farm, which he called the Bouwerie. Through the years, the tranquil country path passing through his farm became first a racy street of saloons, eating houses, and cheap theaters, and by the early twentieth century, a gray and dilapidated avenue of dead-end bars known as the Bowery and a symbol of other American dreams that had somehow gone awry. In recent years, the street has undergone the economic rebirth of gentrification.

The Least You Need to Know

- ✪ The French claimed vast tracts of land but failed to adequately colonize them.

- ✪ Although they set up a lively trade with the Indians, the Dutch likewise failed to create an enduring colony.

- ✪ The cruelty of New Amsterdam's Willem Kieft brought on years of destructive Indian warfare between the Dutch and Indians.

- ✪ The British easily displaced the Dutch in New York, creating the most powerful colonial presence on the East Coast of North America.

A Wilderness Burning (1636-1748)

America has long been a place of hopes and dreams. America has brought out the best of which humanity is capable—a dream of justice, a hope for liberty—and it has brought out the worst. First, it became a battleground on which Native Americans fought against an invasion from Europe. Then it became a battlefield on which the invaders fought one another, invariably embroiling the Native Americans in their conflicts.

New England Bleeds

The only thing certain is that the murder of English Captain John Stone in 1634 was *not* the work of the Pequots. As to the rest of what happened, Indian and English accounts differ sharply.

The Pequots were a powerful Algonquian tribe that settled along the Connecticut River. Resenting the intrusion of Dutch traders in the Connecticut valley, they waged a bitter war against the Dutch. Then, in 1634, Stone was killed as his ship rode at anchor near the mouth of the Connecticut River. Never mind that Stone was a pirate who had tried and failed to hijack a vessel in New Amsterdam, had brandished a knife in the face of the governor of Plymouth Colony, and had been deported from the Massachusetts Bay Colony for drunkenness and adultery. And never mind that the Indians claimed Stone had kidnapped some of their people. New Englanders demanded action against the Pequots for the murder of John Stone.

The Pequot War

For their part, the Pequots wanted no trouble. Although no one accused any Pequot of having laid a finger on Stone, the murder was clearly the work of western Niantics, a tribe nominally under Pequot control. Seeking to avert a war, the Pequots accepted responsibility and signed a treaty with the Massachusetts Bay Colony, promising to surrender those guilty of the murder. They also agreed to pay an exorbitant indemnity, relinquish rights to a vast tract of Connecticut land, and trade exclusively with the English rather than the Dutch. By and by, a portion of the indemnity was paid, but the Pequots claimed that, of the murderers, all were dead (one at the hands of the Dutch, the others of smallpox), except for two, who had escaped.

For two years, the Massachusetts Bay colonists did nothing about what they saw as a breach of treaty. Then, on June 16, 1636, Mohegan Indians warned the English that the Pequots, fearful the colonists were about to take action against them, decided on a pre-emptive strike. A new conference between the Pequots and the colonists was called at Fort Saybrook, Connecticut, and agreements were reached. But word soon arrived of the death of another English captain, John Oldham, off Block Island. This time, the perpetrators were Narragansetts (or a tribe subordinate to them), and although the Narragansett sachems immediately dispatched 200 warriors to avenge the deaths on behalf of the colony, the English sent Captain John Endecott to Block Island with orders to seize the Narragansett stores of wampum, slaughter all the men they could find, and take captive the women and children to sell as slaves in the West Indies.

Anticipating just such an action, the Narragansetts fled before Endecott landed. Apparently of the opinion that an Indian was an enemy regardless of tribe, Endecott paid a visit to the Pequots outside of Fort Saybrook and began burning their villages.

Soon, vast tracts of the Connecticut valley burned, as Indians retaliated by putting to the torch one English settlement after another, and the colonists responded against the Pequots in kind.

The Pequots now suffered defeat at every turn. On September 21, 1638, the Treaty of Hartford divided the Pequot prisoners of war as slaves among the allied tribes— Mohegans, Narragansetts, and Niantics.

King Philip's War

An even more destructive war broke out in New England some four decades later, again over a murder. On June 11, 1675, a farmer saw an Indian stealing his cattle. He killed the Indian. The local Wampanoag chief, whom the Indians called Metacomet and the English called (with contempt) King Philip, sought justice from the local garrison. When he was rebuffed, his followers killed the hot-tempered farmer, his father, and five other settlers. This blew the lid off a war that had been brewing for some time.

VITAL STATISTICS

Among the colonists, 1 in 16 men of military age was killed in King Philip's War. At least 3,000 Indians died; many more were deported and sold into slavery in the West Indies.

Faced with the colonists' insatiable land hunger, King Philip, about 1662, stirred rebellion among Narragansetts, Nipmucks, and his own Wampanoags.

At first, the New Englanders suffered heavy losses. Only after they joined forces as the "United Colonies" did Massachusetts, Plymouth, Rhode Island, Connecticut, Maine, and New Hampshire seize the initiative.

Nevertheless, King Philip's War was a catastrophe for colonists and Indians alike. Between 1675 and 1676, half the region's towns were badly damaged, and a dozen wiped out. The Wampanoags, Narragansetts, and Nipmucks lost a great many of their number. As for the colonists, proportional to the population at the time, King Philip's War stands to this day as the costliest armed conflict in American history.

The French and Indian Wars

The Pequot War and King Philip's War were colonial tragedies. The series of wars that followed them, however, reflected conflicts engulfing Europe.

King William's War

King William III ascended the English throne in 1689 and immediately (May 12, 1689) committed England to the Grand Alliance, joining the League of Augsburg and the Netherlands to oppose French King Louis XIV's invasion of the Rhenish Palatinate. In Europe, this resulted in an eight-year conflict known as the War of the League of Augsburg. In America, the struggle was called King William's War and pitted the French and the Abenaki Indians (of Maine) against the English and their allies among the Iroquois.

The governor of New France, Louis de Buade, comte de Frontenac, proposed not merely a defensive strategy against the English, but an invasion of New York. Lacking sufficient manpower, however, he decided to fight a *petite guerre*, or "little war," consisting not of the mass movement of great battles but of ambushes, murders, and terror, mostly carried out by Indian allies.

In September 1697, the Treaty of Ryswyck ended the War of the League of Augsburg in Europe and therefore officially ended King William's War in America. Yet raids and counter-raids persisted through the end of the seventeenth century.

Queen Anne's War

England, Holland, and Austria had the jitters over an alliance struck between France and Spain when Spain's King Charles II, a Hapsburg (and therefore originally an Austrian), died in 1700, having named a Bourbon (originally a Frenchman) as his successor. The French, naturally, backed Charles's nominee, Philip of Anjou, the grandson of Louis XIV. England, Holland, and Austria threw their support behind the Bavarian archduke Charles, second son of the Hapsburg emperor Leopold I. These nations then formed a new Grand Alliance in 1701, and the War of the Spanish Succession was declared on May 4, 1702, between the Grand Alliance on the one side and France and Spain on the other.

As exported to America, the conflict was called Queen Anne's War. It began on September 10, 1702, when the South Carolina legislature sent an expedition to seize the Spanish-held fort and town of Saint Augustine, Florida. When a combined force of 500 colonists and Chickasaw Indians failed to breach the fort, they settled for burning the town instead.

The act brought counter-raids from Spanish-allied Appalachee Indians, which prompted South Carolina governor James Moore to personally lead militiamen and Chickasaws in a devastating sweep of western Florida during July 1704. The result: 7 villages and 13 Spanish missions (out of 14 in the area) were razed, and the Appalachees were effectively annihilated as a tribe. Strategically, Moore's campaign opened a path into the heart of French Louisiana. Recognizing this, French colonial authorities bribed the Choctaws into an alliance, blocking Moore's advance into Louisiana.

The war raged—from Saint Augustine, Florida, to St. Johns, Newfoundland (captured by the French just before Christmas of 1708)—not in a series of great battles, but in a string of murders, raids, and counter-raids.

In 1713, a war-weary, debt-burdened Louis XIV was ready to end the conflicts in Europe and America. Besides, the 11-year-old Bavarian archduke backed by the Grand Alliance had died, and, uncontested, Louis's grandson Philip of Anjou ascended the Spanish throne by default. The Treaty of Utrecht (July 13, 1713) ended the European and American wars, with Hudson Bay and Acadia becoming English and the St. Lawrence islands becoming French. The Abenakis swore allegiance to the English crown but nevertheless continued to raid English settlements in Maine for years.

Tuscarora and Yemasee Wars

About the time that Queen Anne's War was winding down, colonists in North Carolina engaged in a bloody war with the Tuscarora Indians. North Carolina called on South Carolina for help. In 1713, South Carolina's Colonel James Moore combined 33 militiamen and 1,000 allied Indians with the troops of North Carolina to strike all the principal Tuscarora settlements. This force killed hundreds of Tuscaroras and captured some 400 more, whom the governor sold into slavery to defray the costs of the campaign. A peace treaty was signed in 1715, and those Tuscaroras who managed to escape death or enslavement migrated north, eventually reaching New York. In 1722, they were formally admitted into the Iroquois League as its "sixth nation."

No sooner was the 1715 treaty concluded than the Yemasees of South Carolina rose up against their white neighbors. The military response, led by South Carolina governor Charles Craven, was swift and terrible. With the aid of Cherokee allies, the Yemasees were hunted to the point of tribal extinction.

VITAL STATISTICS

How much was a human being worth? The wholesale price for the Tuscaroras sold on the West Indies slave market was £10 each at a time when £100 per year was considered a handsome living.

King George's War

The death of the Holy Roman Emperor Charles VI in 1740 brought several challenges to the succession of his daughter Maria Theresa as monarch of the Hapsburg lands. It looked as if the Hapsburg territories were ripe for the plucking, and King Frederick the Great of Prussia moved to claim his slice by invading Silesia. France, Spain, Bavaria, and Saxony joined Frederick's fold, while Britain came to the aid of Maria Theresa. Once again, the European conflict spawned an American export: King George's War.

It was fought mainly by New Englanders against the French of Nova Scotia and engulfed the wilderness in flames. Yet the 1748 Treaty of Aix-la-Chapelle, which ended the War of the Austrian Succession, also ended King George's War, restoring the *status quo ante bellum,* "the way things were before the war."

Nevertheless, the *status* was no longer quite *quo*. Enmities and alliances among the French, the Indians, and the English were now not only lines drawn on a map, but scars seared into the souls of all involved. A far bigger, far more terrible war was to come.

The Least You Need to Know

- Wars were fought with the Indians to gain their land.
- Colonies often used Indians as human weapons of terror in violent struggles with one another.
- North America frequently was a theater of wars that originated in Europe.
- King Philip's War (1675-1676) was, in proportion to the population at the time, the most destructive war in American history, killing 1 in 16 colonial men of military age and some 3,000 Indians.

A Woodland World War (1749–1763)

The treaty of Aix-la-Chapelle, which ended King George's War on October 18, 1748, brought no more than momentary peace to the American frontier. On March 27, 1749, King George II granted huge wilderness tracts to a group of colonial entrepreneurs called the Ohio Company, stipulating that, within seven years, the company must construct a 100-family settlement and erect a fort for their protection. The grant and stipulation rekindled the hostility of the French and their Indian allies, who feared an English invasion.

Taking Sides

In August 1749, Jacques-Pierre de Jonquière, marquis de La Jonquière, became governor of New France and began building forts. He also attacked the Shawnees, the most powerful of the Ohio country tribes trading with the English. In the meantime, in 1752, an English trader, Christopher Gist, negotiated a treaty at Logstown (Ambridge), Pennsylvania, between Virginia and the Ohio Company on the one hand and the Six Iroquois Nations (plus the Delawares, Shawnees, and Wyandots) on the other. The treaty secured for Virginia and the Ohio Company deeds to the vast Ohio country. French-allied Indians responded by driving the English out of this wilderness country by year's end. Another governor of New France, Ange Duquesne de Menneville, marquis Duquesne, quickly built a whole chain of forts throughout the Ohio country, from New Orleans to Montreal. Reacting to this, England's Lord Halifax pushed the British cabinet to declare war, arguing that the French had invaded Virginia.

"The Volley Fired by a Young Virginian ..."

In the heat of war fever, Virginia's lieutenant governor, Robert Dinwiddie, secured crown authority to evict the French from the colony. He commissioned a 21-year-old lieutenant colonel of the Virginia militia, George Washington, to deliver an ultimatum to the French interlopers: *Get out or suffer attack.* Washington set out from Williamsburg, Virginia's capital, on October 31, 1753, and handed the message to the commandant of Fort LeBoeuf (Waterford, Pennsylvania) on December 12, 1753. Captain Legardeur refused to decamp. Washington reported to Governor Dinwiddie, who ordered the construction of a fort at the "forks of the Ohio," the junction of the Monongahela, Allegheny, and Ohio rivers (site of present-day Pittsburgh). It was the gateway to the Ohio country, portal to future control of North America.

After patiently watching the construction of Dinwiddie's fort, the French attacked. Badly outnumbered, Ensign Edward Ward, in command of the new outpost, surrendered on April 17, 1754. The French christened the captured structure Fort Duquesne, enlarged it, and occupied it. Unaware of this takeover, Dinwiddie sent Washington with 150 men to reinforce the fort.

A skilled surveyor comfortable in the wild, Washington was building a growing fortune in land. He had no military training but was a natural military leader in that he was charismatic and had a bias for action. When, en route to the fort, he caught sight of a 33-man French reconnaissance party, which holed up in a secluded "bower" (as Washington called it) not far from what was now Fort Duquesne, Washington attacked on May 28.

In the ensuing combat, 10 of the Frenchmen were killed, including Ensign Joseph Coulon de Villiers de Jumonville, whom Washington assumed was the leader of an espionage mission in English territory. This engagement may be seen as the first "battle" of the French and Indian War, which would soon become the North American theater of a much larger conflict, the Seven Years' War, engulfing Europe and many of Europe's other colonies. As the English memoirist and literary letter writer Horace Walpole later put it: "The volley fired by a young Virginian in the backwoods of America set the world on fire."

Washington won the fight, but the French claimed that Jumonville was an "ambassador" leading an "embassy" to talk with English colonial authorities. Washington now realized that, far from intimidating the French, he had enraged them. Realizing they would retaliate in strength, he sought reinforcement from his Indian allies.

A grand total of 40 reluctant warriors answered his call. But it was too late to retreat, so at Great Meadows, Pennsylvania, Washington built a makeshift stockade he aptly named Fort Necessity. On July 3, Major Coulon de Villiers, brother of the man Washington's detachment had killed, led 900 French soldiers, Delawares, Ottawas, Wyandots, Algonquins, Nipissings, Abenakis, and French-allied Iroquois against Fort Necessity. On July 4, somewhat less than half of the outpost's defenders having been killed or wounded holding off a miserable, rain-drenched siege, Washington judged that honor had been served. He surrendered. With the other survivors, he was permitted to leave, save for two hostages, who were taken back to Fort Duquesne.

With the Ohio fort lost and Washington defeated, it was the English, not the French, who had been evicted from the Ohio country. In December 1754, the British crown authorized Massachusetts governor William Shirley to reactivate two colonial regiments. These 2,000 men were joined by two of the British army's shabbiest regiments, commanded by one of its bravest but least imaginative officers, Major General Edward Braddock.

On April 14, 1755, Braddock laid out an attack plan. Brigadier General Robert Monckton would campaign against Nova Scotia, while Braddock himself would capture Forts Duquesne and Niagara. Governor Shirley would strengthen and reinforce, in New York, Fort Oswego and then proceed to Fort Niagara. Another colonial commander, William Johnson, was slated to take Fort Saint Frédéric at Crown Point on Lake Champlain, on what later became the state line between Vermont and New York. George Washington was appointed aide de camp to Braddock.

Monckton and John Winslow (a colonial commander) achieved early success in Nova Scotia, but Braddock found it slow-going with his unwieldy force of 2,500 men. Washington boldly advised him to detach a "flying column" of 1,500 men to make the initial attack on Fort Duquesne. By July 7, the flying column set up a camp just 10 miles from its objective.

French spies out of Fort Duquesne made Braddock's forces sound overwhelmingly impressive. The fort's commandant, Claude-Pierre Pécaudy de Contrecoeur, was prepared to surrender without a fight, but Captain Liénard de Beaujeu talked him into taking the initiative and attacking by surprise.

Liénard de Beaujeu must have been some talker, because all the French had available were 72 marines, 146 Canadian militiamen, and 637 Indians of various tribes. Yet, on the morning of July 9, 1755, they terrorized the British troops, who were poorly trained and unfamiliar with wilderness warfare. They fired wildly, often hitting each other. Many did nothing more than huddle in the road, awaiting slaughter like so many sheep.

Braddock, dull-witted but valiant, had five horses shot from under him as he vainly tried to rally his forces. At last, mortally wounded, he could do nothing more than watch the disaster continue to unfold. Of 1,459 officers and men who had engaged in the Battle of the Wilderness, only 462 returned. As he lay dying, still uncomprehending, Braddock remarked: "Who would have thought it?" They were his last words.

As for Washington, he had his second lesson in defeat—and in survival. He had escaped unscathed, though his coat was shot through with several bullet holes.

Panic, Retreat, and Retrenchment

The British defeat at the Battle of the Wilderness laid open to devastation English settlements up and down the entire frontier.

While the Pennsylvania, Maryland, and Virginia frontiers were convulsed by Indian raids, William Johnson emerged victorious at the Battle of Lake George and built the strategically important Fort William Henry on the lake's south end. Returned from the Battle of the Wilderness, Washington persuaded authorities to build more forts, extending from the Potomac, James, and Roanoke rivers, down into South Carolina. Nevertheless, by June 1756, English settlers in Virginia had withdrawn 150 miles from the prewar frontier.

Seven Years' Bad Luck

For its first three years, the French and Indian War was a North American conflict. In 1756, it became a world war that eventually encompassed more than 30 major battles in Europe and European colonies in India, Cuba, the Philippines, and North America. The expanded conflict was given the generic title of the Seven Years' War.

France sent the dashing, impulsive, but highly capable Louis Joseph, marquis de Montcalm, to take charge of Canadian forces on May 11, 1756. British forces suffered defeat after defeat until, in December 1756, William Pitt the Elder became British secretary of state for the southern department and took command away from incompetent officers chosen only for their political connections and gave it to those with genuine military skill, including colonial commanders.

Pitt chose Brigadier General John Forbes, one of his best commanders, to assault—for the third time in the war—Fort Duquesne. An army of 5,000 provincials, 1,400 Scottish Highlanders, and an ever-diminishing number of Indian allies lumbered toward the stubborn objective at the forks of the Ohio. When the main force bogged down in mud not far from the fort, one of Forbes's subordinates, Colonel Henry Bouquet, lost patience. On September 11, he ordered 800 Highlanders to attack. They were cut down by French and Indians, who killed a third of their number.

It proved a Pyrrhic victory for the French. Losses among their Indian allies were so heavy that most deserted the cause. In October 1758, a treaty concluded at Easton, Pennsylvania, brought peace between the French-allied Delaware and the English.

Before the end of 1758, Forbes retook Fort Duquesne and the gateway to the West. The tide turned in Britain's favor, and 1759 became the "Year of French disaster." It culminated in the siege, battle, and loss of Quebec on September 18, 1759, following a battle in which the war's two most famous commanders—British general James Wolfe and French general Montcalm—fell. The British capture of Quebec effectively ended French power in North America.

Although the war was decided by the surrender of Quebec, fighting continued for the next two years as the British slowly contracted a ring around French Canada.

Spain came late into the fray, during its waning months, siding with France. England declared war on the new combatant on January 2, 1762, and crushed Spain with sea power alone. Secretly, France rushing concluded the Treaty of San Ildefonso with Spain (November 3, 1762), in which it ceded to that country all its territory west of the Mississippi, together with the Isle of Orleans in Louisiana. This offering was intended as compensation for the loss of Spain's Caribbean holdings to the British. On February 10, 1763, the great Treaty of Paris followed, which officially ended hostilities in America and abroad.

The score? France ceded all of Louisiana to Spain and the rest of its North American holdings to Great Britain.

Epilogue in Blood

Within a few days of the Treaty of Paris, on April 27, 1763, Pontiac (ca. 1720–1769), war chief of the Ottawa Indians, called a grand council of Ottawas, Delawares, Senecas, and Shawnees. A brief but terrible coda to the French and Indian War, Pontiac's Rebellion, broke out.

The Least You Need to Know

- ✪ The French and Indian War was the American phase of the Seven Years' War, which historians consider the first "world" war.

- ✪ A young Virginia militia commander, George Washington, destined to become the military leader of the American Revolution and the first president of the United States, initiated the first two battles of the French and Indian War.

- ✪ Although the English had more colonists, the French had more Indian allies and were far better at wilderness combat tactics than the inflexible British regulars.

- ✪ The Ottawa chief Pontiac united several tribes in a short-lived, unsuccessful, but very bloody campaign to stem the tide of English immigration into the Ohio Valley.

PART 2

The World Turned Upside Down

Beginning in the 1960s, a decade of intense American self-questioning, revisionist historians set themselves up in the business of "debunking" American history. It was common then to read about how the American Revolution was about economics rather than such ideals as freedom and equality. Well, to a colonist struggling to make ends meet, economics was freedom and equality. It's true, the roots of the American Revolution were tangled up in money, but they also drew sustenance from an urgent need for justice, for the rights *all* English men and women were entitled to enjoy. Driven by essentially conservative motives—to win traditional rights withheld—the American Revolution ushered in the most radical government the world had ever known, a government founded not on the basis of a monarch's birthright or an allegiance to a tribe, but on a set of glorious ideas. The chapters in this part discuss the origin and course of the war for independence.

Invitation to a Tea Party (1763–1775)

Great Britain won the French and Indian War, but in the process started losing its North American colonies. The colonists had seen two very different sides of the mother country during the conflict. On the one hand, they had experienced the incompetence and arrogance of some British officers and administrators. On the other hand, late in the conflict, they witnessed some examples of inspiring British political and military leadership. Those latter impressions left a stronger mark, so that at the start of the 1760s, except in parts of the frontier and in the urban centers of Massachusetts, Americans' loyalty to Great Britain was at its height.

But colonial participation in the successful war against France and Spain had boosted American self-confidence. The colonies, traditionally competitive with one another, emerged from the French and Indian War feeling stronger bonds among themselves than with what they saw as an increasingly aloof and unfeeling government across the sea.

The King Draws a Line

The Treaty of Easton (Pennsylvania), concluded in 1758, had done much to turn the tide toward the British in the French and Indian War. By agreeing to prohibit white settlement west of the Allegheny Mountains, British authorities persuaded Indian allies of the French that they no longer needed to fear Anglo-American invasion. But another product of the French and Indian War, the road that General John Forbes had hacked through the Pennsylvania wilderness to transport his unwieldy army to battle at Fort Duquesne, ensured that the treaty was almost immediately violated. Even before the war was over, settlers were traveling the Forbes Road, and the Easton agreement was breached before the ink was dry.

With the French neutralized in North America, the British government saw the biggest threat as conflict with the Indians. To prevent this, a royal proclamation was issued forbidding whites from settling beyond the Appalachians, at least temporarily.

Many frontiersmen defied the proclamation, crossed the mountains, and seized the land. The Indian response was violent. When the white trespassers appealed to royal authorities for aid, they were rebuffed. Colonial alienation from the mother country thus increased.

Taxation Without Representation

Fighting any war is expensive, and no war is costlier than one fought far away. During the French and Indian War, the English treasury had incurred a huge debt. Chancellor of the Exchequer George Grenville (who also effectively functioned as prime minister), decided that the colonies must pay their fair share. Grenville pushed through Parliament heavy duties on commodities imported into the colonies, most notably molasses and sugar, and the laws became known collectively as the Sugar Act. Passed in 1764, it was the first time Parliament taxed the colonies. Parliament also decided to enforce the Acts of Trade and Navigation, which had been passed during the 1650s but never been put into effect. The government now used them to raise additional duty revenue.

Already reeling from a business recession caused by the war, colonists were outraged—less by being taxed than by being taxed without representation in Parliament. After the prominent Boston attorney James Otis denounced "taxation without representation," the phrase evolved into a battle cry that spread from Boston to the other colonies. Representative government was not a new or radical idea. On the contrary, colonists were enraged by being denied the rights all *other* English men and women took for granted. Parliament, not the king, had the authority to impose taxes. Because the people were represented in Parliament, taxation was thus a function of the people's will. Take away representation, and taxation became tyranny.

A town meeting in Boston proposed not a violent uprising, but an economic protest. The colonies made a Non-Importation Agreement, pledging to boycott many English imports. Little heeding this protest, Parliament passed the Quartering Act in 1765, requiring colonial governments to furnish barracks and other provisions for royal troops. The next year, the act was extended to require the billeting of soldiers in taverns and inns at the expense of the colonists. Not only did these measures add to the colonies' financial hardship, the Quartering Act was seen as an affront to personal liberty.

Stamps of Tyranny

Parliament had an even more offensive measure in store. In 1765, it passed the Stamp Act, which required that every paper document—from newspapers, to deeds, to playing cards—bear a revenue stamp purchased from royally appointed colonial stamp agents. Worse, violations of the act were to be tried by vice-admiralty courts, in which there were no juries. Not only did the colonists see the stamps as evil, but denial of trial by a jury of one's peers attacked a right as old as the Magna Carta of 1297.

The Stamp Act united the colonies in opposition to tyranny. Secret societies, collectively known as the Sons of Liberty, were formed in many towns, the boycott of English goods intensified, and a Stamp Act Congress was convened in New York in October of 1765. Eight of thirteen colonies sent delegates, who drafted a "Declaration of Rights and Grievances," a step toward revolution.

Parliament repealed the Stamp Act in March of 1766, only to administer a political slap in the face with the Declaratory Act, affirming Parliament's authority to create laws for the colonies "in all cases whatever," even without representation.

Act II

Chancellor of the Exchequer Charles Townshend (1725–1767) next sponsored a new package of acts intended to raise revenue, tighten customs enforcement, and assert imperial authority in America. Passed on June 29, 1767, the Townshend Acts levied import duties on glass, lead, paint, paper, and tea. Additional bills in the bundle authorized "writs of assistance" (blanket search warrants that authorized crown officials to search anyone's home or business at will and without justification), created additional juryless vice-admiralty courts, established a board of customs commissioners with headquarters in Boston, and suspended the New York assembly for its defiance of the Quartering Act of 1765.

Samuel Adams, leader of the Massachusetts Sons of Liberty, sent a "circular letter" to the other 12 colonies calling for renewal of the non-importation boycott.

During 1768 and 1769, all the colonies except New Hampshire boycotted English goods, and the Virginia House of Burgesses, led by Patrick Henry, created the Virginia Association to enforce the boycott. At this, the royal governor of Virginia dissolved the House of Burgesses, thereby further inflaming anti-British passions. However, in April 1770, Parliament again bowed to the pressure and repealed all the Townshend duties—except for a tax on tea.

REMEMBER THIS

First to die in the cause of American liberty was a member of the Boston mob, Crispus Attucks (born about 1723). He was almost certainly a black man, probably a fugitive slave and perhaps partly of Indian descent.

Boston Rising

The British troops sent to Boston at the beleaguered customs officials' request were, to put it mildly, unpopular. On March 5, 1770, an off-duty Redcoat appeared at Grey's ropewalk, a wharfside maker of ship's ropes, looking to supplement his meager income with a part-time job. The presence of one of His Majesty's hated soldiers competing for work rightfully theirs was enough to touch off a small-scale riot.

The melee subsided, but the mob roamed the streets, more people joining them as they walked. By nine that evening, about 60 Bostonians advanced toward the Customs House, one of the despised centers of British authority. They stopped in front of the building and jostled close to a Redcoat sentry named Hugh White. They had heard that White had assaulted one Edward Garrick, apprentice to a local wigmaker, who had complained to White that his company commander stiffed his master for a wig he had ordered. White smashed Garrick in the center of his face with the butt of his musket. Bleeding, Garrick fled, pursued by another soldier at the point of a bayonet.

The mob threatened White, pelting him with hard icy snowballs. Fearing that White would be killed, Captain Thomas Preston mustered seven soldiers and led them to the sentry's rescue. A tense standoff ensued, in which the mob continually taunted the soldiers, pelting them with ice balls, stones, and other missiles.

Suddenly, one of the soldiers fired into the crowd. That set others to shooting.

The first colonist to fall was Crispus Attucks, aged forty years, a fugitive slave from Framingham. Two more Bostonians died instantly and a third was mortally wounded.

Preston had given no order to fire, and only with difficulty regained control of his men. Prudently, British authorities immediately withdrew all the troops from town. But the "Boston Massacre" became the focal point of anti-British propaganda.

Despite the efforts of Sam Adams and other Sons of Liberty to fan the flames of the Boston Massacre into a full-scale revolutionary conflagration, cooler heads prevailed. Some of the Redcoats and their captain were put on trial in a colonial court and, thanks to the principled and brilliant defense of attorneys John Adams and Josiah Quincy, they were either acquitted of murder or punished for lesser offenses. Colonial justice was shown to be superior even to vaunted British justice. Indeed, Anglo-American relations actually improved—albeit briefly.

Tearing Down, Building Up

By 1773, the only tax remaining from the Townshend Acts was the duty on tea. Doing without tea was never a viable option for *English* men and women. Moreover, in the eighteenth century, tea was an extremely valuable trade commodity—practically a second currency. The East India Company, England's chief tea producer, was vital to British government interests because it had extensive political and economic influence in India at a time when the British Empire was consolidating its control of much of that nation.

The East India Company played a vital role in the expansion of the British Empire, but it was close to bankruptcy. To evade paying duties on English tea, colonists smuggled in Dutch tea. Parliament sought to rescue the company by suspending the tax it paid on tea in England while retaining the import tax on tea sold in the colonies. This made East India tea cheaper than the smuggled Dutch product, and Townshend hoped this would put an end to colonial protest. It did not, especially after the government ruled that the company could sell its tea directly to government-appointed agents at a set price rather than at wholesale to colonial merchants at public auction.

VITAL STATISTICS

The protesters dumped 342 chests of tea into Boston Harbor. The cargo weighed 92,616 pounds and was valued at approximately a pound per pound: £92,659. This was a tremendous amount of money in a day when a man earning £100 a year was considered moderately wealthy.

The committees of correspondence worked overtime to impose an absolute boycott on tea. After the royal governor of Massachusetts rejected colonists' demands that he send three recently arrived tea ships back to England, a band of Bostonians—rather lamely disguised as Indians—boarded the vessels in Boston harbor on the night of December 16, 1773. They seized and then dumped three full cargoes of tea chests overboard. The act triggered similar "tea parties" in ports up and down the coast.

Some Intolerable Acts

During the period immediately preceding the American Revolution, King George III of England (1738–1820) relied on the advice of his autocratic prime minister, Lord North. After the Boston Tea Party, North sponsored a series of laws he called the Coercive Acts and colonists denounced as the Intolerable Acts.

The first of these, the Boston Port Act (March 31, 1774), closed the harbor to commerce until Boston paid for the destroyed tea. Next, the Massachusetts Government Act (May 20) gave the crown the power to appoint members of the legislature's upper house, expanded the royal governor's powers, and further abridged the right of trial by a jury. The act banned most town meetings.

Intended to restore order in Massachusetts, the Intolerable Acts backfired, leading to the convention of the First Continental Congress.

Continental Congress

The Congress met in Philadelphia during September 1774, and only Georgia failed to send delegates. The 56 delegates who convened ranged from radicals who wanted to sever all ties with England, to conservatives who wanted to find a way to heal the breach. At this point, those favoring independence were in the minority. The Massachusetts delegation produced the Suffolk Resolves, which the radicals supported, calling for the people to arm, to disobey the Intolerable Acts, and to collect their own *colonial* taxes. The moderates countered with a formal plan of union between England and the colonies. With modifications, the Suffolk Resolves were adopted by a margin of six to five. The Intolerable Acts were declared unconstitutional (with respect to the British constitution), and the non-importation boycott was given teeth by creating a colonial association to enforce it.

Following the Continental Congress, Thomas Jefferson (in his pamphlet, *Summary View of the Rights of British America*) and John Adams (in a series of published letters he signed "Novanglus," Latin for New Englander) proposed colonial self-government. Parliament rejected this idea as too radical, but liberals in the English government formulated a plan of conciliation in 1775, which would have granted some self-government to the colonies. The House of Lords rejected it, however, and Parliament declared Massachusetts to be in rebellion. Thus, it was the British Parliament, not the American rebels, that "declared" the American Revolution.

The Shot Heard 'Round the World

Massachusetts responded to the Parliamentary declaration by organizing a special militia that could be ready for battle on a minute's notice. They were called—what else?—the *Minutemen*.

General Thomas Gage, commander of British regulars, dispatched Lieutenant Colonel Francis Smith with a column from Boston to seize gunpowder and arms stored at the Massachusetts Provincial Congress in Concord. On the morning of April 19, 1775, Smith's troops dispersed a company of Minutemen at Lexington, unintentionally killing several in an unauthorized burst of musket fire. Smith reached Concord but found only a small portion of the gunpowder still there. He had not reckoned on the resourcefulness of a small band of swift Patriot riders.

Paul Revere (1735–1818) was a prosperous silversmith from Charlestown, Massachusetts. Revere was a leader of the Sons of Liberty and had been a participant in the Boston Tea Party. A courier for the Massachusetts Committee of Correspondence, he rode from Charlestown to Lexington on the night of April 18, alerting the populace to the approach of British troops. In Lexington, he also warned John Hancock and Samuel Adams, leaders of the Massachusetts rebels, to flee. Accompanied by two other riders, Charles Dawes and Samuel Prescott, Revere rode on to Concord, but was intercepted by a British patrol. Although Prescott was the only one who reached Concord, it was Revere whom Henry

Wadsworth Longfellow celebrated in his famous—if fanciful—poem of 1863, "Paul Revere's Ride."

The Minutemen at Concord were far more effective than those at Lexington. The British were driven out of town and sent on their way back to Boston. All along the retreat route, the Redcoat column was harassed by gunfire from Patriot snipers, resulting in the deaths of 73 British soldiers and the wounding of an additional 174. Fifty-three were reported missing, presumably having deserted under fire.

The pattern of battle would prove typical of the war. Trained to fight European-style, open-field battles, the Redcoats would often win the formal "set-piece" battle, only to be cut up piecemeal afterward by colonial guerrilla groups.

Washington Signs On

Soon after the battles at Lexington and Concord, colonial militia forces from all over New England converged on Boston and laid siege to the British soldiers in the city. In May 1775, a hard-drinking, irascible, and irreverent Vermont landowner named Ethan Allen led a militia outfit he had organized—the Green Mountain Boys—against Fort Ticonderoga, situated between Lake Champlain and Lake George in New York. After seizing the fort from the meager British garrison that manned it, Allen took the British fort at Crown Point, on the western shore of Lake Champlain. Despite these early triumphs, anyone who assessed the situation with a cold eye would have put their money on the Brits, an established imperial power, with deep pockets, a tested army, and the most powerful navy in the world. Moreover, while the *colonies* had acted in unity, the *colonists* were hardly unanimous in the desire to rebel. Each colony contained a large "Loyalist" population as well as many other colonists who just wanted to be left alone.

Forty-three-year-old George Washington, now a prosperous Virginia planter, was accustomed to long odds. In the French and Indian War he had fought in three battles, scored one victory, and suffered two defeats. On June 15, 1775, at the suggestion of John Adams of Massachusetts, the Second Continental Congress asked Washington to lead the as-yet non-existent Continental Army. Washington accepted.

A Misnamed Battle Near Bunker Hill

The colonies' new general set off for New England to take command of the Minutemen and the rest of the militia. Before Washington arrived, however, British General Thomas Gage (who had been reinforced on May 25 by fresh troops from Britain and additional generals, John Burgoyne, William Howe, and Henry Clinton) offered peace, granting amnesty to everyone except Sam Adams and John Hancock, the chief troublemakers. In response, the Massachusetts Committee of Public Safety ordered General Artemus Ward to fortify Bunker Hill on Charlestown Heights, overlooking Boston harbor. Ward instead sent Colonel William Prescott with 1,200 men to occupy nearby Breed's Hill, which was lower, flatter, and easier to fortify, but also more vulnerable to attack.

Gage opened up on Breed's Hill with a naval bombardment at dawn on June 17, 1775. Then he launched an amphibious attack with 2,500 men under General Howe. Twice, the superior British force attempted to take the hill, and twice it was repelled. In a third assault, with fixed bayonets, the British succeeded only after the colonials had run out of ammunition. Misnamed for Bunker Hill, the battle was a tactical defeat for the colonists, but it was a tremendous psychological victory for them because they inflicted very heavy casualties on the British.

VITAL STATISTICS

Of the 2,500 British troops engaged at Bunker Hill, 1,000 perished, a devastating casualty rate of 42 percent—the heaviest loss the British would suffer during the long war.

The Olive Branch Spurned, a Declaration Written

The Second Continental Congress made its own final attempt to stop the revolution by sending to King George III and Parliament the so-called Olive Branch Petition. Meanwhile, Washington formed the first parade of the Continental Army on Cambridge Common in Cambridge, Massachusetts, on July 3, 1775. In September, the crown spurned the Olive Branch Petition. Georgia, the final holdout from the Second Continental Congress, joined that assembly and the Revolution. By December 1775, Virginia and North Carolina militias defeated the forces of the royal governor of Virginia and destroyed his base at Norfolk.

With the rebellion in full swing, it was time to create a feeling of historical purpose to catch up with the rush of events. In January 1776, Thomas Paine, a recent immigrant to Philadelphia from England, anonymously published a modest pamphlet called *Common Sense*. In brilliant prose, Paine outlined the reasons for breaking free from England, portraying the American Revolution as an epoch-making step in the history of humankind.

With the colonies united as never before, the next great document to emerge from the gathering storm was a formal declaration of independence. On July 1, 1776, Richard Henry Lee, one of Virginia's delegates to the Continental Congress, presented a draft proposal for a document asserting that "these United Colonies are, and of a right ought to be, free and independent States." Congress adopted the resolution on July 2, and Thomas Jefferson of Virginia was selected to draft a formal declaration of independence.

Inspired by the great English political philosopher John Locke (1632–1704), Jefferson listed the "unalienable rights" of humankind. These included life and liberty, but where Locke had listed *property* as the third right, Jefferson specified "the pursuit of happiness." The purpose of government, Jefferson declared, was "to secure these rights," and the authority of government to do so derived "from the consent of the governed." When a government ceased to serve its just purpose, it was the right and duty of "the governed" to withdraw their allegiance from it. And that is precisely what the colonies had done. The Second Continental Congress edited Jefferson's draft, eliminating, among other things, his condemnation of slavery, and then adopted the Declaration of Independence on July 4, 1776. That is the date we celebrate as Independence Day, although the Declaration was not signed by the congressional delegates until August 2.

The Least You Need to Know

- ✪ Unfair taxation, limits on westward settlement, and the involuntary quartering of British soldiers united the colonies in rebellion.

- ✪ The American Revolution began well before there was general agreement among the colonies that outright independence from Britain should be the goal of the war; many colonists wanted nothing more than relief from taxes and other British laws they believed unjust.

- ✪ Thomas Paine (*Common Sense*) and Thomas Jefferson (the Declaration of Independence) helped elevate a colonial revolution to the status of a momentous world event.

Kindling the Flames of Liberty (1776–1783)

Momentous as it was, there is much the Declaration of Independence failed to do. It did not deal with the issue of slavery, and it did not specify just how the separate colonies, each with its own government and identity, were supposed to unite as a single nation. Throughout the early years of the Revolution, the Continental Congress struggled with this issue and finally produced, in November 1777, the Articles of Confederation.

A timid and tentative document, the Articles nevertheless served the struggling nation through the American Revolution.

Boston Besieged

Most of the king's troops were bottled up in Boston, to which Washington's forces laid siege. Try as they might, the British were unable to break out of the city. When Washington displayed his artillery on Dorchester Heights, the British evacuated by sea in March 1776 and reestablished its headquarters at Halifax, Nova Scotia, far removed from the revolutionary hotbeds of Massachusetts and Virginia.

Southern Exposure

While His Majesty's forces were being humiliated in New England, Sir Henry Clinton sailed with his troops along the southern coast. His purpose was to rally property-rich Loyalists against the upstart ragtag rabble of the newly established "American" governments in the Carolinas and Georgia. Seeking to establish a base for concerted Loyalist resistance, Clinton bombarded Charleston's harbor fortifications as a prelude to capturing the city. A stockade constructed of stout palmetto trunks held against the British cannonballs, which harmlessly bounced off the barrier—and the flag of South Carolina, a palmetto tree beneath a crescent moon, has commemorated this stubborn resistance ever since. Patriot forces drove off the British by June 28, 1776. It was a valuable triumph, which stalled British activity in the South for more than two years.

A Pale Flush of Victory

In its first 12 months, the war had gone far better for the Patriots than anyone would have predicted. The British had been forced out of New England and the South. One key American hope had been dashed, however. The French-speaking citizens of Quebec refused to make common cause with the American rebels against the British. Washington understood that, as long as the British conducted the war from far-off London, the Patriot enjoyed a great advantage. But if they used nearby Canada as the staging area for an invasion of the colonies, that advantage would evaporate. He therefore authorized an invasion of Canada.

An army under General Richard Montgomery marched from upper New York and captured Montreal on November 10, 1775. Simultaneously, troops commanded by Colonel Benedict Arnold advanced through the wilderness of Maine to unite with Montgomery's units in an attack on the walled city of Quebec. The invaders were beaten back, and Montgomery was killed on December 30. American forces maintained a blockade of the city through May 1776, but the offensive in the rest of Canada petered out.

The British Lion Roars

Beginning in the summer of 1776, British forces wrested the initiative from the Patriots. British general Guy Carleton, the very able governor of Quebec, was ordered to chase the Americans out of Canada and down through the region of Lake Champlain and the Hudson River. This action would sever the far northern tier of colonies from the southern tier. Simultaneously, a much larger army led by General William Howe, who had replaced Gage as supreme commander of Britain's North American forces, was assigned to capture New York City and its strategically vital harbor.

Howe hurled against New York City the largest single force the British would ever field in the Revolution: 32,000 troops, 400 transport vessels, and 73 warships (commanded by his vice admiral brother, Richard Howe, with whom he shared the American supreme command).

General Washington saw that, militarily, the situation in New York was hopeless. Congress, fearing that the loss of a major city would dispirit Patriots throughout the colonies, ordered Washington to defend the city. Inevitably, he was defeated on Long Island on August 27, 1776, and took up positions on Manhattan Island.

He never surrendered but fought a series of brilliant rearguard actions against Howe on Manhattan Island, which cost the British time, money, men, and energy. It took Howe from August to November to clear Washington's forces from New York City and, at the Battle of White Plains (October 28, 1775), Westchester County to the north.

Howe doggedly pushed Washington across New Jersey, hoping to force the Continental Army to a stand for a fight to the finish. Instead, Washington crossed New Jersey and escaped across the Delaware River into Pennsylvania on December 7, 1776.

AMERICAN ECHO

"These are the times that try men's souls. The summer soldier and sunshine patriot will, in this crisis, shrink from the service of his country; but he that stands it now, deserves the love and thanks of man and woman. Tyranny, like hell, is not easily conquered."

—Thomas Paine, *The American Crisis* (December 23, 1776)

Recrossing the Delaware

"These are the times that try men's souls," Thomas Paine wrote on December 23, 1776, and they were times that had transformed Washington's men into a determined and disciplined—albeit much reduced—army. To Howe, it seemed clear that Washington had been crushed. Certainly, he had no business striking back, especially not in winter. Howe was a competent European general. In Europe, the proper seasons for a fight were spring, summer, and fall, not winter. But Washington understood: this was not Europe. Collecting his scattered regulars and militiamen, Washington led his army back across the Delaware River, from Pennsylvania to New Jersey.

Crossing the icy river during Christmas night, he surprised and overran a garrison of the vaunted Hessian mercenaries at Trenton, New Jersey on December 26, 1776, and then marched on to another important victory at Princeton, January 3, 1777.

Encouraged by these seemingly miraculous victories, Congress rejected the peace terms the Howe brothers proposed. The revolution hadn't been won, but it hadn't been lost, either.

Saratoga Sunrise

Wearily, the British laid out plans for a new assault on the northern colonies. Major General John Burgoyne was in charge of Britain's Canadian-based army, but thanks in part to the incompetence of Lord Germain, the British minister in charge of the war, he and Howe failed to work out a plan for coordinating their two forces. Burgoyne led his army down the customary Lake Champlain-Hudson River route, while Howe decided not to support Burgoyne's offensive at all. Instead, he left a garrison under Sir Henry Clinton in New York City and transported the bulk of his army by sea to attack Philadelphia. Howe reasoned that, as the seat of the Continental Congress and capital of the rebellion's government, Philadelphia was a more valuable objective than anything in the North. The consequences for Burgoyne were disastrous.

Popularly known as "Gentleman Johnnie," Burgoyne was so confident of victory that he invited his officers to bring wives and mistresses on the campaign. He staged sumptuous dinner parties for all engaged in the grand work of teaching the rebels a lesson they would never forget. He recaptured Fort Ticonderoga on July 5, 1777, but moved so slowly that Patriot forces had plenty of time to regroup for guerrilla combat in the frontier woodlands of upstate New York.

The Americans harassed Burgoyne's lumbering columns and, near Saratoga, New York, attacked with forces commanded by Horatio Gates and supported by Benedict Arnold and Daniel Morgan.

During the Saratoga Campaign, Burgoyne charged the Americans twice, on September 19 (at Freeman's Farm) and on October 7, 1777 (at Bemis Heights), only to be beaten back with heavy losses both times. By the end of the Battle of Bemis Heights, Burgoyne was cut off and surrendered his 6,000 regulars and Loyalist auxiliaries to the Patriot forces on October 17, 1777. His was the first British army to be given up to the Americans.

Trouble in the City of Brotherly Love

Despite the triumphs at Saratoga, the news was not all good for the Americans. Howe landed on upper Chesapeake Bay, 57 miles outside of Philadelphia. He advanced against the principal city of North America, defeated Washington's gallant but clumsy attempt to stop him at the Battle of Brandywine (September 11, 1777), and captured Philadelphia on September 26, 1777.

Howe had paid dearly for the prize he now held: Burgoyne's entire army was lost. Howe held the capital of the revolution, but the Continental Congress had evacuated to York, Pennsylvania. The rebellion continued. Even more important, the French were impressed by the American victory at Saratoga and the resolve with which Washington had fought at Germantown (October 4, 1777) in a vigorous but unsuccessful effort to retake Philadelphia. He may have lost Philadelphia, but the French had seen him fight like a lion.

Vive la France!

As early as 1776, Louis XVI's foreign minister, the Comte de Vergennes, persuaded his king to aid—albeit secretly—the American cause. From the French perspective, the American Revolution was a proxy war against Britain but Vergennes had no desire to risk involving France in a *losing* war with its traditional rival. The victory at Saratoga, Washington's performance at Germantown, and the extraordinary diplomatic skills of Benjamin Franklin (whom Congress had installed in Paris as its representative during this period) finally propelled France openly into an American alliance on February 6, 1778. France granted diplomatic recognition to the "United States of America." Shortly after the alliance was signed, Spain, a French ally, also declared war on Britain.

A Hard Forge

France was an ally. The winter of 1778 was not. The ill-clad, poorly sheltered Continental Army, encamped at Valley Forge, Pennsylvania, suffered mightily. Yet on the frigid anvil of that terrible winter, a stronger army was forged, in large part through the efforts of Baron von Steuben (1730–1794), a Prussian officer who trained American troops to European standards. (A number of Europeans played valiant roles as volunteers in the service of the American Revolution. In addition to Baron von Steuben, these included Johann, Baron de Kalb [1721–1780]; a German in the French army; and two Polish patriots, Tadeusz Kosciuszko [1746–1817] and Kasimierz Pulaski [ca. 1747–1779]. Most famous of all was a Frenchman, the Marquis de Lafayette [1757–1834], a youthful but brilliant commander fiercely loyal to Washington.)

Spring brought Washington new recruits and the promise of French army and naval forces. The Howe brothers, having failed to crush the revolution, returned to England. Sir Henry Clinton assumed principal command in North America and evacuated his army from Philadelphia, which proved a prize of no military value. He concentrated his forces at New York City, and dispatched troops to the Caribbean in anticipation of French action there.

Washington pursued Clinton through New Jersey, fighting him to a stand at Monmouth Courthouse on June 28, 1778. If Monmouth was not decisive, it nevertheless marked the third year of a war in which the British had no positive results to show.

White War, Red Blood

The American Revolution was really two wars. Along the eastern seaboard, it was a contest of one army against another. Farther inland, the fighting resembled that of the French and Indian War. Both sides employed Indian allies, but the British recruited more of them and used them as agents of terror to raid and burn outlying settlements. From the earliest days of the war, the royal lieutenant governor of Detroit, Henry Hamilton, played a key role in stirring the Indians of the Indiana-Illinois frontier to wage ferocious war on Patriot settlers. Hamilton's Indian nickname tells the tale: they called him "Hair Buyer," because he paid a bounty on Patriot scalps. In 1778, young George Rogers Clark (1752–1818), a hard-drinking Kentucky militia leader, overran the British-controlled Illinois and Indiana region and took "Hair Buyer" prisoner. Even more celebrated in the western campaign—albeit less militarily significant—were the exploits of the intrepid frontiersman Daniel Boone.

Bloody though the Kentucky frontier was, conditions were even worse on the New York–Pennsylvania frontier, which was terrorized by the Mohawks and other Iroquois tribes. Washington dispatched Major General John Sullivan into western New York with instructions to wipe out tribal towns wherever he found them. Nevertheless, the Indians persisted in raiding, and the western frontier smoldered and rekindled periodically for the rest of the war.

More Action in the South

In the lower South, the British found effective Indian allies in the Cherokees, who raided the Patriot frontier.

As the war ground on, the British regular army, which had neglected the South following early failures there, shifted attention to the region by late 1778.

In December 1778, British forces pacified Georgia, and during 1779, fought inconclusively along the Georgia–South Carolina border. A Franco-American attempt to recapture British-held Savannah, Georgia, was defeated. In February of 1780, Sir Henry Clinton arrived in South Carolina from New York with 8,700 fresh troops and laid siege to Charleston. In a stunning defeat, Charleston was surrendered on May 12 by American General Benjamin Lincoln, who gave up some 5,000 soldiers as prisoners of war. Quickly, Patriot general Horatio Gates led a force to Camden in upper South Carolina but was badly defeated on August 16, 1780, by troops under Earl Cornwallis.

With the coastal Tidewater towns in British hands, the inland Piedmont shouldered the task of carrying on the resistance. Such legendary guerrilla leaders as the "Swamp Fox" Francis Marion and Thomas Sumter cost the British a great deal. On October 7, 1780, a contingent of Patriot frontiersmen destroyed a force of 1,000 Loyalist troops at the Battle of King's Mountain on the border of the two Carolinas.

The Victory at Yorktown

Fresh from his seaboard conquests, Cornwallis now found himself pinned down by frontier guerrillas. An American army under Major General Nathanael Greene coordinated with the South Carolina guerrillas. Dividing his small army, Greene dispatched Brigadier General Daniel Morgan into western South Carolina, where he decimated the "Tory Legion" of Lieutenant Colonel Banastre Tarleton at the Battle of the Cowpens on January 17, 1781. Breaking free of the guerrillas, Cornwallis pursued Morgan, who linked up with Greene and the main body of the Southern army. Together, Morgan and Greene led Cornwallis on a punishing wilderness chase into North Carolina and then turned about and fought him to a draw at Guilford Courthouse on March 15, 1781.

Effectively neutralized, Cornwallis withdrew to the coast. Greene returned to South Carolina, where he retook every British-held outpost except for Charleston and Savannah. Although the enemy would hold these cities for the rest of the war, their possession was of negligible military value because the occupying garrisons were cut off from the rest of the British forces.

Cornwallis had withdrawn to Virginia, where he joined forces with a raiding unit led by the most notorious turncoat in American history, Benedict Arnold. Cornwallis reasoned that Virginia was the key to possession of the South. Therefore, he established his head-quarters at the small tobacco port of Yorktown on Virginia's Yorktown peninsula.

General Washington combined his Continental troops with the French army of Comte de Rochambeau and laid siege to Yorktown on October 6, 1781. Simultaneously, a French fleet under Admiral de Grasse prevented Cornwallis's army—bottled up on the Yorktown peninsula—from either escaping or being reinforced by sea. Recognizing the gravity of the situation, General Clinton dispatched a British naval squadron from New York to the Chesapeake, only to be driven off by de Grasse. Washington and Rochambeau relentlessly bombarded Yorktown. Cornwallis decided to surrender his 8,000 troops, 214 cannons, 24 transport vessels, and thousands of muskets to the allies' 17,000 men on October 19, 1781.

The surrender did not officially end the war—that would not come until 1783—but it marked the collapse of the British will to continue fighting against colonial independence.

The Least You Need to Know

- ✪ George Washington's greatest accomplishments were to hold his armies together during a long, hard war; to exploit British strategic and tactical blunders; and to make each British victory extremely costly.

- ✪ The American Revolution did not end in Patriot victory, so much as in the defeat of England's will to continue to fight.

- ✪ The Battle of Yorktown, the symbolic (but not official) end of the American Revolution, was as much a French victory as an American one.

PART 3

Building the House

With independence achieved, the citizens of the new United States were faced with the tasks of building a nation, of creating laws without reviving tyranny, of representing the will of the majority without trampling the rights of the minority, and of proclaiming liberty without bringing down the curse of anarchy upon themselves. Then, having created a strong Constitution, the new nation took its place among the other nations of the world—barely surviving the War of 1812 in the process. Following that conflict, as the United States pushed westward, a new kind of leader emerged, hailing not from the patrician ranks of the Tidewater states, but from the western frontier. The "Age of Jackson" saw the nation's expansion and democracy's growth. But this age also doomed Indian men, women, and children to march along a bitter Trail of Tears, and, through the first in a series of tortured compromises, it grappled with the survival of slavery in a land of liberty. Here is a narrative of the years that proved the United States a viable nation.

From Many, One (1787-1797)

Two of America's four treaty commissioners did not negotiate with the British. John Adams went to Holland to negotiate a loan for the infant republic. John Jay was delayed in Madrid, wrangling with Spain, which had proved a most difficult ally. Instead of directly helping the United States, Spain used the American Revolution to expand its North American territories, overrunning much of British Florida by 1781 and launching raids from Spanish Texas across the Mississippi River.

While Adams and Jay were occupied with Dutch and Spanish affairs, commissioner Benjamin Franklin boldly broke with America's most important ally, France, because he recognized that the French government was less interested in supporting the new United States than it was in promoting the claims of its ally Spain in the New World. Almost entirely on his own—and without consulting France—Franklin obtained not only British recognition of American independence, but also cession of the vast region from the Appalachians to the Mississippi River as part of the United States. (The fourth American treaty commissioner, Henry Laurens, had been a British prisoner of war since 1780, when he was captured en route to Europe. He was not present for most of the negotiations.)

The peace agreement Franklin negotiated gained British acknowledgment of American independence and made navigation of the Mississippi free to all signatories (France, Spain, and Holland), restored Florida to Spain and Senegal to France, and granted to the United States valuable fishing rights off Newfoundland. The Treaty of Paris was signed on September 3, 1783, and was ratified by the Continental Congress on January 14, 1784.

Bound by a Rope of Sand

Drafted in 1777 and ratified by the states in 1781, the Articles of Confederation became the first constitution of the United States. The document John Dickinson (1732–1808) conceived in 1776 provided for a strong national government but was soon diluted by states clamoring for more rights. Instead of a nation, the revised Articles created a "firm league of friendship" among 13 sovereign states.

The Articles did provide for a permanent national congress, which was charged with conducting foreign relations, declaring war, making peace, maintaining an army and navy, and so on, yet was ultimately powerless because it had no power to enforce the laws it enacted. The states, one by one, either chose to comply or not. Even more important, the states held the purse strings and therefore determined whether or not any act of the congress would be implemented.

The Articles held the states together during the last years of the American Revolution but lawmakers called it "a rope of sand."

Northwest Ordinance

Under the Articles of Confederation, Congress managed to pass one momentous piece of legislation. The Northwest Ordinance (July 13, 1787) spelled out how territories and states were to be formed from the western lands gained in the revolution. What was then called the Northwest—the vast region bounded by the Ohio and Mississippi rivers and by the Great Lakes—was to be divided into three to five territories. Congress was empowered to appoint a governor, a secretary, and three judges to govern each territory. When the adult male population of a territory reached 5,000, elections would be held to form a territorial legislature and to send a nonvoting representative to Congress. When its adult male population reached 60,000, the territory could write a constitution and apply for statehood.

Of equal importance, the Ordinance was the first federal stand against slavery. The law prohibited slavery in the territories.

We the People ...

Despite the bold Northwest Ordinance, the impotence of Congress under the Articles of Confederation was demonstrated almost daily. For example, the federal government was powerless to intervene when Massachusetts faced an insurrection by farmer Daniel Shays, who led an assault on the state judiciary. Nor could it intervene when Rhode Island issued a mountain of worthless paper currency. A 1786 convention in Annapolis, Maryland, to discuss interstate commerce problems recognized that the issue could be addressed only by a sweeping revision of the Articles of Confederation. The Annapolis delegates called for a constitutional convention, which met in Philadelphia in May 1787. By the end of the month, the delegates agreed that Americans needed a genuine national government, not a confederation of states.

A Fresh Start and New Compromise

Fifty-five delegates convened in Philadelphia and elected George Washington president of the convention.

While some delegates held out for a simple revision of the Articles of Confederation, the Virginia delegation, led by Edmund Randolph, introduced the Virginia Plan. It proposed a central federal government consisting of a *bicameral* legislature, an executive branch and a judicial branch. Citizens would elect the members of the legislature, who, in turn, would choose the nation's chief executive. The Virginia Plan specified that representation in both legislative chambers would be proportionate to state population, which naturally upset representatives of the smaller states.

WHAT'S THE WORD?

Bicameral literally means "two-chambered" and refers to a type of legislature consisting of two groups of representatives. In the British Parliament, the two houses are the House of Lords and the House of Commons; in the U.S. Congress, they are the Senate and the House of Representatives.

As debate raged over the Virginia Plan, William Paterson of New Jersey introduced an alternative. The so-called New Jersey Plan retained most of the Articles of Confederation and gave each state equal representation, but added a separate, independent Supreme Court.

Connecticut Compromise

Into the debate stepped Roger Sherman, delegate from Connecticut, who offered a compromise between the Virginia and New Jersey plans. The "Connecticut Compromise" called for a bicameral legislature—whose upper house—the Senate—provided each state with equal representation while the lower house—the House of Representatives—provided representation proportionate to each state's population. Moreover, neither chamber would choose the chief executive. An Electoral College would make that choice.

The Connecticut Compromise created a strong central government leavened by a system of checks and balances. The legislative and executive branches counterbalanced each other, and, within the legislative branch, the innately more conservative Senate moderated the popular representation of the House of Representatives. The full power of the judicial branch was implicit in the Constitution but was not implemented until Chief Justice John Marshall introduced the concept of judicial review in the 1803 case of *Marbury* v. *Madison* (see "Supreme Court Reigns Supreme" in Chapter 12).

Three-Fifths of a Person

The Connecticut Compromise left unaddressed the thorniest issue: apportioning representation in the House of Representatives. The more representatives a state claimed, the more influential it would be in the federal government. If representation was to be proportional to population, the South wanted its slaves counted as population. The North objected, arguing that a slave could not be both property and person.

A peculiar-sounding solution was reached. Embodied in the Constitution as Article I, Section 2, the "Three-Fifths Compromise" weaseled out of using the word *slave* altogether: "Representation and direct taxes will be apportioned among the several states according to respective numbers determined by adding to the whole number of free persons including those bound to service for a set number of years and excluding Indians not taxed three-fifths of all other persons."

Federalist Hard Sell

With the compromises in place, William Johnson (secretary of the Convention), Alexander Hamilton, James Madison, Rufus King, and Gouverneur Morris wrote the actual Constitution document. When 38 of the 55 Convention delegates approved the document, it was sent to Congress, which submitted it to the states for ratification.

So began an uphill battle. Those who supported the proposed Constitution were called Federalists; those opposed, Anti-Federalists. Although Delaware, Pennsylvania, and New Jersey instantly ratified the document, a total of nine states had to ratify before the Constitution became law. The process was hotly contested in many states, and nowhere more than in Virginia and New York. To convince New York voters to ratify, Alexander Hamilton, James Madison, and John Jay collaborated on a series of essays collectively called *The Federalist Papers,* published during 1787 and 1788 in various New York newspapers.

Together, the *Federalist* essays are a brilliant defense of the Constitution. Perhaps the single most important essay is the tenth, which pierced the heart of the most compelling Anti-Federalist argument: the nation was simply too big and diverse to be regulated by a central government. Madison argued that precisely because the nation was so large and diverse, governance demanded a strong central government to prevent any single special interest from taking control even as the power of the government would be checked by the multitude of interests and points of view. Essay 51, by Madison, distilled the argument for internal checks and balances: "In framing a government ... administered by men over men … you must first enable the government to control the governed; and in the next place oblige it to control itself … by so contriving [its] interior structure [so] that its several constituent parts may, by their mutual relations, be the means of keeping each other in their proper places."

VITAL STATISTICS

Of the 85 *Federalist* essays, most scholars agree that Hamilton wrote 52; Madison, 28; and Jay, 5.

Virginia ratified the Constitution by a close vote of 89 to 79, but only after the framers promised to add a "Bill of Rights," a kind of Magna Carta to address the rights of individuals. In the meantime, *The Federalist Papers* tipped the balance in New York by a close vote of 30 to 27.

Father of His Country

When New Hampshire became the ninth state to ratify the Constitution on June 21, 1788, the document became law and was put into effect on March 4, 1789. The next month, the Senate counted ballots cast by members of the Electoral College for the first president of the United States. The result surprised no one. George Washington had been unanimously elected, and John Adams became his vice president.

The new president was inaugurated in New York City on April 30, 1789. Even with a Constitution in place, it was up to Washington to create much of the American government and, above all, to shape the office of president. He formulated and installed the key executive departments, naming Thomas Jefferson as Secretary of State, Henry Knox as Secretary of War, Alexander Hamilton as Secretary of the Treasury, Samuel Osgood as head of the Post Office, and Edmund Randolph as Attorney General.

Washington became the prototype for the presidency, and the chief quality he introduced into the office was restraint. He avoided conflict with Congress, believing it was not the chief executive's duty to propose legislation. He opposed the formation of political parties, although by the time of his second term, two opposing parties had been formed: the conservative Federalists, headed by John Adams and Alexander Hamilton, and the liberal Democratic-Republicans, headed by Thomas Jefferson. (The party labels were created by historians, not the parties themselves.)

Washington's most eloquent expression of the refusal to become a post-revolutionary tyrant was his decision not to stand for a third term of office. The two-term presidency thereafter became an inviolable tradition until the twin crises of the Depression and World War II prompted the nation to elect Franklin Delano Roosevelt to a third and a fourth term. (Although the nation was grateful to FDR, it also approved the Twenty-Second Amendment to the Constitution on February 26, 1951, restricting future presidents to no more than two elected terms.)

The classical Romans reserved one title for their greatest leaders—*Pater Patriae,* Father of His Country—and almost immediately, a grateful nation accorded this epithet to George Washington.

Glorious Afterthought: The Bill of Rights

The framers of the Constitution had no desire to deny individual rights but believed the Constitution created a government of "enumerated powers" only. The government could assume no authority except as explicitly provided for ("enumerated") in the Constitution. Anti-Federalists, however, demanded a separate bill of individual rights. The Federalists agreed to provide it, and, in 1789, Congress authorized James Madison to formulate the required amendments. Madison produced 12 amendments, 10 of which directly guaranteed individual rights (the other two dealt with different issues and were not offered for ratification at the time). Distilled within the Bill of Rights, an afterthought to the Constitution, is the very essence of all that is most valuable in American law.

Hamilton Gets the Credit

Most unapologetic among the Federalists was Alexander Hamilton, the most influential member of Washington's. As secretary of the treasury, he not only developed a strong financial program for the infant nation, he used finance to unify the United States and to elevate federal authority over that of the states. He proposed a controversial plan whereby the federal government would assume all debts incurred by several states during the Revolution and pay them at par value rather than at the reduced rates some states had already negotiated on their own. Hamilton reasoned that this policy would demonstrate the nation's financial responsibility, ultimately improving its standing among other nations. It would also show the world that the federal government, not the states, was in charge.

Also controversial was Hamilton's proposal to create the Bank of the United States. Fearing that it would concentrate too much power in the central government, Thomas Jefferson, Washington's secretary of state, led the opposition against it, arguing that the bank violated the Tenth Amendment, which gave the states and the people all powers not explicitly enumerated as federal.

Jefferson's view of the Constitution became known as "strict construction." Hamilton, in contrast, supported the constitutional view that became known as "loose construction," arguing in support of the "implied powers" doctrine. Explaining that the Constitution's framers could not anticipate all future contingencies, it was impossible for them to list all the powers the federal government may assume. Regarding the Bank of the United States, Hamilton held that the Constitution grants the federal government the power to tax, and taxation *implies* the creation of a place to keep the revenue collected—namely, a bank.

The dispute between Jefferson and Hamilton is the foundation of the American two-party political system, with either party mostly defined by its view of the federal government. Jefferson's Democratic-Republican Party believed in a central government that conceded much of its authority to individuals and states; Hamilton's Federalists stood for a powerful and active central government.

The Least You Need to Know

⊛ The Treaty of Paris (1783) ended the Revolution and gained British recognition of American sovereignty.

⊛ After the crisis of the Revolution had ended, the Articles of Confederation's weaknesses became acutely apparent, and a Constitutional Convention was convened.

⊛ In addition to the nation's first president, George Washington, the defining personalities of the early republic were Thomas Jefferson (who favored the forces of liberal democracy) and Alexander Hamilton (who favored a powerful central government).

Growing Pains (1798–1812)

When Washington delivered his Farewell Address in March 1797, the United States was recognized by the world as a nation. In his speech, the outgoing president advised his fellow Americans to avoid what some have called "foreign entanglements" (though he did not use the phrase) to preserve the nation's good credit, and to beware the divisive dangers of political parties.

Good advice, but the presidential election of 1796 had already shown that political parties were indeed dividing the nation. John Adams, a Federalist, was elected with 71 votes in the Electoral College. In those days—before the Twelfth Amendment (ratified in 1804) charged the Electoral College to vote separately for president and vice president—the runner-up in a presidential election became vice president. In 1796, that was Thomas Jefferson, leader of the emerging Democratic-Republican Party, with 68 electoral votes. Thus, the president and vice president held significantly different governing philosophies. A believer in a strong central government, Adams was significantly less radical than his fellow revolutionary Jefferson, who favored empowering the states and the people.

Foreign Affairs

During Washington's second term, intense friction developed between Britain and the United States. Despite having agreed to do so in the Treaty of Paris, the British refused to evacuate the frontier forts in the Old Northwest—roughly the area corresponding to today's upper Midwest, east of the Mississippi River. Worse, many Americans believed that British traders and officials were encouraging Indian attacks on settlers. Finally, British naval vessels were boarding American merchant ships on the high seas and *impressing* their sailors into the British service to fight its war against revolutionary France.

WHAT'S THE WORD?

Impressment was the practice, common in England during the eighteenth and early nineteenth centuries, of compelling—even kidnapping—individuals to serve in the military, especially the navy.

Anxious to avert a new war with Britain, Washington commissioned Chief Justice John Jay to conclude a treaty, signed on November 19, 1794, to secure the British evacuation of the frontier forts and refer debt and boundary disputes to settlement by joint U.S.–British commissions. This amicable solution alarmed the French, who feared that their former ally, the United States, would now unite with Britain against them. It was true that most Americans recoiled in horror from the excesses of the French Revolution (1789–1799). Just a year before the Jay Treaty was concluded, Washington rebuffed the overtures of Edmond Charles Edouard Genèt (1763–1834), a French diplomat sent to the United States to secure American aid for France in its war with England. "Citizen Genèt"—as he styled himself in the new French republican manner—defied Washington by plotting with American privateers (in effect, pirates for hire) to prey on British vessels in U.S. coastal waters. The president asked the French government to recall Genèt.

In France, however, a new and more violently radical revolutionary party, the Jacobins, had replaced the Girondists, the party to which Genèt belonged. The Jacobin government asked Washington to extradite Genèt. Observing strict neutrality, Washington refused, whereupon Genèt chose to become a citizen of the United States.

As Easy as XYZ

The Genèt episode, combined with the Jay Treaty, brought Franco-American relations to the verge of war. After the French Directory, the body that governed France for a time following the French Revolution, refused to receive U.S. minister Charles Cotesworth Pinckney, the new president, John Adams, sent a commission consisting of Pinckney, John Marshall, and Elbridge Gerry to heal the breach by concluding a new treaty of commerce. French prime minister Charles Maurice de Talleyrand-Périgord (1754–1838) sent three agents to greet the American commissioners in Paris in October 1797. They told the Americans that before they could even discuss a treaty, the United States would have to loan France $12 million *and* pay Talleyrand a personal bribe of $250,000.

On April 3, 1798, an indignant President Adams submitted to Congress the correspondence from the commission, which designated the French agents as "X," "Y," and "Z." Congress, equally indignant, published the entire portfolio, and in this way the public learned of the "XYZ Affair." An outraged nation mobilized for war with its erstwhile ally. Indeed, an undeclared naval war (often called the Franco-American Quasi-War) was fought sporadically from 1798 to 1800. Fortunately, that conflict was limited to a few naval engagements (all but one of which the embryonic United States Navy emerged victorious). International tempers cooled as the French Revolution and its immediate aftermath came to an end.

John Adams on Power

Yet something far more sinister than another war was brewing. In the summer of 1798, in response to the Genèt episode, the XYZ Affair, and the escalating war fever, the Federalist-dominated Congress passed the Alien and Sedition Acts. These included the Naturalization Act (June 18, 1798), raising the residence prerequisite for citizenship from 5 to 14 years; the Alien Act (June 25, 1798), authorizing the president summarily to deport, without trial or hearing, all aliens he regarded as dangerous; and the Alien Enemies Act (July 6, 1798), authorizing the president, in time of war, to arrest, imprison, or deport subjects of any enemy power, again without resort to trial or hearing. Most tyrannical of all, the Sedition Act (July 14, 1798) prohibited assembly "with intent to oppose any measure of the government" and forbade printing, uttering, or publishing anything "false, scandalous, and malicious" against the government. What made the dangerous Alien and Sedition Acts even more insidious in the fledgling democracy was the fact that many of the leading Democratic-Republicans, the political party opposed to the Federalists, were recent refugees from Europe. The acts were aimed directly at neutralizing their power by extending the residency requirement for citizenship.

Adams had neither written nor instigated passage of the Alien and Sedition Acts, but he did sign them. Adams believed that democracy gave the people "too great" power and that it was the role of the central government to provide an "equal power" to check it.

In contrast to Adams, Jefferson believed that philosophy and morality (if not religion) were sufficient to create good government. He deplored the Alien and Sedition Acts and he and his political protégé, James Madison, took steps to counter them by writing resolutions for Virginia (Madison in 1798) and Kentucky (Jefferson in 1799) opposing the acts as unconstitutional and therefore, not binding on the states. Jefferson argued that any state had the right to judge the constitutionality of acts of Congress and to *nullify* those it determined to be unconstitutional.

WHAT'S THE WORD?

Nullification would become a major issue in the decade before the Civil War, when South Carolina's John C. Calhoun echoed Jefferson and asserted that the states could override ("nullify") any federal laws they judged unconstitutional. Nullification attacked the foundation of American nationhood.

Thanks to the Virginia and Kentucky resolutions, most provisions of the Alien and Sedition Acts were short-lived. The idea of nullification, however, proved more durable.

The Age of Jefferson

Public disgust with the Alien and Sedition Acts helped oust the Federalist Adams in 1800, but the Electoral College voted a tie between the two Democratic-Republican candidates, Thomas Jefferson and Aaron Burr. As prescribed by the Constitution, the tied election was sent to the House of Representatives for resolution. Hamilton, no friend of Jefferson but very much Burr's implacable enemy, persuaded fellow Federalists to support Jefferson, who was elected on the *36th* ballot. Runner-up Burr became vice president.

Historians speak of an "Age of Jefferson" but not an "Age of Adams." Perhaps the reason is that, despite Federalist objections to most of Jefferson's policies, the people made them key elements of the American agenda. Internal taxes were reduced; the military budget was cut; and the Alien and Sedition Acts were variously repealed, unenforced, or allowed to expire. The greatest triumph of Jefferson's first term was the momentous expansion of the nation through the Louisiana Purchase.

Supreme Court Reigns Supreme

Jefferson commenced his first term by manipulating the law to prevent a group of Federalist judges, appointed by John Adams, from assuming office. After his inauguration, Jefferson discovered that, during his final days as president, Adams had signed a number of judicial appointments, but had not "distributed" (formally delivered) them. Not wanting to place Federalists in important court positions, Jefferson decided *never* to distribute the signed appointments.

One of the Adams appointees, William Marbury, petitioned the Supreme Court for a writ of mandamus—an order to Jefferson's secretary of state James Madison to distribute his commission as justice of the peace for Washington, D.C. This put Chief Justice John Marshall in a tough spot. If he issued the writ, he would put the court in direct opposition to the president, but if he denied the writ, he would dilute the power of the Supreme Court by appearing to bow to the president's wishes. Refusing to be impaled on the horns of the dilemma, Marshall held that Marbury had been wrongfully deprived of his commission but also declared that Section 13 of the Judiciary Act of 1789, under which Marbury had filed his suit, was unconstitutional. The Supreme Court is first and foremost a court of appeal—its jurisdiction is "secondary." By allowing the Supreme Court to hear a case that should have been heard by a lower court, Section 13 gave the court improper "original" jurisdiction and was therefore unconstitutional. Marbury's suit was thrown out, a political crisis averted, and—most important of all—the mighty Supreme Court function of "judicial review" was established, by which the high court has the final word on whether a law or other government action is constitutional. Thus, *Marbury* completed the establishment of the constitutional "checks and balances" system. Thanks to Marshall's decision, all three branches of government wielded equal power.

A Purchase and a Grand Adventure

Following the French and Indian War, France ceded the Louisiana Territory to Spain. However, in 1800, Napoleon Bonaparte reacquired the territory by secret treaty in exchange for parts of Tuscany, which Napoleon pledged to conquer on behalf of Spain. Napoleon also promised to maintain Louisiana as a buffer between Spain's North American settlements and the United States. After the secret treaty was signed, Napoleon abandoned his Tuscan campaign and refused to maintain the promised buffer. Spain and France fell to disputing, and in 1802, Spain effectively held the United States hostage to its dispute by closing the Mississippi to American vessels.

VITAL STATISTICS

The Louisiana Purchase added 90,000 square miles of trans-Mississippi territory to the United States. Purchased at a cost of 60 million francs (about $15 million), it was a great real estate bargain at 4 cents an acre.

Jefferson could not tolerate an end to western trade, but neither did he relish the notion of Napoleon at his back door. To resolve the crisis, he sent James Monroe to France to make an offer to buy New Orleans and a portion of Florida.

Monroe found himself in precisely the right place at precisely the right time. One of Napoleon's armies was caught up in a losing struggle against a Haitian war for independence led by Toussaint Louverture. Seeking to cut his losses in the Caribbean and instead focus his conquests exclusively in Europe, Napoleon directed his minister Talleyrand to offer America not just New Orleans and Florida, but the entire Louisiana Territory. Negotiations proceeded as soon as Monroe arrived, and the bargain was concluded for 60 million francs, about 4 cents an acre for 90,000 square miles of trans-Mississippi territory.

Struggle for Sovereignty

Doubling the nation's territory, the Louisiana Purchase was overwhelmingly popular and catapulted Jefferson to a second term in the 1804 election. The new term began promisingly with a favorable peace in the Tripolitan War, putting an end to intimidation by the Barbary pirates of Tripoli, Algiers, Morocco, and Tunis.

Alas, the rest of Jefferson's second term was plain awful, cursed by a crippling economic crisis resulting from a failure of foreign policy.

In Europe, the Wars of the French Revolution had segued into the Napoleonic Wars. When neither the English nor the French could score a decisive victory, they turned to attacks on the commerce of noncombatant nations, including the United States, in the hope of damaging one another's economy. The English resumed the practice of impressing sailors on American merchant ships. They also seized American vessels attempting to enter French ports. Jefferson retaliated with the Non-Importation Act, which prohibited the importation of many English goods.

The simmering crisis came to full boil on June 22, 1807, when the British man-of-war *Leopard,* off Norfolk Roads, Virginia, fired on the U.S. frigate *Chesapeake.* The British boarded the frigate and seized four men they claimed to be deserters from His Majesty's navy. The incident infected the nation with war fever. Jefferson resisted and instead pushed through Congress the Embargo Act of December 22, 1807, prohibiting all exports to Europe and restricting imports from Great Britain.

Intended as an alternative to war, the Embargo was a self-inflicted economic wound, which provoked outrage and despair from American farmers and merchants.

Tecumseh Raises the Hatchet

While Jefferson was dealing with Barbary pirates and the depredations of England and France, the American frontier erupted into violence. In 1794, the major tribes of the Old Northwest were defeated by General "Mad Anthony" Wayne at the watershed Battle of Fallen Timbers (August 20). After almost a decade of relative peace on that frontier region, President Jefferson in 1803 directed the territorial governor of Indiana, William Henry

Harrison (1773–1841), to obtain "legal" titles to as much Indian land as possible. Over the next three years, Harrison acquired 70 million acres by negotiating with whatever chiefs and tribal leaders were willing to sign deeds. The problem was that for every Indian leader who claimed authority to sell land, another rose up to challenge the sale.

The most prominent, brilliant, and charismatic of the challengers was the Shawnee Tecumseh (ca. 1768–1813), who organized a united resistance against white invasion, while cultivating an alliance with British interests. Westerners feared Tecumseh and other British-backed Indians. They demanded chastising the Indians and the British, who (they said) incited the Indians to war, thereby damaging western American shipping and commerce. The West was spoiling for a war, and William Henry Harrison and Tecumseh would give it one.

The Least You Need to Know

- The Democratic-Republican "Age of Jefferson" swept away the repressive Alien and Sedition Acts of the Federalists and expanded the United States with the Louisiana Purchase.

- Chief Justice John Marshall defined the Supreme Court's function and established its power with his decision in the Marbury v. Madison case.

- The Shawnee leader Tecumseh emerged with a dream of once and for all uniting Native America in resistance to the expansion of white civilization.

1812: The Decision for War (1812–1814)

Late in the summer of 1811, Tecumseh left the Ohio country for the South to enlarge his network of alliances by reaching out to the Chickasaws, Choctaws, and Creeks. Except for a militant Creek faction known as the Red Sticks, these groups wanted no part of Tecumseh's enterprise. Worse for Tecumseh, William Henry Harrison used the Indian leader's absence to move against his headquarters at Tippecanoe (modern Battle Ground, Indiana). Having assembled a ragtag army of 1,000 men—including 350 U.S. regulars, raw Kentucky and Indiana militiamen, and a handful of Delaware and Miami Indian scouts—Harrison attacked outside Tippecanoe on November 7, 1811. Losses were heavy on both sides—about 50 whites and 50 Indians were slain—but the battle cost Tecumseh's followers their headquarters and prompted many of them to desert their leader. Thus, the western settlers had their first victory. They would get more than their fill of fighting during the next three years.

The War Hawks Roost

Nineteenth- and early twentieth-century schoolbook histories teach that the War of 1812 was fought because of the Royal Navy's impressment of sailors, who were abducted from U.S. vessels on the high seas and at mouths of cannon. Actually, the United States declared war on June 19, 1812, three days *after* the British had agreed to halt impressment.

The true urge behind the war was not to be found on the ocean, but in the trans-Appalachian West. In Congress, that region was represented by a group of land-hungry "War Hawks," spearheaded by Representative Henry Clay of Kentucky. They saw combat with Britain as an opportunity to clear "hostile" Indians from the frontier areas, opening them to white settlement. Also up for grabs was so-called Spanish Florida, which extended from modern Florida west to the Mississippi River. Because Spain was allied with Britain against Napoleon, the War Hawks reasoned that victory over Britain would result in the acquisition of its ally's territory.

But President James Madison, elected to his first term in 1808, did not want war. He renewed the diplomatic and economic initiatives Jefferson had introduced (mainly the ineffectual and self-destructive Embargo) to avoid armed conflict. Facing a tough re-election battle in 1812, however, he yielded to the War Hawks and asked Congress for a declaration of war. He got it.

Three-Pronged Flop

One reason for fighting the American Revolution was to escape the perceived evil of maintaining a standing army. Since winning independence, the United States had done without a large standing force. In 1812, the U.S. Army consisted of just 12,000 regular troops. The nation's navy had better leaders, but it, too, was puny. Ignoring these realities, American strategists laid out a three-pronged invasion of Canada: a penetration from Lake Champlain to Montreal; another across the Niagara frontier; and a third into Upper Canada from Detroit. Thoroughly uncoordinated, all three prongs failed.

The West at Risk

The surrender of Detroit on August 16, 1812, and the collapse of the Canadian campaign laid the West open to Indian raids and British invasion. Suffering inflicted along the frontier was brutal, but neither the British nor their Indian allies capitalized decisively on their gains.

Stranglehold

In miraculous contrast to the dismal American performance on land were the operations of the U.S. Navy. The British brought to bear 1,048 vessels to blockade U.S. naval and commercial shipping to strangle the nation's war effort. Opposed to this vast armada were the 14 seaworthy vessels of the U.S. Navy and a ragtag fleet of privateers. They prevailed in several ship-on-ship engagements, the most famous of which were the battles between the USS *Constitution* ("Old Ironsides") and the British frigates *Guerriere,* off the coast of Massachusetts on August 19, 1812, and *Java,* off the Brazilian coast on December 29, 1812. Yet the Royal Navy tightened its blockade, and the American economy verged on collapse.

Triumph of an Inland Navy

During 1813, renewed American attempts to invade Canada were again unsuccessful. In the West, however, the situation brightened. William Henry Harrison managed to rebuild—and even enlarge—his army, so that by late summer of 1813, he fielded 8,000 men. In the meantime, a dashing young naval officer named Oliver Hazard Perry (1785–1819) cobbled together an inland freshwater navy. On September 10, Perry engaged the British on Lake Erie and destroyed their entire freshwater squadron.

Perry's triumph cut off British supply lines and forced the abandonment of Fort Malden, as well as a general retreat eastward from the Detroit region. On October 5, 1813, Harrison overtook the retreating British and their Indian allies at the Battle of the Thames.

O, Say Can You See

The American victories in the West, so long in coming, might have turned the tide of the war had it not been for Napoleon's defeat in Europe. With Napoleon out of the way, at least temporarily, the British turned their attention to North America. They planned to attack in three principal areas:

- New York, along Lake Champlain and the Hudson River, to sever New England from the rest of the Union
- New Orleans, thus blocking the vital Mississippi artery
- The Chesapeake Bay, a diversionary maneuver that would draw off U.S. manpower from the New York–New England and southern fronts

Late in the summer of 1814, American resistance to the attack in Chesapeake Bay folded. The British, under Robert Ross, invaded Washington, D.C., and burned the major public buildings, including the Capitol and the White House, as President Madison and most of the government fled into the countryside.

By the fall of 1814, the United States was flat broke. New Englanders even started talking about seceding from the Union.

Ross next set his sights on Baltimore, bombarding Fort McHenry in Baltimore Harbor during the night of September 13–14, 1814. A young Washington lawyer, Francis Scott Key (1779–1843), witnessed the event while he was detained on a British warship. Peering anxiously through the long night, Key saw at dawn that the "Star-Spangled Banner" yet waved; the fort had not fallen to the British, who, giving up, withdrew. Key was moved to write a poem that eventually became the lyrics to our national anthem.

Deliverance on Lake Champlain

While Washington burned and Baltimore fell under attack, 10,000 British troops descended into the United States from Montreal. On September 11, 1814, U.S. Navy captain Thomas MacDonough (1783–1825) defeated and destroyed the British fleet on Lake Champlain. Deprived of a waterborne means of communication and supply, the British aborted their invasion and retreated.

The failure of the British offensive along Lake Champlain added some high cards to the hand of American peace negotiators meeting with their British counterparts in the Flemish city of Ghent. The war-weary British decided to forego territorial demands. The United States let up on its demand that Britain recognize American neutral rights. The Treaty of Ghent, signed on December 24, 1814, restored the *status quo ante bellum*—the way things were before the war—and the document was unanimously ratified by the U.S. Senate on February 17, 1815.

WHAT'S THE WORD?

The Latin phrase **status quo ante bellum** is common in treaties and underscores the utter futility of much combat. The phrase means "the way things were before the war."

An American Hero Is Born

In 1814, trans-Atlantic communication traveled at the speed of sail. Word of the Treaty of Ghent had not reached either General Andrew Jackson or British Major General Edward Pakenham when the two clashed at the Battle of New Orleans during January 8-18, 1815.

Jackson's forces consisted of 3,100 Tennessee and Kentucky volunteers, in addition to New Orleans militiamen and a motley mob of locals (for a total of 4,732), which the general wisely kept well to the rear. Jackson's numerically inferior forces withstood a fierce artillery bombardment and repulsed two British assaults on their defensive positions. The British force of 7,500 veterans of the Napoleonic Wars withdrew on January 8, having suffered heavy losses, including the death of Pakenham and his two senior subordinates. By January 18, the entire available British force, some 14,000 men, totally evacuated the field.

The War of 1812 may have ended in December 1814, but Jackson's victory the following year made Americans feel they had won the war.

Whatever the United States lost in the War of 1812, it had stood up against the most powerful military force in the world. And, in Andrew Jackson, the war created a brand-new military and political hero, a "Westerner" born and bred far from the traditional seaboard seats of power. Like Jefferson before him, Andrew Jackson would lend his name to an entire era.

The Least You Need to Know

- ⊙ The War of 1812 was provoked by Westerners, who were eager to expand the territory of the United States.

- ⊙ The War of 1812, which the Treaty of Ghent brought to an end, was effectively a draw, restoring the status quo ante bellum.

- ⊙ Although the war brought great hardship to the United States, it ultimately reinforced the bonds of national unity by demonstrating that America could stand up to the most powerful nation on the planet.

Fanfare for the Common Man (1814–1836)

Casualties of the War of 1812 included many soldiers, settlers, Indians, and the U.S. economy. Another casualty was the Federalist Party. Federalists, who had opposed the war and, in extreme cases, even advocated dissolution of the union because of it, were now seen as unpatriotic. Democratic-Republican James Monroe handily won the 1816 presidential election.

Good Feelings

One of the great misnomers in American history describes this nation in the years following the War of 1812 as the "Era of Good Feelings." A Federalist newspaper sarcastically coined the phrase following Monroe's re-election in 1820. Monroe was personally popular, but he presided over a country that, although proud of its nationhood after the war, was torn by bitter sectional rivalries and disputes over the interpretation of the Constitution.

Monroe broke with Jefferson and supported the rechartering of the Bank of the United States, brainchild of Washington's Federalist secretary of the treasury Alexander Hamilton. The bank was popular with the East Coast establishment. The perpetually struggling Westerners, who needed easy credit to expand and establish themselves, bitterly opposed it.

Those Westerners also argued for a loose interpretation of the Constitution, particularly the phrase in the Preamble, "to promote the general welfare." These words, Secretary of War John C. Calhoun and Henry Clay (powerful Congressman from Kentucky) argued, obliged the federal government to build the roads the West so badly needed. Monroe vetoed road-building bills on Constitutional grounds but did support a high tariff on imports, which aided the industrialized Northeast at the expense of the rural South and West. The tariff increased sectional strife.

A Monumental Ditch

Monroe's opposition to federally built roads for the West did not impede—and might even have actually stimulated—development of the nation's first great commercial link between the East Coast and the vast inland realm, the Erie Canal, from New York City to Buffalo, on the shore of Lake Erie. The New York legislature approved the project in 1817, and it was completed in 1825. Running 363 miles, the canal was a spectacular engineering achievement and a testament to American labor. It was also a stunning commercial triumph, which quickly repaid the $7 million in state and private investment it had cost to build and soon returned an average of $3 million in annual profits.

The Erie Canal inaugurated the commercial opening of the West and touched off a canal-building boom that linked the Northeast with the western system of natural waterways.

A Place in the Family of Nations

The completion and success of the Erie Canal justifiably puffed the nation's pride, even if its economy was still shaky and the jarring demands of sectionalism were increasingly strident. Monroe's secretary of state John Quincy Adams negotiated the Rush-Bagot Agreement and the Convention of 1818 with Britain. The first document established the U.S. border with Quebec, which established the enduring precedent of an unfortified border between the United States and Canada.

The Convention of 1818 addressed the issue of the disputed Oregon Territory (the land west of the Rocky Mountains, north of the forty-second parallel to the 54°42' line). The Convention specified joint U.S. and British occupation of the area—not only a temporary solution to a hot dispute, but also a demonstration that England now took American sovereignty seriously.

On February 12, 1819, Adams concluded a treaty with Luis de Onís, Spain's minister to Washington, which secured both western and eastern Florida for the United States. With the acquisition of Florida, a prime objective of the War of 1812 was belatedly realized. A thornier problem was the establishment of the border between the United States and Mexico, at the time a part of the Spanish empire. J. Q. Adams wanted a border that would pull Texas into American territory. To get Florida, however, he sacrificed Texas and agreed on a boundary at the Sabine River, the western border of the present-day state of Louisiana. The United States renounced all claims to Texas.

That renunciation was short lived. After the Texas War for Independence in 1836, U.S. rights to the territory became a cause of war between Mexico and the United States.

Yet one more treaty was concluded, this one with the czar of Russia, who had asserted a claim to the California coast as far south as San Francisco Bay. Secretary Adams talked Czar Alexander I into a position north of the 54°42' line, so that Russia would no longer be a contender for the Oregon Territory. The czar did retain his claim to Alaska, a barren and frozen land, which—at the time—nobody in the United States could imagine ever wanting.

Monroe Doctrine

The cornerstone of Monroe's foreign policy was laid in 1823. The origin of the "Monroe Doctrine" is found in the turbulent years of the Napoleonic Wars. These conflicts touched South America, sparking widespread revolutions there. After peace was re-established in Europe in 1815, Spain began making noises about reclaiming its South American colonies. President Monroe responded in his 1823 message to Congress with the four principles now known as the Monroe Doctrine:

1. The Americas were no longer available for colonization by any power.

2. The political system of the Americas was essentially different from that of Europe.

3. The United States would consider any European interference in the Americas a direct threat to U.S. security.

4. The United States would not interfere with existing colonies or with the internal affairs of European nations, nor would the United States participate in European wars.

Bad Feelings

The so-called Era of Good Feelings was filled with plenty of distinctly *bad* feelings, a mixture of present financial hardships and an anxiety-filled foreboding of political and civil calamity just over the horizon.

A Panic

From 1811, when constitutional challenges prevented rechartering the Bank of the United States, until 1816, the year the bank was revived under Monroe, a host of shabby state banks scrambled to provide credit to practically all comers. Then, when the War of 1812 broke out, all the state banks (except for those in New England) suspended the practice of *specie payments*—converting on demand paper bank notes to gold or silver. The value of all that paper money so recklessly loaned now plummeted. Banks failed, investors collapsed, and businesses went belly up.

WHAT'S THE WORD?

Specie payments are payments in gold and silver, rather than paper money.

Monroe's Second Bank of the United States stepped in with a plan to stabilize the economy by sharply curtailing credit and insisting on the repayment of existing debts in specie. This plan preserved the Bank of the United States but devastated much of the nation. "The Bank was saved," one pundit observed, "but the people were ruined." In the West and South, individuals were especially hard hit, and these states passed laws to provide debt relief, but not before 1819, when the panic peaked.

The nation weathered the Panic of 1819, but the crisis created lasting resentment against the Bank of the United States, which Missouri senator Thomas Hart Benton called "The Monster."

A Desperate Compromise

The deepening gulf between the northern and southern states gaped its widest thus far in 1818 and 1819. At that point, the Senate consisted of 22 senators from northern states and 22 from southern states. Since the era of the American Revolution, the balance between the free North and the slave-holding South had been precariously preserved with the addition of each state, a slave state always balancing a free state. Now the territory of Missouri petitioned Congress for admission to the Union as a slave state, and the balance threatened suddenly to shift.

Representative James Tallmadge of New York responded to Missouri's petition by introducing an amendment to the statehood bill calling for a ban on the further introduction of slavery into the state—but persons who were slaves in the present territory would remain slaves after the transition to statehood. The amendment also called for the emancipation of all slaves born in the state when they reached 25 years of age. Thus, gradually, slavery would be eliminated from Missouri. The House passed the Tallmadge amendment, but the Senate rejected it and then adjourned without reaching a decision on Missouri statehood.

When the Senate reconvened, a long and tortured debate began. Not until March 1820 was a complex compromise reached. Missouri would be allowed to join the Union as a slave state, but Maine (hitherto a part of Massachusetts) would be admitted simultaneously as a free state. Looking toward the future, the Missouri Compromise drew a line across the Louisiana Territory at latitude 36°30'. North of this line, slavery would be forever banned, except in the case of Missouri.

The Missouri Compromise held the fragile Union together for another three decades.

The Age of Jackson

The single strongest candidate in the 1824 presidential election was Andrew Jackson (1767–1845), or "Old Hickory" and "The Hero of New Orleans," the candidate of the people. However, Jackson did not win the election.

The Rise of Old Hickory

As the façade of the Era of Good Feelings crumbled away, no party had risen to replace the Federalists in opposition to the Democratic-Republicans. In 1824, Jackson received 99 electoral votes, J. Q. Adams 84, William Crawford 41, and Kentucky's Henry Clay 37. Because none of the candidates had a majority, the election was sent to the House of Representatives to choose from among the top three. Illness forced Crawford out of the running, and the choice was therefore between Adams and Jackson. The House voted Adams into office over Jackson, who had received the greater number of electoral votes. Charging a corrupt bargain, Jackson's supporters split from the Democratic-Republican Party and became simply Democrats.

Adams had a tough time as a "minority president." His support of canals and other internal improvements, his call for the establishment of a national university, and his advocacy of scientific explorations were rejected by Congress, which focused on expansion and frontier individualism. This attitude swept Jackson into office in his second bid for the presidency in 1828.

Common Man or King Andrew?

Jackson, seventh president of the United States, was the first who had not been born in patrician Virginia or New England. By the political geography of the day, this Tennessean was a "Westerner" and, though wealthy, was one of the common folk.

There can be no doubt that Jackson's two terms as president—from 1829 to 1837—brought a greater degree of democracy to American government. During the Jackson years, most states abandoned property ownership as a prerequisite for the right to vote. This move broadened the electorate and made elected officials act in a way that was more fully representative of the people who had put them in office. Although this transformation nurtured democracy, it also encouraged demagoguery.

Jackson reserved his most potent venom for the Second Bank of the United States. When the bank's charter came up for renewal, Jackson vetoed the recharter bill. After winning re-election in 1832, he issued an executive order summarily withdrawing all federal deposits from the bank. The bank fizzled, finally closing its doors when its charter expired in 1836. Credit became more plentiful, and westward settlement accelerated. But for the rest of the nineteenth century, the easy-credit American economy was doomed to a punishing voyage over tumultuous seas, riding the crest of each boom, only to be nearly drowned in the trough of every bust.

The Least You Need to Know

- ☼ James Monroe was a popular leader, who nevertheless presided over a period of great economic hardship and bitter sectional rivalries.

- ☼ The Erie Canal, completed in 1825, threw open commerce and communication between the East Coast "establishment" and the developing civilization of the burgeoning West.

- ☼ The Missouri Compromise of 1820 was a desperate bid to stave off civil war over the slavery issue by maintaining the precarious balance of congressional representation between slave states and free states.

- ☼ The "Age of Jackson" brought with it a vast expansion of the concept of democracy. However, this period also sacrificed some of the reason and restraint that had characterized the nation under the Founding Fathers.

Trails of Tears (1817–1842)

The "Age of Jackson," like Jackson the man, was full of contradiction and paradox. Bringing to the United States its first full measure of undiluted democracy, "Old Hickory" was also derided as "King Andrew," a tyrant. A believer in individual rights, Jackson made the federal government—and the president in particular—more powerful than ever. A frontier Southerner, he didn't want to threaten the institution of slavery, yet he turned against the South when that region threatened the supreme authority of his government. A military hero who had built much of his reputation by fighting Indians, he espoused what many considered at the time the most enlightened approach to the "Indian problem"—relocation from the East ("removal") to new lands in the West.

Enlightened? The great "removal" opened the darkest chapter of Indian-white relations in the United States and forever stained the administration of Andrew Jackson.

Liberty and Union, Now and Forever

In 1828, as the John Quincy Adams administration drew to a close, Congress passed the latest in a long series of tariff laws designed to foster American manufacturing by levying duties on imported manufactures. The rapidly industrializing Northeast loved the tariff. The agricultural South hated it. Among the South's best customers were the European nations, especially England, which bought raw cotton and turned it into fabric and clothing, which it exported to the United States. If tariffs made it too costly for Americans to buy European goods, Europe would need less cotton.

Southerners denounced the 1828 measure as the "Tariff of Abominations." Led by South Carolinian John C. Calhoun, vice president under both J. Q. Adams and Jackson, Southerners called the act economically discriminatory and unconstitutional. Calhoun wrote the *South Carolina Exposition and Protest* in 1828, arguing that any state could deem the federal tariff unconstitutional and declare it "null and void."

A showdown over the Tariff of Abominations was deferred by the 1828 election of Andrew Jackson, who pledged tariff reform. When Jackson's reforms in the Tariff Act of 1832 proved too modest, South Carolina called a convention, which passed an Ordinance of Nullification on November 24, 1832, forbidding collection of duties in the state.

Calhoun bet that, as a Southerner, Jackson would yield on the tariff. Instead, the president responded on December 10 with a declaration upholding the tariff's constitutionality, denying the power of any state to block enforcement of any federal law, and threatening to enforce duties collection with arms. He secured from Congress passage of a Force Act, authorizing the use of federal troops.

Civil war suddenly seemed likely. But 1833 also saw passage of a compromise tariff. South Carolina accepted the new tariff, which rendered nullification moot. Civil war was averted, but nullification remained a powerful influence on southern political thought.

The Seminoles Say No

The political fabric was not the only aspect of the Union showing signs of wear during the Age of Jackson. Violence between settlers and Indians reached acute proportions during the War of 1812 and did not subside thereafter. During the war, General Jackson scored a major triumph against the Red Stick Creeks in the lower Southeast, extorting from them the cession of vast tracts of tribal lands. Closely allied politically and by intermarriage with the Creeks were the Seminoles of Florida and Alabama. The Creek cessions made the Seminoles all the more determined to hold on to their own homelands.

In 1816-1817, Jackson, still a general at the time, conducted military campaigns to push the Seminoles off land in Florida, Georgia, and Alabama. Late in 1817, the Seminole chief Neamathla warned Jackson's subordinate Brigadier General Edmund P. Gaines to keep whites out of his village, Fowl Town. In response, Gaines sent a detachment of 250 to arrest Neamathla. The chief escaped, but the troops attacked the town, and the First Seminole War was underway.

Andrew Jackson led 800 regulars, 900 Georgia militiamen, and a large contingent of friendly Creeks through northern Florida, bringing destruction to the Seminole villages he encountered and even capturing Spanish outposts in the process. The taking of Pensacola on May 26, 1818, created a diplomatic crisis—resolved when Spain abandoned Florida and ceded the territory to the United States.

With that, many more settlers rushed into the region, overwhelming the battered Seminoles and their remaining Creek allies. A minority signed treaties in 1821, 1823, and 1825, turning over 25 million acres to the United States. The Seminoles were ordered to a reservation inland from Tampa Bay. Most of the Creeks repudiated the land cessions, but were persecuted under the policies of Georgia governor George Troup. When the Creeks appealed to Andrew Jackson—now president—for justice, he advised them to move to "Indian Territory" west of the Mississippi. Some did.

The Defiance of Black Hawk

In the meantime, the so-called Old Northwest was also racked with violence. The end of the War of 1812 and the death of Tecumseh failed to bring peace as white settlers pushed into present-day Ohio, Indiana, and Illinois. A group of Indian militants rallied behind Black Hawk (1767–1838), charismatic chief of the closely allied Sac and Fox tribes (today sometimes called the Meskwaki-Sauk or Mesquakie tribe).

Throughout 1832, Black Hawk skillfully led resistance against white settlement in Illinois, but by the end of the summer, he and his followers had been defeated.

Indian Removal

As seen by later generations, Andrew Jackson is one of our most controversial chief executives. Even his most enthusiastic admirers have difficulty justifying his role in passage of the Indian Removal Act of May 28, 1830. This law evicted the major tribes from land east of the Mississippi and consigned them to "Indian Territory" in the West. The act did not seize the land, but exchanged western for eastern territory and, by way of additional compensation, paid tribal annuities.

Hollow Victory

In law, Indian "removal" was a voluntary exchange of eastern lands for western lands. In practice, Indians were coerced or duped into making the exchange.

Some went quietly. Others, including the Seminoles, fought. Still others, including numbers of Cherokees, holed up in the Appalachian Mountains to evade removal. A politically sophisticated tribe long integrated into white society, the Cherokees also took legal action. The tribe's majority party, called the Nationalist Party, appealed to the U.S. Supreme Court in 1832 to protest state-sanctioned seizures of property and prejudicial treatment in state and local courts, all intended to pressure the Indians into accepting the "exchanges" mandated by the Removal Act. In *Worcester* v. *Georgia* (1832), Chief Justice John Marshall found that the federal government had no power to strike down Georgia's laws, but he held that the Cherokees were a "domestic, dependent nation" existing under the guardianship of the United States. This gave tribal leaders hope that the federal government "guardians" would intervene against Georgia. Instead, Jackson told the local military commander, Brigadier General John Coffee, that the court "cannot coerce Georgia to yield its mandate." Popular lore put different words in the president's mouth: "John Marshall has made his decision; now let him enforce it."

The chief executive who had asserted federal superiority over South Carolina during the Nullification Crisis, now claimed that the U.S. government was powerless to interfere in the affairs of an individual state. Once again, he advised the Indians to resolve their difficulties by accepting removal.

In the meantime, the president directed federal officials to negotiate a removal treaty with the compliant minority faction of the Cherokees (called the Treaty Party), who represented perhaps a thousand out of 17,000 Cherokees living in the Southeast. The resulting Treaty of New Echota (December 29, 1835) bound *all* Cherokees to removal. Jackson barred the Cherokee National Party from holding meetings to discuss the treaty or alternative courses of action, but, under the leadership of John Ross, the Nationalists delayed the major phase of the removal until the fall and winter of 1838 and 1839.

A Man Called Osceola

While the Cherokees were being subdued and removed, federal authorities turned their attention to the always-troublesome Seminoles. Like the Cherokees, the Seminoles suffered abuse from state and local governments; their afflictions were compounded in 1831 by a devastating drought. Faced with annihilation, Seminole leaders signed a provisional treaty on May 9, 1832, agreeing to removal pending tribal approval of the site designated for resettlement. Accordingly, a party of seven Seminoles traveled westward. But before they returned, John Phagan, a federal Indian agent, coerced representatives into signing a final treaty, binding the Seminoles to leave Florida by 1837. Not only did the tribe rescind the signatures as fraudulent, but even the government acknowledged the wrongdoing by removing Phagan from office. Nevertheless, Jackson transmitted the treaty to the Senate for ratification and troops were sent into Florida to begin organizing the removal.

By early winter 1835, growing troop strength made it clear to Seminole leaders that war was in the offing. During this period, Osceola (1803–1838)—called Billy Powell by the whites—emerged as a charismatic Seminole leader. He negotiated delay of removal until January 15, 1836, hoping to buy sufficient time to prepare for combat. Osceola set about organizing Seminole and Red Stick Creek resistance.

Beginning in December 1835, Osceola initiated guerrilla warfare. Generals Edmund Gaines, Duncan Clinch, Winfield Scott, Robert Call, Thomas Jesup, and Zachary Taylor all failed to bring the Second Seminole War to a conclusion.

Osceola was finally captured on October 21, 1837, when General Jesup requested a "truce" conference in Osceola's camp—and treacherously abducted him. Imprisoned at Fort Moultrie, South Carolina, Osceola contracted "acute quinsy" (a severe complication of tonsillitis). He died on January 30, 1838.

Despite Osceola's death, the war continued from 1835 to 1842, a period during which 3,000 Seminoles did submit to removal, but at the average cost of one soldier killed for every two Indians "removed." The war never really ended. It petered out through mutual exhaustion, becoming reactivated between 1855 and 1858 as the Third Seminole War. The last Seminole holdouts refused to sign treaties with the United States until 1934.

"The Cruelest Work I Ever Knew"

During the summer of 1838, Major General Winfield Scott began a massive roundup of Cherokees. Per the fraudulent Treaty of New Echota, the Cherokees were bound for "Indian Territory," an area encompassing present-day Oklahoma and parts of Nebraska, Kansas, and the Dakotas. They were herded into hastily built concentration camps to await removal. Here they endured a long, hot, disease-plagued summer.

During fall and winter 1838-1839, the Cherokees were marched under armed escort along the 1,200-mile route to Indian Territory. Cold, short of food, and subject to abuse at the hands of their military guards (including theft, rape, and murder), 4,000 of the 15,000 who started the journey perished before reaching its end. Many years later, a Georgia soldier recalled: "I fought through the Civil War and have seen men shot to pieces and slaughtered by thousands, but the Cherokee removal was the cruelest work I ever saw." The Cherokees forever afterward called the experience the "Trail of Tears."

Welcome to Indian Territory

What awaited the Native Americans removed from the East was a tract of bleak and forbidding western land. The hardships of soil and climate, combined with the inefficiency and corruption of the federal system obligated by treaty to aid and support the "resettled" Indians, killed many. Yet, over time, many among the removed tribes made the best of their grim situation and, in varying degrees, even prospered.

Contrary to treaty agreements, the Kansas-Nebraska Act of 1854 unilaterally reduced the area of Indian Territory. During the Civil War, many Cherokees, Creeks, and others allied themselves with the Confederates in the hope of getting a better deal from that government. In 1866, the victorious Union forces punished "Confederate Indians" by contracting Indian Territory to the area encompassed by present-day Oklahoma.

The Least You Need to Know

- ✪ In the Nullification Crisis, "states' rights" confronted federal authority in a prelude to civil war.

- ✪ Osceola (among the Seminoles) and Black Hawk (among the Sac and Fox) emerged as formidable leaders of Native American resistance against the expansion of white settlement into Indian lands.

- ✪ The Indian Removal Act was an attempt to separate Indians and whites by means of land exchanges.

PART 4

The House Divided

Just as you can find people who'll tell you that the American Revolution was all about money and had little or nothing to do with liberty, there are still plenty of folks who'll argue that the Civil War was about states' rights or about the North wanting to achieve economic domination over the South. These things certainly figured in the nation's great conflict, but the irreducible fact is this: if it hadn't been for slavery in the South, and the opposition to it in the North, there would have been no Civil War. This part of the book tells the story of how the "peculiar institution" of slavery divided the country. It also describes how the question of whether a "nation conceived in liberty and dedicated to the proposition that all men are created equal can long endure" was finally answered by the bloodiest, costliest, and most destructive war in American history.

CHAPTER 16

A Nation in Chains (1724–1857)

IN THIS CHAPTER

- ✪ A nation divided over the slavery issue
- ✪ Abolition movements, the Underground Railroad, and rebellion
- ✪ Compromises on the slavery issue
- ✪ Bleeding Kansas and the Dred Scott decision

By the early 1700s, slavery had caught on in a big way throughout the Southern colonies. In places like South Carolina, it was perceived as essential to the economy, and slaves soon outnumbered whites in that colony. The Declaration of Independence declared no slave free, and although the Constitution (Article 1, Section 9) gave Congress the option of ending the slave trade—the foreign importation of slaves—after the last day of 1807, it both sanctioned and protected slavery itself.

Against the American Grain

From the beginning, many white Americans opposed slavery. The first organized opposition came from the Quakers, who issued a statement against the institution as early as 1724.

During the colonial period, slave markets were active in the North as well as the South. The agricultural economy of the northern colonies, however, was built upon small family farms rather than large plantations. While some Northerners were passionately opposed to slavery on moral grounds, it is also true that the region lacked economic incentives for slavery. Following independence, some states outlawed the institution altogether. Rhode Island, traditionally a seat of tolerance, abolished slavery in 1774, and the Northwest Ordinance of 1787 excluded slavery from the nation's vast Northwest Territory.

Many of the founding fathers owned slaves. Recent scholarship shows that Washington engaged in a deep moral struggle with slavery and wrote an eloquent passage in his will stipulating that his slaves were to be emancipated immediately upon the death of his wife, Martha. Few of Washington's slave-holding contemporaries were willing to relinquish such a valuable legacy as human property.

Eli Whitney's Slave Machine

Even in the South, there was reason to believe that slavery would eventually die out. As the free laboring population grew, there was a decreasing need for slaves, and so it was hoped that the slavery question would ultimately answer itself.

But an invention appeared that changed everything. A young New Englander working as a tutor in Georgia, Eli Whitney (1765–1825) observed that planters were vexed by a problem with the short-staple cotton raised in the inland region of the lower South. Unlike the long-staple cotton that grew near the coast, the inland variety had stubborn seeds that required extensive handwork to remove. Even performed by slaves, the labor was so time-consuming that large-scale production was unprofitable.

Whitney decided to solve the problem. By April 1793, he had fashioned a machine that used a toothed cylinder to separate the cottonseed from the cotton fiber. Each *cotton gin* could turn out 50 pounds of cleaned cotton a day—far more than what manual labor could produce.

WHAT'S THE WORD?

Cotton gin sounds to us like a peculiar form of booze, but late-eighteenth-century ears would have immediately recognized "gin" as a shortened form of the word "engine." Two hundred years ago, a gin was any labor-saving device, particularly one intended to help move heavy objects.

The gin caught on fast. Cultivating short-staple cotton was suddenly extremely profitable. "King Cotton" soon displaced tobacco, rice, and indigo as the primary Southern export crop. With increased production came a greatly increased demand for slave labor to feed the ever-churning cotton gins.

Underground Railroad

Just as individuals in the late eighteenth century had been fascinated by inventions like the cotton gin, Americans in the late 1820s and 1830s were enthralled with railroads, which had just begun to appear in the United States. The railroad seemed nothing less than a miracle of technology. Maybe because abolitionists were in search of a moral miracle, they called the loosely organized, highly stealthy network developed in the 1830s to help fugitive slaves escape to the North or Canada—the *Underground Railroad.*

The Underground Railroad was a group of committed whites and free blacks, including escaped slaves ("conductors") and safe houses ("stations") dedicated to the covert delivery and deliverance of slaves ("passengers" or "freight") out of the slave states bordering the North. Prior to the Civil War, 50,000 to 100,000 slaves found freedom via the Underground Railroad.

Southern slave-holders did not suffer the Underground Railroad gladly. "Conductors" were menaced, assaulted, and even killed. Fugitive slaves, when retaken, were often severely punished as an example to others. When the Supreme Court ruled in 1842 (*Prigg v. Pennsylvania*) that states were not required to enforce the Fugitive Slave Law of 1793 (which provided for the return of slaves who escaped to free states), southern opposition to the Underground Railroad intensified.

The Liberator and the Narrative

William Lloyd Garrison (1805–1879) was a genteel New England abolitionist, a native of Newburyport, Massachusetts, who became co-editor of a moderate periodical called *The Genius of Universal Emancipation*. But the injustice of slavery soon ignited a fiercer fire in Garrison's belly. On January 1, 1831, he published the first issue of *The Liberator,* a radical abolitionist periodical that declared slavery an abomination in the sight of God and demanded the emancipation of all slaves, without compromise or delay.

The Liberator galvanized the abolitionist movement. Three years after the first issue was printed, Garrison presided over the founding of the American Anti-Slavery Society. He believed that slavery would be abolished when a majority of white Americans experienced a "revolution in conscience."

With each passing year, Garrison grew more radical. In 1842, he declared that Northerners should renounce allegiance to the Union because the Constitution protected slavery.

If *The Liberator* was the most powerful white voice in support of abolition, a gripping account of slavery and liberation by an escaped Maryland slave named Frederick Douglass was the most compelling African American voice. Published in 1845, *Narrative of the Life of Frederick Douglass* was widely read and discussed. Not only did the book vividly portray the inhumanity of slavery, it also made manifest the intense humanity of the slaves, especially as evidenced in the author, the brilliant and self-educated Douglass. An active lecturer in the Massachusetts Anti-Slavery Society, Douglass parted company with Garrison over the issue of breaking with the Union. Douglass wanted to work within the Constitution.

The Tortured Course of Compromise

The Missouri Compromise, negotiated in 1820, was awkward and strained and began to buckle and break in 1848. In that year, California was officially transferred to the United States by the Treaty of Guadalupe Hidalgo, which ended the U.S.–Mexican War on February 2, 1848. Would California be admitted as a slave state or free state?

In 1846, when Congress was seeking a means of bringing the war with Mexico to a speedy conclusion, it debated a bill to appropriate $2 million to compensate Mexico for "territorial adjustments." Pennsylvania congressman David Wilmot introduced an amendment to the bill, called the Wilmot Proviso, which would have barred the introduction of slavery onto any land acquired as a result of the war. Southern opposition to this limitation of slavery was articulated by Senator John C. Calhoun of South Carolina. He presented four resolutions:

1. Territories, including those acquired as a result of the war, were the common and joint property of the states.

2. Congress, acting as agent for the states, could make no law discriminating between the states and depriving any state of its rights with regard to any territory.

3. The enactment of any national law regarding slavery would violate the Constitution and the doctrine of states' rights.

4. The people have the right to establish their state government as they wish, provided that its form is republican.

Calhoun warned that failure to maintain a balance between the demands of the North and the South would surely lead to "civil war."

1850: A Compromise New and Doomed

Over the next three years, Congress labored to bolster the 1820 compromise. Thanks to abolitionists such as Garrison and Douglass, most Northerners were no longer willing to allow slavery to extend into any new territory, whether it lay above or below the line drawn by the Missouri Compromise. To break the dangerous stalemate, Michigan Senator Lewis Cass advanced the doctrine of "popular sovereignty," proposing that new territories would be organized without any mention of slavery one way or the other. When the territory applied for admission as a state, the people of the territory would vote to be slave or free. As to California, it would be directly admitted to the Union instead of going through an interim of territorial status.

Southerners cringed. They assumed that California would vote itself free, as would—down the line—New Mexico. Senators Henry Clay of Kentucky and Daniel Webster of Massachusetts worked out a new compromise. California would be admitted to the Union as a free state. The other territories acquired in the U.S.–Mexican War would be subject to "popular sovereignty." In addition, the slave auction market in the District of Columbia (long an embarrassment in a city that hosted foreign diplomats) would be closed. To appease the South, a new ironclad Fugitive Slave Law was passed, strictly forbidding Northerners to grant refuge to escaped slaves.

As with the Missouri Compromise, the Compromise of 1850 passed, but it satisfied no one.

Kansas-Nebraska Act

Many observers saw the flaming handwriting on the wall: The Union was coming apart. In 1854, the Nebraska and Kansas territories applied for statehood. In response, Congress repealed the Missouri Compromise and passed the Kansas-Nebraska Act, which left the question of slavery entirely to "popular sovereignty." There was no doubt that Nebraskans would vote themselves a free state, but Kansas was up for grabs. Pro-slavery Missourians suddenly flooded across the border, elected a pro-slavery territorial legislature, and then—mission accomplished—returned to Missouri. Anti-slavery Iowans likewise poured in, but they decided to settle permanently. Soon a chronic state of civil warfare developed between pro- and anti-slavery factions in Kansas. Violence was so commonplace that the territory was branded "Bleeding Kansas."

The anti-slavery faction set up its headquarters in the town of Lawrence. In 1856, pro-slavery "border ruffians" raided Lawrence, setting fire to a hotel and a number of houses and destroying a printing press. Several townspeople perished. During the night of May 24, John Brown, a radical abolitionist who had taken command of the territory's

"Free Soil Militia," led four of his sons and two other followers in an assault on pro-slavery settlers along the Pottawatomie River. Brown and his men hacked five to death with sabers. Brown pronounced the act payback for the sack of Lawrence.

The Dred Scott Disgrace

In 1857, at the height of the Kansas bloodshed, the United States Supreme Court weighed in with a decision in the case of Dred Scott. A fugitive slave, Scott had belonged to John Emerson of St. Louis. An army surgeon, Emerson had been transferred first to Illinois and then to Wisconsin Territory, with his slave in tow. When Emerson died in 1846, Scott returned to St. Louis and sued Emerson's widow for his freedom, arguing that he was a citizen of Missouri who was now free by virtue of having lived in Illinois (where slavery was banned by the Northwest Ordinance) and in Wisconsin Territory (where the terms of the Missouri Compromise made slavery illegal). The Missouri state court decided against Scott, whereupon his lawyers (financed by prominent abolitionists) appealed to the Supreme Court.

The high court was divided along regional lines. The anti-slavery Northern justices sided with Scott, but the pro-slavery Southerners upheld the Missouri state court decision. Chief Justice Roger B. Taney, son of wealthy Maryland slave-holders, had the final word. He ruled that neither free blacks nor enslaved blacks were U.S. citizens and therefore, neither could sue in federal court.

That ruling settled the case, but Taney went further. He held that the Illinois law banning slavery had no force on Scott after he returned to Missouri, a slave state. The law that stood in Wisconsin was likewise null and void, Taney argued, because the Missouri Compromise was (he declared) unconstitutional. According to Taney, the Compromise violated the Fifth Amendment, which bars the government from depriving an individual of "life, liberty, or property" without due process of law.

Why did Chief Justice Taney issue such a broad ruling? Shortly after his election in 1856, then President-elect James Buchanan unethically if not illegally lobbied the Supreme Court to make just such a ruling. Buchanan supported the South's desire to gain the admission of Kansas to the Union as a slave state, whereas antislavery forces favored popular sovereignty. Buchanan believed that if the Supreme Court, final arbiter of law, decided against Dred Scott, the constitutional protection of slavery where it existed would be affirmed and a civil war thereby permanently averted—and his own presidency made much easier.

Buchanan could not have been more mistaken.

The Dred Scott decision outraged abolitionists and galvanized their cause. No longer was the slavery issue a question of how the nation could expand westward while maintaining a balance in Congress. It was now Fifth Amendment issue of property. Justice Taney had put slavery beyond compromise. Only a constitutional amendment abolishing slavery would resolve the issue to the abolitionists' satisfaction. But that required ratification by two thirds of the states—an impossibility without the armed coercion of civil war.

The Least You Need to Know

- ⚙ Opposition to slavery in America came early; the first organized efforts to abolish it began in 1724.

- ⚙ Labor-intensive cotton cultivation made the Southern economy dependent on slavery, especially after the invention of the cotton gin.

- ⚙ A series of compromises staved off civil war for three decades, as Northern opposition to slavery grew stronger and Southern advocacy of it became increasingly strident.

- ⚙ The Dred Scott decision made slavery an issue transcending individual states; therefore, it made compromise impossible and civil war inevitable.

Westward the Course (1834–1846)

Two cancers consumed the American body politic: chronic war between whites and Indians, and the continued existence of slavery. The symptoms were bloody. Add to this two major wars with foreign powers—the War of 1812 and the U.S.–Mexican War—and America, in the years leading up to mid-century, seemed a pretty unhealthy place.

Yet as the cliché has it, it's all relative. Between 1800 and the 1850s, Europe was in a virtually continuous state of war. So, despite their own problems, Americans understood that they had one powerful peace-keeping asset Europe lacked: space. The West, open clear to the Pacific, surely meant America had room enough for everybody.

The Plow and the Reaper

Land aplenty was one thing; actually, *living* on it and making a living *from* it was quite another. Like the South, the West offered the prospect of large-scale farming, but most western territories and states barred slavery. Moreover, most immigrants who settled on the western lands were culturally and morally disinclined to keep slaves. Without cheap labor, how would a big piece of land be worked?

Labor wasn't the only problem. In most of the new territories, prairie soil was hard. It did not yield to the plow, but clogged it, making cultivation all but impossible. Was the nation destined to cling to its East Coast?

As would happen time and again in American history, technology changed everything.

Cyrus McCormick

By the time he was 22, Cyrus McCormick (1809–1884) had come up with a practical prototype of a horse-drawn reaper. It was equipped with a cutting bar, a reel, a divider, guards over reciprocating knives, and a platform on which the grain was deposited after having been cut. Everything was driven and synchronized by a single gear wheel. Perfected and patented in 1834, the device was an important step toward making large-scale farming possible with a minimal labor force.

VITAL STATISTICS

Before the advent of the reaper, it took 20 hours to harvest an acre of wheat. By the time the McCormick device was fully perfected, about 1895, the same task consumed less than an hour.

John Deere

The reaper solved only half the problem of large-scale farming on the stubborn prairies of the Midwest and West. While McCormick was perfecting his reaper, John Deere (1804–1886) hammered out a new kind of plow. Made of stout steel, the plow was beautifully shaped, calling to mind the prow of the graceful clipper ships of the period. It was much stronger than a conventional plow. The combination of sleek, ship-like design and steely strength made it ideal for breaking up and turning over the tough prairie soil without ever clogging.

Armed with the McCormick reaper and the John Deere plow, wave upon wave of immigrants pushed the frontier farther west with each passing year.

Martyrdom in Texas

As the prairie voids of the northern Midwest and West began to fill in, the Southwest— still territory belonging to the Republic of Mexico—was being settled by an increasing number of American colonists.

That colonization had started in 1820, when Moses Austin secured a grant from the Spanish government to establish an American colony in Texas. He fell ill and died in 1821, before he could begin the project of settlement. On his deathbed, Moses asked his son, Stephen F. Austin, to carry out his plans. Mexico, in the meantime, had won independence from Spain in the revolution of 1821. Under terms established in 1824 by an act of the new Mexican republic, along with additional agreements negotiated in 1825, 1827, and 1828, Austin brought more than 1,200 American families to Texas. By 1836, 50,000 Americans and only 3,500 Mexicans lived in the colony.

The American majority soon chafed under Mexican rule. Violent outbreaks between settlers and Mexican military garrisons were frequent. Austin repeatedly negotiated peace with the increasingly unstable Mexican government, but after Mexican president Antonio López de Santa Anna treacherously imprisoned him for two years, Austin, in 1835, urged Texans to support a Mexican revolt against Santa Anna. This appeal triggered the Texan War of Independence.

Seeking to crush the rebellion, Santa Anna led troops into Texas during January 1836 and reached San Antonio in February. There, against the advice of independence leader Sam Houston (1793–1863), militia colonel William B. Travis led a force of 189 to 257 Texans (scholars differ on the exact count), intent on making a defensive stand. They holed up behind the walls of a decayed Spanish mission formally called San Antonio de Valero but nicknamed "the Alamo" because it was close to a stand of poplars (*álamos* in Spanish).

The Texas band, which included such renowned frontier figures as Jim Bowie and Davy Crockett, held off some 1,800 Santa Anna troops for 10 days. They hoped desperately that the American nation would rally to their aid. It did not.

On March 6, the Mexican troops finally breached the mission's wall and slaughtered almost everyone inside. This Mexican tactical "victory" turned out to be a strategic disaster for Santa Anna. Sam Houston rallied Texans under the battle cry "Remember the Alamo!" and brilliantly led his ragtag army against the Mexican leader at the Battle of San Jacinto on April 21.

Defeated and captured, Santa Anna was given the choice of signing the hastily drawn up Treaty of Velasco, which granted Texas independence, or being shot. He signed, and Texas became a republic.

Westering

During the 1830s and well into the 1840s, before the McCormick reaper and the Deere plow had transformed them, the western plains were known as the Great Desert, and they remained largely unsettled as pioneers set their sights on the Far West beyond. By the early 1830s, Americans were beginning to settle in California, many of them "mountain men"— fur trappers—who turned from that profession to ranching and mercantile pursuits.

Overland Trail

Early mountain men and other explorers carried back to the East tales of the wondrous and potentially bountiful lands that lay in the direction of the sunset. Throughout the 1830s, America's westward dreams simmered. At last, on February 1, 1841, 58 settlers living in Jackson County, Missouri, met at the town of Independence to plan the first fully organized immigrant wagon train to California. By the time it assembled across the Missouri River at Sapling Grove, the party had grown to 69, including more than 20 women and children, under John Bartleson's leadership. The prominent Catholic missionary Father Pierre-Jean de Smet and the mountain man Thomas Fitzpatrick also joined the train of 15 wagons and 4 carts.

The trek consumed five months, three weeks, and four days. The following year, some 20 wagons carrying more than 100 persons made the trip. Other journeys followed each year thereafter until the completion of the transcontinental railroad in 1869 made the Overland Trail and the other trans-West routes obsolete.

Oregon Fever

Until gold was discovered in California during 1848–1849, Oregon was the strongest of the magnets drawing immigrants westward. In 1843, a zealous missionary named Marcus Whitman led 120 wagons with 200 families in the "Great Migration" to Oregon. Soon, stories of a lush agricultural paradise touched off "Oregon fever," bringing many more settlers into the Northwest.

Oregon was a hard paradise. The climate could be brutal, and diseases ranged from endemic to epidemic. Whitman worked as a missionary and a physician, ministering in both capacities to the Cayuse Indians in the vicinity of Walla Walla (in present-day Washington State). A narrow and overbearing man who insisted that the Indians accept none but the Christian God, Whitman fell afoul of the Cayuse during a measles epidemic that killed half their number. Blamed for the sickness, he and his pretty blonde wife, Narcissa, were massacred on November 29, 1847.

"What Hath God Wrought?"

In 1819, the Danish scientist Hans C. Oersted (1777–1851) noticed that a wire carrying an electric current deflected a magnetic needle. After this discovery, a number of scientists began experimenting with telegraphs, but it was a struggling American painter, Samuel F. B. Morse, who created the first practical device in the 1830s.

Morse developed a simple electromagnetic transmitter and receiver, and also created "Morse Code" to translate the alphabet into combinations of dots and dashes. He secured a patent in 1837 and, six years later, successfully lobbied Congress to fund a 40-mile demonstration line between Baltimore and Washington, D.C. On March 4, 1844, he debuted his magnetic telegraph by sending the message "What hath God wrought?" from the capital to a remote station in Baltimore.

Morse's transmitter, receiver, and code system were widely adopted. Within a single decade, the single 40-mile line had multiplied into 23,000 miles of wire networking the nation. In a burst of keystrokes, Morse compressed vast distance and gave the nation a technology that would help bind East to West.

The Least You Need to Know

- ✪ Vast spaces were always America's greatest resource and heaviest burden; a large nation was difficult to unify and govern.

- ✪ A group of American entrepreneurs colonized the Mexican frontier state of Texas, and then fought a brief, decisive war to achieve independence.

- ✪ Technology played a key role in westward expansion. The McCormick reaper and Deere plow made farming the plains practical, and Morse's telegraph made the vastness of the West less daunting.

Destiny Manifested (1846–1860)

Phrases enter and exit the American language as through a revolving door, but one phrase used in 1845 by *New York Post* editor John L. O'Sullivan to describe America's passion for the new lands of the West arrived and lingered. "It is our *manifest destiny*," O'Sullivan wrote, "to overspread and to possess the whole of the continent which Providence has given us for the development of the great experiment of liberty and federated self-government entrusted to us." Under the quasi-religious banner of "manifest destiny," the American West would be won—the obstinacy of prairie soil, the harshness of the elements, the lives and culture of the Indians, and the claims of Mexico notwithstanding.

After Texas gained its independence in 1836, the United States was reluctant to accept the newborn republic's bid for annexation. To accept Texas into the Union would not only add a slave state but would surely ignite war with Mexico. When France and England made overtures of alliance to the Republic of Texas, however, outgoing President John Tyler urged Congress to adopt an annexation resolution. Under Tyler's successor, James K. Polk, Texas was admitted into the Union on December 29, 1845.

In the meantime, England and France also seemed to be eyeing California, held so feebly by Mexico that it looked to be ripe and ready to fall into whatever hands were there to catch it.

Halls of Montezuma

Polk was moved to action. He offered Mexico $40 million for the California territory. The Mexican president turned down the offer and refused even to see President Polk's emissary. Thus rebuffed, Polk authorized the U.S. consul at Monterey (California), Thomas O. Larkin, to organize California's small American community into a separatist movement sympathetic to U.S. annexation. In the meantime, John Charles Frémont, a military officer and intrepid western explorer, marched onto the stage with the so-called Bear Flag Rebellion, in which California's independence from Mexico was proclaimed.

For Mexico, the independence of California merely added insult to injury. Mexico's most intense dispute with the United States was over the boundary of the new state of Texas. President Polk dispatched troops to defend Texas and its boundary on the Rio Grande. On May 13, 1846, after Mexican troops advanced across the river, the president asked Congress for a declaration of war.

By this time, Mexican forces had already laid siege against Fort Texas—present-day Brownsville. General Zachary Taylor, marching to the relief of the fort, faced 6,000 Mexican troops with a mere 2,000 Americans. Nevertheless, he emerged victorious in the May 8 Battle of Palo Alto.

In the meantime, early in June, official U.S. action commenced against the Mexicans in California as Stephen Watts Kearny led the "Army of the West" from Fort Leavenworth, Kansas, to California via New Mexico. Near Santa Fe, at steep-walled Apache Canyon, New Mexico's governor Manuel Armijo set up an ambush to destroy Kearny's column, but the governor's ill-disciplined troops panicked and dispersed without firing a shot. Kearny passed through the canyon unopposed and took Santa Fe. On August 15, New Mexico was annexed to the United States.

General Taylor attacked Monterrey (Mexico) on September 20, 1846, taking the city after a four-day siege. Always cautious, Taylor allowed Mexican forces to withdraw. In the meantime, Antonio López de Santa Anna, who had been living as an exile in Cuba after a rebellion had ended his dictatorship of Mexico, made a proposal to the U.S. government. He pledged to help the nation win the war, to secure a Rio Grande boundary for Texas, and to secure a California boundary through San Francisco Bay. In return, he wanted $30 million and safe passage to Mexico. American officials withheld the cash but allowed Santa Anna to return to his homeland. No sooner did he arrive than he mustered an army to defeat Zachary Taylor.

By January 1847, Santa Anna had gathered 18,000 men, about 15,000 of whom he hurled against Taylor's 4,800-man force at Buena Vista. After two days of bloody battle, Taylor forced Santa Anna's withdrawal on February 23. Despite this brilliant victory, President Polk was distressed by Taylor's repeated reluctance to pursue the defeated enemy. The president was even more worried that Taylor's victories would transform him into a military celebrity and therefore, a potential political rival. So, for both military and political reasons, Polk replaced Taylor with General Winfield Scott, hero of the War of 1812.

On March 9, Scott invaded Veracruz, beginning with the first-ever amphibious assault in U.S. military history. He laid siege against the city's fortress for 18 days, forcing Santa Anna to withdraw to the steep Cerro Gordo Canyon with 8,000 of his best troops.

Scott cannily declined the frontal attack the Mexicans expected. Instead, he sent part of his force to cut paths up either side of Cerro Gordo and Santa Anna in a pincers movement, sending his troops into retreat all the way to Mexico City.

Scott showed himself willing to take the kind of gamble Taylor would have found unthinkable. He purposely detached his rapidly pursuing army from its slower-moving supply lines to press the pursuit of Santa Anna's force. On September 13, Chapultepec Palace, the seemingly impregnable fortress guarding Mexico City, fell to Scott. On September 17, Santa Anna surrendered.

The Mexican War ended with the hastily concluded Treaty of Guadalupe Hidalgo, which was ratified by the Senate on March 10, 1848. Mexico ceded New Mexico (which also included parts of the present states of Utah, Nevada, Arizona, and Colorado) and California renouncing claims to Texas above the Rio Grande. In return, the Mexican government received a payment of $15 million.

Of God and Gold

The Mexican War was controversial. Citizens in the Northeast, especially in New England, saw it as an immoral Southern-backed land grab. Southerners and Westerners were thrilled by the war, which did add much land to the nation.

The Mormons' Trek

War was not the only engine that drove "manifest destiny." The West likewise lured seekers of God and those who lusted after gold. In the late 1820s, Joseph Smith, Jr., living in Harmony (modern Oakland), Pennsylvania, began transcribing a text he said was engraved on golden plates that had been buried near Palmyra, New York, and revealed to him by an angel named Moroni. On March 26, 1830, Smith published the text through a Palmyra printer as *The Book of Mormon*. One month later, he founded a church based on the book, which had been written by Moroni's father, the angel Mormon. It told of a struggle between two tribes—one good, the other evil—which took place in the New World long before Columbus's arrival. Moroni emerged as the sole survivor of the tribe of the good. Whoever dug up *The Book of Mormon* would be charged with restoring to the world the true Church of Christ.

At first, Smith's church had six members. By 1844, 15,000 members of the Church of Jesus Christ of Latter-Day Saints—popularly called Mormons—were settled in Nauvoo, Illinois. Persecuted wherever they went, the Mormons always lived apart in separatist villages. Outraged by Mormon polygamy, a mob murdered Joseph Smith and his brother on June 27, 1844. Smith's second-in-command, Brigham Young, decided the Mormons had to move somewhere so remote that no one would ever bother them again. Over the next two years, Young planned and executed the Mormon Trek to the Great Salt Lake in Utah.

Throughout the 1840s and 1850s, "Saints"—as Mormons called themselves—poured into the region, Young overseeing the construction of a magnificent town. He and his followers introduced into the arid Salt Lake Valley irrigation on a scale unprecedented in American agriculture. By 1865, 277 irrigation canals watered 154,000 square miles of what had been desert.

Chasing the Glitter

Johann Augustus Sutter was a bankrupt German merchant who fled his creditors, settling in Mexican California in 1838 and building a sprawling ranch in the region's fertile central valley.

On January 24, James Wilson Marshall, one of Sutter's employees, discovered gold flakes in the "race" (water course) of a new mill on the ranch. Within a month and a half of the discovery, all of Sutter's employees had deserted him in the quest for more gold. Sutter's ranch faltered and failed. Worse, his claims to the land at and around the mill were found invalid.

Sutter lost everything but, in the meantime, word of the gold strike spread east. Men dropped their tools where they stood and made the long journey—overland or around Cape Horn by sea—to California.

The trip paid off for a very few. Most prospectors found lives that were hard and, often, short.

Most men made the mistake of looking for their fortune on or in the ground. The real money was made by those who sold groceries, hardware, real estate, liquor, finance, and other necessities to the '49ers. Collis Huntington and Mark Hopkins, small merchants, made a fortune in mining supplies. Charles Crocker used the profits from his dry goods store to start a bank. Leland Stanford parlayed modest mercantile pursuits into a political career culminating in the governorship of California. Together—as the "Big Four"—Huntington, Hopkins, Crocker, and Stanford provided the major financing for the Central Pacific Railroad, the western leg of the great transcontinental railroad completed in 1869.

WHAT'S THE WORD?

People who participated in the great California Gold Rush of 1849 earned the name '49er or Forty-niner.

The California Gold Rush lasted through the eve of the Civil War and populated much of California. When gold was subsequently discovered in Nevada, Colorado, and the Dakotas, even more of the frontier West was settled. Thanks to the gold and silver rushes, the bonds of union grew stronger between East and West while those uniting North and South disintegrated. Even as it basked in the reflected glory of western gold, America was entering its darkest hours.

The Least You Need to Know

- ⚙ Although controversial, the war with Mexico greatly expanded the western territory of the United States.

- ⚙ The Mormon Trek, begun in 1847, was both the most spectacular and best-organized mass migration to the vast lands of the American West.

- ⚙ The lure of gold brought unprecedented numbers of fortune seekers to California beginning in 1849.

A Strange Flag over Sumter (1859–1862)

Abraham Lincoln was born on February 12, 1809, in a log cabin in Hardin (now Larue) County, Kentucky. In 1816, the family moved to Indiana and, finally, to Illinois in 1830. He ran for the Illinois state legislature, losing his first bid, but subsequently serving four consecutive terms (1832–1841). After setting up a successful law practice in Springfield, the state capital, he served a term (1847–1849) in the U.S. House of Representatives.

Then, admitting he "was losing interest in politics," Lincoln returned to law—until passage of the Kansas-Nebraska Act in 1854. Its doctrine of popular sovereignty potentially opened vast new territories to slavery. Lincoln admitted that the Constitution protected slavery, but he personally hated it. He ran unsuccessfully for the U.S. Senate in 1855. The following year, he left the Whig Party to join the newly formed Republicans.

In 1858, Lincoln again ran for the Senate against the Illinois incumbent, Stephen A. Douglas, accepting his party's nomination (June 16, 1858) with a powerful speech suggesting that Douglas, Chief Justice Roger B. Taney, and Democratic presidents Franklin Pierce and James Buchanan had conspired to nationalize slavery. He declared that the Kansas-Nebraska Act was a compromise doomed to fail. The nation would become either all slave or all free. "A house divided against itself," he paraphrased Mark 3:25, "cannot stand."

John Brown's Body

Lincoln soon found himself transformed from an obscure Illinois politician to his party's standard bearer. He challenged Douglas to a series of debates that captured the attention of the national press. Although Lincoln failed to win a seat in the Senate, he emerged as an eloquent, morally upright, thoroughly balanced embodiment of prevailing sentiment in the North. Radical Southerners warned that the election of any Republican, even the relatively moderate Lincoln, would mean civil war.

While Lincoln and other politicians chose the stump and the rostrum as their forums, others took more direct action.

John Brown was born on May 9, 1800, in Torrington, Connecticut, but he grew to adulthood in Ohio. He drifted from job to job but by the 1850s found his calling as an abolitionist.

Brown and his five sons settled in "Bleeding Kansas," where they became embroiled in the violence between pro-slavery and anti-slavery forces for control of the territorial government. Brown assumed command of the local Free-Soil militia. After pro-slavery forces sacked the Free-Soil town of Lawrence, Brown, with four of his sons and two other followers, retaliated with sabers, hacking to death five unarmed pro-slavery settlers along the Pottawatomie River during the night of May 24, 1856.

Brown next became obsessed with emancipating America's slaves by inciting a mass slave rebellion. He persuaded a group of Northern abolitionists to finance his scheme to capture the federal armory at Harpers Ferry, Virginia (present-day West Virginia). Using the weapons liberated from the armory, he would establish a base of operations in the mountains and direct the rebellion.

On October 16, 1859, Brown and 21 others, sixteen whites and five blacks, seized the town and broke into the armory and the nearby Hall's Rifle Works. They hunkered down, holding hostage some sixty locals, among whom was the great-grandnephew of George Washington. Brown sent two of his black "troops" to recruit local slaves, confident that these two men would raise a spontaneous army of thousands.

Combat commenced on the 17th, as local militia surrounded the armory and opened fire. As for the rebellion, not a single slave answered the call, and when the shooting started, the first civilian Brown's men killed was a free black man.

President James Buchanan sent the nearest contingent of U.S. regular troops, a company of Marines, and put them under the nearest experienced officer, U.S. Army Colonel Robert E. Lee. When Brown refused to surrender, Lee ordered the Marines to charge. In three minutes, the battle was over. Two of Brown's men fell to the Marines' bayonets, Brown was wounded by a Marine's saber, all but four of the raiders were killed, and four of the 60 hostages, including the mayor of Harpers Ferry, also died.

The wounded Brown and other survivors were arrested and tried for "treason" against the state of Virginia.

"Now, if it is deemed necessary that I should forfeit my life for the furtherance of the ends of justice," he said at his trial, "and mingle my blood further with the blood of my children and with the blood of millions in this slave country whose rights are disregarded by wicked, cruel, and unjust enactment—I submit; so let it be done."

Found guilty, he was sentenced to hang. Among those bearing witness to his execution on December 2, 1859, were a cadet class from the Virginia Military Institute taught by Professor Thomas Jackson, who, within two years, would be far better known as "Stonewall" Jackson, and a raven-haired idol of the American stage, John Wilkes Booth.

Bleak Transition

Lincoln, nominee of the brand-new Republican Party, faced Democrat Stephen A. Douglas, who had defeated Lincoln in the race for the Senate. The Democrats were fragmented, and Lincoln won a plurality of 180 electoral votes against 123 for his combined opponents.

News of a "black Republican" victory pushed the South to secession. First to leave the Union was South Carolina, on December 20, 1860; Mississippi followed on January 9, 1861; Florida on January 10; Alabama on January 11; Georgia on January 19; Louisiana on January 26; and Texas on February 1. Four days later, delegates from these states met in Montgomery, Alabama, where they wrote a constitution for the Confederate States of America and named Mississippi's Jefferson Davis provisional president. As the Union crumbled about him, lame duck president James Buchanan fretted, feebly protesting his powerlessness.

Lincoln's objective was to preserve the Union. He was even willing to consider protecting slavery where it existed, by constitutional amendment, if necessary. He believed the Fugitive Slave Act should be enforced. But his refusal to speak out until his inauguration conveyed the impression that he was opposed to *any* compromise on slavery.

VITAL STATISTICS

The popular vote was much closer than the electoral vote. Lincoln received only 1,866,452 votes against 2,815,617 votes for his combined opponents.

April 12, 1861, 4:30 A.M.

After Lincoln was sworn in on March 4, 1861, the Confederate president, Jefferson Davis, and Confederate Congress authorized an army and navy and began seizing federal civil and military installations throughout the South. Fort Sumter, which guarded Charleston harbor, was especially important. If the Confederacy could not control the key international port on the coast of South Carolina, it could not claim sovereignty.

Jefferson Davis ordered Brigadier General Pierre Gustave Toutant Beauregard to capture Fort Sumter. Beauregard accordingly laid siege to the fort, hoping to starve out post commandant Major Robert Anderson and his men.

Beauregard offered Anderson, his former West Point artillery instructor, generous surrender terms, including withdrawal with all military honors. Anderson apologetically refused, and the first shot of the Civil War was fired at 4:30 A.M. on April 12, 1861.

The ensuing bombardment lasted 34 hours before Anderson, satisfied that he had done his duty, surrendered. Incredibly, this first engagement of the war, in which some 4,000 rounds were fired, produced no casualties. The first battle of the Civil War, it was the last without bloodshed.

VITAL STATISTICS

The population of the South in 1861 was about nine million people, including three million slaves (who were not considered military assets, except as laborers). The North had 22 million people.

From Bull Run to Antietam

During the spring of 1861, Virginia, North Carolina, Tennessee, and Arkansas joined the seven original Confederate States. Yet even that number put the odds at 11 Southern states versus 23 Northern. The North had a far more extensive industrial base than the South and more than twice as many miles of railroad. As far as foodstuffs production, Northern agriculture was better organized. The entire South could scrape together no more than $27 million in specie (gold and silver), whereas the North commanded far more wealth and, with extensive diplomatic relations, could secure international credit.

The next major battle after Fort Sumter took place at Manassas Junction, Virginia, near Bull Run Creek, about 25 miles southwest of Washington. Newspapers had freely published the Union army's plan of action, and Confederate sympathizers in Washington supplied General Beauregard with more intel. He was well prepared for the Union advance and erected defenses near the Junction. There, across Bull Run Creek, his men—ultimately about 18,000 actually engaged—faced a like number of Yankees under the command of an earnest but mediocre Brigadier General Irvin McDowell.

The battle began well for the North, as McDowell pushed the rebels out of their initial positions. But then the Southern forces rallied with the arrival of a Virginia brigade led by Thomas J. Jackson. He held his ground at Henry House Hill, and Confederate commander Barnard Bee exclaimed, "There is Jackson standing like a stone wall." The epithet, Stonewall, has stuck to this day.

Inspired by Jackson and his Virginians, the Confederates rallied, breaking through the Union lines and sending, panicked Northern troops in retreat all the way to Washington.

The First Battle of Bull Run stunned the capital, which trembled in anticipation of a Confederate invasion that never came.

Seven Days

Justifiably dismayed by McDowell's performance at Bull Run, President Lincoln called on Major General George B. McClellan to take command of the main Union force, the Army of the Potomac, created in the wake of the battle. Jefferson Davis combined Beauregard's troops with those of General Joseph E. Johnston, who was given senior command of Confederate forces in Virginia. Now the major action centered in Virginia as McClellan set about building up his army with the objective of capturing Richmond, which was proclaimed the Confederate capital in May.

Timing is everything in war, and McClellan repeatedly put off his big assault on Richmond, delaying so often and so long that he lost the initiative altogether. He settled into an arduous campaign on the Virginia peninsula. The principal series of battles, called the Seven Days (June 26 through July 2, 1862), saw the loss of more men than in all the Civil War battles fought elsewhere during the first half of 1862, including another encounter that became a byword for slaughter, Shiloh (April 6 and 7, 1862).

Shiloh pitted Brigadier General Ulysses S. Grant's Army of the Tennessee and Don Carlos Buell's Army of the Ohio—about 63,000 men total—against 40,335 Confederates under Albert Sidney Johnston. Grant lost 13,047 who were killed, wounded, captured, or missing, and the Confederates lost more than 10,699, including Johnston, who was killed in action. Narrowly a Union tactical victory, the battle resulted in a strategic stalemate on the war's western front.

Back in Virginia, the Seven Days saw the placement of Robert E. Lee at the head of the South's major army, which he renamed the Army of Northern Virginia. Lee led his forces in a brilliant offensive against the overcautious McClellan, launching daring attacks at Mechanicsville, Gaines Mill, Savage's Station, Frayser's Farm, and Malvern Hill. Although Lee lost twice as many men as his adversary, he won a profound psychological victory. McClellan withdrew back up the peninsula, all the way to the James River. Richmond remained unscathed.

Back to Bull Run

Appalled and heartbroken by McClellan's repeated failure to seize the initiative, Lincoln cast about for a general to replace him. On July 11, he appointed Henry W. Halleck, whose unflattering nickname among the troops was "Old Brains." Into Virginia, Halleck sent a newly organized force, the Army of Virginia (which included three corps of the Army of the Potomac) under the pompous Major General John Pope. Lee met him with more than half the Army of Northern Virginia. At Cedar Mountain on August 9, "Stonewall" Jackson drove Pope back toward Manassas Junction, and then Lee sent the "Stonewall Brigade" to flank Pope and outmarch him to Manassas. After destroying Pope's supply depot, Jackson took a position near the first Bull Run battlefield. Pope lumbered into position to attack Jackson on August 29 just as Lee sent a wing of his army, under James Longstreet, against Pope's left flank on August 30.

The action at this Second Battle of Bull Run (August 28-30, 1862) was devastating and sent Pope reeling back across the Potomac. Union forces were effectively swept out of Virginia, and the Confederates went on the offensive. It was the low point of the war.

Perryville and Antietam

Lee audaciously conceived a double offensive. In the West, he would invade Kentucky; in the East, he would invade Maryland. Neither of these so-called border states had seceded, yet both were slave states, and capturing them would significantly expand the Confederacy. Moreover, if Louisville, Kentucky, fell to the Confederates, Indiana and Ohio would be open to invasion, with Confederate control of the Great Lakes possible. If all came to pass, the Union would be defeated.

VITAL STATISTICS

Although Antietam was a Union victory, McClellan lost more troops than Lee: 12,000 versus 10,000.

But it didn't go this way.

Inept and disputatious, Confederate general Braxton Bragg dithered and was defeated at Perryville, Kentucky, on October 8, 1862. In Maryland, Lee's invasion went well—until a copy of his orders detailing troop placement fell into the hands of George McClellan (restored to command of the Army of the Potomac after Pope's disastrous performance at Second Bull Run). McClellan massed close to 90,000 troops in front of Lee at Sharpsburg, Maryland, along Antietam Creek. On September 17, in the bloodiest single day of fighting up to that time, McClellan drove Lee back to Virginia. Indeed, only the belated, last-minute arrival of a division under A. P. Hill saved Lee's forces from total annihilation.

Emancipation Proclaimed—More or Less

Bloody—McClellan's casualties numbered 12,410; Lee's, 10,316—Antietam was a tactical draw, which Lincoln turned into a strategic victory by seizing it as the platform from which to issue his "preliminary" Emancipation Proclamation.

The President's Dilemma

Lincoln did not enter the war committed to emancipation. He personally hated slavery ("As I would not be a slave, so I would not own slaves," he once declared), but, as president, he was sworn to uphold the Constitution, which protected slavery in the slave states. More pragmatically, he feared that emancipation would propel the four slave-holding border states into the Confederate fold.

In August 1861, Lincoln prevailed on Congress to declare slaves in the rebellious states "contraband" property. As such, they could be seized by the federal government, which could then refuse to return them. Congress, dominated by abolitionist Radical Republicans, was always several jumps ahead of the president when it came to emancipation. In March 1862, Congress passed a law *forbidding* army officers from returning fugitive slaves. In July, it enacted legislation freeing slaves confiscated from owners "engaged in rebellion." With these acts, Congress edged Lincoln closer to emancipation.

The President's Solution

Secretary of State William H. Seward warned that a proclamation of emancipation would ring hollow down the depressingly long corridor of Union defeats. It was not until Antietam that Lincoln felt confident enough to issue the preliminary proclamation on September 23, 1862. This document set not a single slave free. Rather, it warned slave owners living in states "still in rebellion on January 1, 1863," that their slaves would be declared "forever free." When that deadline came and passed, Lincoln issued the "final" Emancipation Proclamation, which freed only those slaves in areas of the Confederacy that were not yet under the control of the Union army. Areas under Union military control were no longer, technically, in rebellion. Their slaves were not emancipated. Nor were slaves in the border states.

Timid as the Emancipation Proclamation may seem from a modern perspective, it served to galvanize the North by elevating the war to a higher moral plane. Slavery was now the central issue of the great Civil War, which, for many Northerners, assumed the stature of a holy crusade.

The Least You Need to Know

- ✪ John Brown's October 16, 1859, raid on Harpers Ferry energized the abolitionist movement and suggested that war between the North and the South was inevitable.
- ✪ Plagued by cautious or inept commanders, the Union army performed poorly in the first months of the war.
- ✪ The Emancipation Proclamation was a fairly timid document, which reflected Lincoln's first priority: to preserve the Union, not necessarily to free the slaves.

CHAPTER 20

The Bloody Road to Appomattox and Beyond (1863–1876)

Through the long, murderous summer of 1862, Abraham Lincoln despaired. His generals, Don Carlos Buell and George B. McClellan, failed to press their gains toward decisive victories. Frustrated, Lincoln removed Buell from command of the Army of the Ohio and replaced him with William S. Rosecrans in late October 1862. The next month, he put Ambrose E. Burnside in McClellan's place as commander of the Army of the Potomac. Rosecrans scored a very costly victory at Murfreesboro, Tennessee (December 31, 1862–January 3, 1863), forcing Braxton Bragg out of Tennessee. Burnside suffered a terrible defeat at Fredericksburg, Virginia. He tried to regain the initiative for the Union by renewing a drive on Richmond but faltered at the Rappahannock River and was mauled by Lee's army. On December 13, Burnside hurled a series of fruitless charges against the Confederate defenses at Fredericksburg. He not only failed to penetrate the Confederate lines, but he also lost 12,653 men—killed, wounded, captured, or missing—in the process.

A month after Fredericksburg, Lincoln replaced Burnside with "Fighting Joe" Hooker, who led the Army of the Potomac at Chancellorsville (May 1 through 3, 1863), again aiming to take Richmond. Hooker was defeated by Stonewall Jackson, who lost his life in the campaign, accidentally shot by one of his own troops. Lincoln replaced Hooker with George Gordon Meade on June 29, 1863, just two days before Union and Confederate forces clashed at an obscure Pennsylvania hamlet called Gettysburg.

Four Score and Seven

Anxious to move the war into Union territory and thereby undermine the Northern will to continue the fight, Lee invaded Pennsylvania with his Army of Northern Virginia (between 71,000 and 75,000 men). He had not planned to do battle at Gettysburg, a village distinguished only in that it was positioned at an important crossroads, but Lieutenant General A. P. Hill's corps of Confederates needed supplies, and the prosperous little college town looked to offer good foraging. Nearing Gettysburg on June 30, Hill came under fire from cavalry under Union Brigadier General John Buford. He regarded the crossroads as strategic and was determined to hold the high ground on the periphery of central Gettysburg.

The battle began in earnest the next day, July 1. At first, it did not go well for the Union. Hill's troops killed the dashing and much-loved Major General John F. Reynolds, commander of the Union I Corps, almost as soon as he came onto the field. Despite shock and confusion, his troops held their ground until reinforcements arrived. In the afternoon, Hill and Lieutenant General R. S. Ewell joined forces in an attack that routed the Federals through the town of Gettysburg. The forces regrouped and rallied on Cemetery Ridge, where they were joined by fresh troops from the south and east. The Confederates arrayed their forces in an encircling position, encompassing Seminary Ridge, parallel to Cemetery Ridge.

VITAL STATISTICS

Of 104,256 Union troops "present for duty" at Gettysburg, 3,155 died on the field, 14,529 were wounded (many of these subsequently died), and 5,365 were listed as captured or missing. Confederate figures are less reliable. Of 17,000-75,000 troops engaged, 3,903 were killed outright, 18,735 were wounded (a large percentage mortally), and 5,425 were listed as missing.

Thus, the field was set for the second day. Robert E. Lee attacked on July 2 and inflicted heavy casualties but was unable to outflank and destroy the Union forces.

Lee still held the initiative on the third day of battle, July 3. Persuaded that a triumph at Gettysburg, well into Northern territory, would turn the war decisively in the Confederacy's favor, Lee ordered a direct attack—across open country—on the Union's center.

Twelve thousand five hundred Confederate troops advanced against the Union position on Cemetery Ridge in "Pickett's Charge"—so called, even though Major General George Pickett commanded but three of the nine brigades involved. Attacking uphill is almost invariably a fatal proposition, and the Confederate attackers, pounded by artillery and musket fire, lost half their number.

Watching the survivors return from the failed assault that awful third day, Lee said to a subordinate: "It is all my fault." Hoping to win the war at Gettysburg, Lee had made an uncharacteristic tactical blunder and suffered a terrible defeat.

Indeed, the losses on both sides were staggering but hardest on the Confederates. For the North, with more men, hardware, and money than the South, could spend more of all three and still go on fighting. As Lee said, the Battle of Gettysburg *was* a turning point, but it did not turn the war in his favor. Lee would never again bring offensive war into Union territory.

Vicksburg and Chattanooga

While the attention of the Northern public focused most sharply on Gettysburg, Union forces under General Ulysses S. Grant were concluding a long and frustrating campaign against Vicksburg, Mississippi, the Confederacy's seemingly impregnable stronghold on the Mississippi River. The prize here was not only a fortress, but control of the great river. If the South lost the Mississippi, the Confederacy would be cut in two, the western states unable to supply or reinforce the East.

Grant campaigned against Vicksburg during the fall and winter of 1862 to 1863. On July 4, 1863, after a long siege, which inflicted great suffering on the townspeople, he finally took the prize and turned next to Chattanooga, Tennessee.

The city occupied a critical position in a bend of the great Tennessee River. Union forces under William S. Rosecrans had ousted Braxton Bragg from Chattanooga in early September 1863; but, reinforced, Bragg returned to engage Rosecrans at the Battle of Chickamauga on September 19 and 20. Bragg fielded 65,000 men against Rosecrans's 60,000. By the second day of this bloody struggle along Chickamauga Creek in northwestern Georgia, the Confederates had driven much of the Union army, in disarray, from the field.

Complete disaster was averted by Major General George H. Thomas, who heroically held the Union left flank and was for this dubbed the "Rock of Chickamauga." Moreover, Bragg failed to lay full siege to Chattanooga. He also detached troops to attack Knoxville. By failing to act with sharp focus, Bragg allowed Grant sufficient time to arrive on October 23 and reinforce the Army of the Cumberland (now under Thomas's command). Sixty thousand Union troops faced Bragg's reduced forces, about 40,000 men, in two battles set in the rugged terrain overlooking Chattanooga.

The Battle of Lookout Mountain (November 24) was called the "Battle Above the Clouds" because it was fought at an elevation of 1,100 feet above the Tennessee River and above a thick blanket of fog. The Battle of Missionary Ridge followed (November 25). In these two engagements, Thomas and Grant decisively defeated Bragg, resulting in Tennessee and the Tennessee River falling into Union hands.

To Richmond

In contrast to Meade and so many other Union commanders, Ulysses S. Grant demonstrated a willingness to fight and then fight some more. So, with the war entering its fourth year, Lincoln finally found the great general he had been searching for. In March 1864, the president named Grant general in chief of all the Union armies.

Grant's strategy was starkly simple: exploit the North's superiority of industrial strength and population. He assigned William Tecumseh Sherman command of the so-called western armies. Meade retained command of the Army of the Potomac—albeit under Grant's watchful eye. Using these two principal forces, Grant relentlessly pressed the South's Army of Tennessee and the Army of Northern Virginia.

Retreat in Reverse

The Wilderness Campaign (May through June 1864) was the first test of Grant's attrition strategy. Grant directed Meade, leading a force in excess of 100,000, to attack the 60,000 to 65,000 men of Lee's Army of Northern Virginia in a tangled woodland just 50 miles northwest of Richmond. The Battle of the Wilderness (May 5 and 6) cost 17,666 Union casualties to Lee's 11,033. Undaunted, Grant ordered Meade southeast to Spotsylvania Courthouse, where more than 118,399 Union soldiers became casualties between May 8 and 20. Still, Grant pushed, attacking Lee's right at Cold Harbor, just north of Richmond. Nearly 13,000 Union troops were killed, wounded, captured, or went missing between May 31 and June 12.

The Wilderness and Cold Harbor were Union defeats; but, instead of doing what a defeated general is supposed to do, retreat, Grant sidestepped Lee and advanced. This forced Lee to stretch his very limited resources thinner and thinner to defend the approach to Richmond.

Beginning in July 1864, Grant laid siege to Petersburg, Virginia, as he closed in on Richmond. The Siege stretched for nearly a year. It hemmed Lee in and wore him down but proved costly to both sides. Lee attempted to draw off some of Grant's strength by detaching Jubal Early with the late Stonewall Jackson's old corps, in a surprise assault against Washington, D.C., in July, but Early was quickly driven off. Union general Philip

Sheridan pursued Early into the Shenandoah Valley, defeating him at the Battle of Cedar Creek on October 19, 1864.

Just three weeks later, Lincoln was elected to a second term by a comfortable margin. Clearly, the North was prepared to continue the fight, and Petersburg's Confederate defenders—starving, sick, and exhausted—at last broke in March 1865. On April 2, Lee evacuated the Richmond front. Jefferson Davis and the entire Confederate government fled the Southern capital.

The March to the Sea

While Grant concentrated on taking Richmond, William Tecumseh Sherman invaded Georgia with forces varying from 81,758 to 112,819 men, after leaving Chattanooga in early May 1864. Sherman was opposed by Joseph P. Johnston's army of 60,000, which repeatedly fell back during the onslaught, although Johnston scored a victory at Kennesaw Mountain on June 27 when a headstrong Sherman made the mistake of launching an assault uphill. By early July, Johnston had assumed a position defending the key rail center of Atlanta. However, President Jefferson Davis, disappointed by Johnston's many retreats, brashly replaced him with General John B. Hood. A heroic but foolhardy commander, Hood attacked Sherman and lost. By September, Hood abandoned Atlanta, and the Union army's occupation of this major city greatly boosted Union morale even as it deprived the South of a key industrial center and rail hub.

After the fall of Atlanta, Hood invaded Tennessee, hoping that Sherman would turn away from the Southern heartland to pursue him there. Instead of personally pursuing Hood, however, Sherman detached General George H. Thomas to do that. Then, with about 60,000 men of his available forces, Sherman marched out of Atlanta, which was razed by a blaze for which Sherman was blamed, but which was at least partly the work of Confederates who wanted to leave Union soldiers no prizes to seize.

Sherman headed to the Atlantic Coast. The "March to the Sea" burned a broad, bitter swath of destruction all the way to Savannah. Sherman was intent on demonstrating to the people of the South that their government was incapable of protecting them.

AMERICAN ECHO

"War is at best barbarism .... Its glory is all moonshine. It is only those who have neither fired a shot, nor heard the shrieks and groans of wounded who cry aloud for blood, more vengeance, more desolation. War is hell."

—William Tecumseh Sherman, address to the graduating class of the Michigan Military Academy, June 19, 1879

In the meantime, General Hood was defeated at Franklin, Tennessee, on November 30, and General Thomas triumphed at Nashville on December 15-16, 1864, sending the ragged remnants of Hood's army limping back toward Georgia. Confederate General Joseph P. Johnston, now in command of the greatly reduced Army of Tennessee, engaged Sherman several times as the Union army stormed through the Carolinas in the spring of 1865. On April 13, 1865, Sherman occupied Raleigh, North Carolina, and on April 26 at Durham Station, Johnston formally surrendered his army.

Mr. McLean's House

Although sporadic fighting continued west of the Mississippi until the end of May 1865, the principal land campaign of the Civil War ended at Durham Station on April 26. An earlier event, however, is traditionally considered the symbolic end of the Civil War.

Following the collapse of Petersburg and the evacuation of Richmond, Robert E. Lee's Army of Northern Virginia desperately foraged for food, arriving in this quest at Appomattox Courthouse, about 25 miles east of Lynchburg, Virginia. Lee's forces, which now stood at perhaps no more than 28,000, was surrounded by some 150,000 troops of the Army of the Potomac under General George Meade.

After heavy skirmishing on the morning of April 9, Lee concluded that his was a lost cause. He and General Grant met in the parlor of a farmhouse belonging to Wilmer McLean. In a brief and cordial conference, the two generals came to terms. Lee agreed to surrender of the Army of Northern Virginia, and Grant agreed to feed his starving men and to release them, "on parole," to return to their homes.

With Malice Toward Some

Confident now of ultimate victory, President Lincoln delivered a gentle, healing message in his Second Inaugural Address on March 4, 1865, calling for a consummation of the war with "malice toward none" and "charity for all" in an effort to "bind up the nation's wounds." Weary and careworn beyond imagining, Lincoln nevertheless looked forward to peace. On the evening of Good Friday, April 14, 1865, he and his wife, Mary Todd, sought a few hours of diversion in a popular comedy called *Our American Cousin*. The play was being presented at Ford's Theatre, a short distance from the White House.

The President Attends a Comedy

John Wilkes Booth was the popular scion of America's foremost theatrical family. He conspired with a small band of followers, George A. Atzerodt, David Herold, and a former Confederate soldier who called himself Lewis Paine (his real name was Louis Thornton Powell). They plotted to murder Lincoln, Vice President Andrew Johnson, and Secretary of State William H. Seward.

On April 14, Atzerodt suddenly backed out of his assignment to kill Johnson. In the meantime, Herold held Paine's horse while Paine broke into Seward's residence. He stabbed and clubbed Seward, an aged and infirm man who was recuperating from severe injuries suffered in a carriage accident. It was a bloody scene: Seward, his son Augustus, and his daughter Fanny were all injured, as were a State Department messenger and a male nurse, but none of them died.

Booth was deadlier. He walked into Ford's Theatre, entered the president's box from behind, raised his derringer, pointed it between Abraham Lincoln's left ear and spine, and squeezed off a single shot. He then leaped from the presidential box onto the stage, shouting "Sic semper tyrannis!"—Thus ever to tyrants—the state motto of Virginia. But his right spur had caught on the Treasury Regiment banner festooning the president's box, and he hit the stage full force with his left foot, which snapped just above the instep.

As audience and actors stared in stunned silence, Booth limped across the boards and made a clean getaway into Maryland and then Virginia. He was not found until April 26, when he was cornered in a barn near Fredericksburg. Intending to smoke him out, Union soldiers set fire to the barn. Seeing the actor's form silhouetted by the flames, Sergeant Boston Corbett, acting without orders, fired a shot that fatally wounded the assassin.

Reconstruction Deconstructed

On the night of the assassination, the president was carried, comatose, to a house across the street from the theater. There Abraham Lincoln died at 7:22 A.M. the next morning. With him died any hope of "malice toward none" and "charity for all." Booth murdered Lincoln to avenge the South. In fact, the South became the most thoroughly brutalized victim of the assassination.

As the war was winding down, President Lincoln had formulated plans to set up loyal governments in the Southern states as quickly as possible. New governments had already been formed in Louisiana, Tennessee, and Arkansas, but Congress refused to recognize them. Radical Republicans, wishing to delay the restoration in part to keep Democrats out of power, passed the Wade-Davis Reconstruction Bill. This would have put off the process of readmission to the Union pending the signature of loyalty oaths. Lincoln had "pocket vetoed" the measure—declining to sign it before the end of the congressional session and thereby effectively killing it, at least until it might be reintroduced in the next session of Congress.

After Lincoln was assassinated, Vice President Andrew Johnson modified the Wade-Davis plan by issuing amnesty to anyone who took an oath pledging loyalty to the Union now and in the future. Johnson also required that the states ratify the Thirteenth Amendment (which freed the slaves), explicitly abolish slavery in their own state constitutions, repudiate debts incurred while in rebellion, and formally declare secession null and void. By the end of 1865, all the secessionist states, except for Texas, had complied.

Congress, however, complained that Johnson's program returned power to the very individuals who had brought rebellion in the first place. Moreover, the readmitted states persisted in keeping former slaves in subservience. To correct this problem, Congress passed in 1866 the Freedman's Bureau Act and the Civil Rights Act, both intended to ensure African American equality under the law. When Johnson vetoed these acts, Republicans responded by refusing to recognize the legitimacy of the Southern states and overrode the veto.

Republicans also introduced the Fourteenth Amendment, declaring African Americans to be citizens and prohibiting states from discriminating against any class of citizen. When the Southern state governments created under Johnson's plan refused to ratify the Fourteenth Amendment, Congress passed a series of Reconstruction Acts in 1867, placing the South under military occupation.

The military governments installed in the former Confederacy quickly enfranchised African Americans, and Congress forced acceptance of the Fourteenth Amendment by refusing to recognize new state governments until those governments had ratified it. Former Confederate leaders were explicitly barred from participating in the creation of the new governments.

Articles of Impeachment

In defiance of Congress, Johnson deliberately interfered with enforcing the reconstruction laws. Johnson was against slavery, but, like many white people of the period, he believed the "African race" to be naturally inferior to the white race.

In 1868, when Johnson dismissed Secretary of War Edwin M. Stanton, House Republicans charged him with violating the Tenure of Office Act. Passed in 1867, this act (later found unconstitutional by the Supreme Court) barred a president from removing, without the Senate's approval, any officeholder who had been appointed with the Senate's consent. The House impeached Johnson, but the Senate acquitted him by a single vote after a trial spanning March through May 1868.

Hail to "His Fraudulency"

Although Andrew Johnson remained in the White House, his authority was effectively neutralized. Acting in the resulting vacuum, the Radical Republicans imposed a harsh reconstruction program on the South. Intentions of great nobility were tainted by a spirit of vengeance and motives of political advantage. Reconstruction provisions included:

- Equal rights for African Americans
- The creation of state-supported free public-school systems
- Revision of labor laws to make them fairer to workers
- Revision of tax laws to make them generally more equitable

Laudable as these objectives were, radical reconstruction also imposed a punitive tax burden on the South and created conditions that led to widespread, ruinous corruption. In many places, uneducated former slaves were thrust into high-level government positions for which they were wholly unprepared. Northern white opportunists took advantage of the South's prostration through loan sharking and buying up distressed properties on the cheap.

Deprived of power by the federal government, Southern whites set up shadow governments and established the Ku Klux Klan and other white-supremacist vigilante groups. During the early 1870s, white resistance to reconstruction often turned violent.

In this tumultuous atmosphere, the presidential election of 1876 resulted in a majority of popular votes going to Democrat Samuel J. Tilden. However, the Republicans challenged and reversed the *electoral* vote tally in the three Southern states they still controlled under Reconstruction legislation. The Republicans effectively stole the election from Tilden and gave it to their candidate, Rutherford B. Hayes.

After months of bitter dispute, both sides agreed to send the matter to a special congressional commission. It ruled Hayes the winner after a secret bargain was struck with Democrats, whereby the Republicans pledged to immediately end Reconstruction in exchange for the White House. Southern blacks were now entirely at the mercy of Southern whites; freed from slavery, they entered a new period of oppression. As for Hayes, a cynical press dubbed him "His Fraudulency." He served a single term as best he could but was doomed to be regarded as one of the nation's less effective presidents.

The Least You Need to Know

- ✪ Victory in the Civil War was the result of numbers: The North had more men, more money, and a higher manufacturing capacity than the South.

- ✪ The 1868 impeachment of Lincoln's successor, President Andrew Johnson, was a measure of how bitterly divided the nation remained after the Civil War.

- ✪ Republicans and Democrats struck a backroom deal that elevated Rutherford B. Hayes to the presidency in 1876 in exchange for Republican abandonment of Reconstruction.

PART 5

Rebuilding the House

The years following the Civil War saw the full-scale settlement of the American West and increased pressure on the Indians, whose tribes were broadcast across the plains and mountains. War between settlers and Native Americans, chronic since the days of Columbus, now became acute, and the U.S. Army was called upon to fight three decades of "Indian Wars." Against this background, the West produced real-life legends: cattle barons, cowboys, outlaws, fortune seekers, and fortune makers. The late nineteenth century was an era marked by technological triumphs, by the creation of financial empires, and by the corrupting force of crooked politics. Good and bad, all seemed bigger than life, as you'll see in the chapters that follow.

Sea to Shining Sea (1862–1878)

Armies, money, and the will to continue the fight won the Civil War and restored the Union. Something else ensured final victory: call it the "American Dream."

Even amid the awful carnage of a war that tore them apart, Americans looked west. There, it seemed, was refuge from the war. There was a place for new beginnings. There was the future. And what is the future, if it is not a dream?

Home Sweet Homestead

On May 20, 1862, President Lincoln signed into law the Homestead Act, which granted 160 acres of public land in the West as a homestead to "any person who is the head of a family, or who has arrived at the age of 21 years, and is a citizen of the United States, or who shall have filed his declaration of intention to become such."

The Homestead Act was a bold experiment in public policy and was shaped by years of hard experience with the distribution of unsettled land. Traditionally, such territories had drawn unscrupulous speculators, who figured out ways to come into control of vast acreage and make quick fortunes. The new law sought to avoid such abuses and aspired to a high degree of democracy. The Homestead Act opened the West to hundreds of thousands of American families.

VITAL STATISTICS

Under the Homestead Act, some 600,000 farmers received clear title to approximately 80 million acres of formerly public land by the end of the nineteenth century.

By Rut and by Rail

Transportation and westward movement have always been a chicken-and-egg proposition in this country. Farmers and others clamored for better and cheaper transportation, while freight carriers did what they could to promote a level of settlement that would make service to the outlying regions profitable. The earliest western transportation was by river, with shallow-draft flatboats abounding on the muddy Missouri and its tributaries. Then, spurred by the discovery of gold in California, stagecoach and freight entrepreneurs took the plunge, investing in coaches, livestock, and road improvements.

By the 1850s, Adams Express Company and Wells, Fargo & Company were engaged in cutthroat competition for California freighting. The success of California overland operations prompted others to establish routes elsewhere in the West, often with government subsidy in the form of postal contracts. By 1854, William H. Russell and William B. Waddell merged with their principal competitor, Alexander Majors, to create a freighting empire that endured until the Civil War.

The Great Iron Road

After the success of the Erie Canal, completed in 1825 and linking New York City with the Great Lakes, other eastern seaport cities rushed to build canal systems. Baltimore was an exception and chose instead to invest in a brand-new transportation technology: the railroad. Begun in 1828, the Baltimore and Ohio Railroad reached the Ohio River, principal artery to the West, by 1852. At about this time, railroads were also being built in the Midwest. The Chicago and Rock Island Railroad (later called the Chicago, Rock Island, and Pacific Railroad, but far better known as the Rock Island Line) became the first rail route to the Mississippi River in 1854. By 1856, the route bridged the river and penetrated the fertile farmlands of Iowa. Other midwestern lines soon followed.

In 1853, Congress authorized Secretary of War Jefferson Davis to conduct detailed surveys of potential transcontinental rail routes. The result of the hasty surveys was, again, inconclusive (although they added significantly to the general knowledge of the West). Besides, Davis—the Mississippian who would become president of the Confederacy with the outbreak of civil war—had stacked the deck in favor of a southerly route. He wanted the transcontinental line to pass through his part of the country.

The wrangling over the choice of routes might have gone on forever had it not been for one remarkable man. Theodore Dehone Judah (1826–1863), son of an Episcopal clergyman in Bridgeport, Connecticut, was a civil engineer with a genius for building railroads. In 1854, Colonel Charles Wilson, president of California's Sacramento Valley Railroad, commissioned Judah to survey a right-of-way from Sacramento to the gold-mining town of Folsom. Judah reported to Wilson that this stretch of track could serve as something far more significant than a link to little Folsom. The track was ideally suited to be the Pacific end of a transcontinental railroad. Wilson and other backers were very excited, but then the gold petered out at Folsom, and the rail line went no farther.

Judah did not stop, however. He lobbied Washington, even as he continued searching for a viable pass across the Sierra Nevada. Judah rounded up seven backers, including four whose fortunes were destined to be made by the railroad: Collis P. Huntington and Mark Hopkins, partners in a hardware store; Leland Stanford, wholesale grocer; and Charles Crocker, dry goods merchant. Returning to Washington, D.C., Judah successfully lobbied for passage of the Pacific Railway Act of 1862, authorizing the Central Pacific and the Union Pacific railroads to begin construction of a transcontinental line. The Central Pacific would build from the West Coast eastward, and the Union Pacific would build westward from Omaha, Nebraska.

With the North and South torn apart by war, President Lincoln and Congress were eager to bind the northern part of the nation together along its east-west axis. They were so eager, in fact, that they provided railway entrepreneurs with unprecedented amounts of government subsidy. The Railway Act granted huge tracts of land to the railroad, along with massive construction loans. Additionally, at the behest of Abraham Lincoln, multimillionaire congressman Oake Ames and his brother Oliver created one corporation to build the railroad and another corporation to finance the construction. The latter was named Crédit Mobilier, after the company that had successfully financed the French railway system 10 years earlier. The Ames brothers made investors an offer they couldn't refuse: Crédit Mobilier, run by the directors (principal investors) of the Union Pacific, was paid by the Union Pacific to build the Union Pacific. The directors made a profit on the railroad as well as on the cost of building it. The scheme was an open door to fraud, and construction bills were routinely padded.

In the end, scandal and greed could take nothing away from the heroism and wonder of what it meant to build a transcontinental railroad, especially in an age when earth was moved and iron rails laid not by machines, but by human muscle.

Under the leadership of Grenville Mellon Dodge and another ex-army general, John Stephen Casement, the Union Pacific began laying prodigious lengths of track—266 miles in 1866 alone. The tracks were set into place mostly by unskilled Irish immigrants, who received room and board in addition to their pay. On the Central Pacific, the bulk of the work force was Chinese, who were paid at about the same rate as the Irish but who had to furnish their own tent accommodations and their own food.

Taskmasters drove the laborers relentlessly, heedless of life and limb, because, although they would be joined, the Central Pacific and Union Pacific companies were actually in fierce competition with one another. The volume of their government land grants was directly proportional to the amount of track that was laid. In fact, in the absence of an officially predetermined meeting point for the converging tracks, survey parties laid out some 200 miles of overlapping, parallel, entirely redundant right-of-way. U.S. Secretary of the Interior Orville H. Browning belatedly intervened, naming Promontory Summit, 56 miles west of Ogden, Utah, as the meeting point. (Many histories of the West confuse Promontory Summit with nearby Promontory Point.)

A Golden Spike at Promontory

The ceremonial union of the two lines at Promontory Summit was set for May 8, 1869. Leland Stanford of the Central Pacific almost failed to arrive because of a train wreck. Thomas C. Durant of the Union Pacific was kidnapped en route and held hostage by tie cutters his company had not paid for months, delaying the ceremony by two days. Durant telegraphed for money and was released.

On May 10, 1869, workers and executives alike were at last prepared to savor their finest moment. But the event did not go quite as planned.

Chinese laborers, acutely aware of how Caucasians felt about them, were lowering the last rail into place when a photographer hollered, "Shoot!" The laborers dropped the quarter-ton rail and ran.

Then there was elegantly frock-coated Leland Stanford, who took upon himself the honor of joining the last eastbound and westbound rails with a single commemorative Golden Spike. It was wired to the telegraph, so that each blow would be transmitted across the nation.

Stanford raised the heavy sledge, brought it down—and clean missed. After another embarrassing try, laborers in shirtsleeves lent a hand, and the deed was done. From sea to shining sea, the United States was bound by bands of iron.

The Least You Need to Know

- The Homestead Act of 1862 populated and cultivated the space between the Mississippi and the Pacific and brought to the West an unprecedented degree of family- and community-based settlement.

- Construction of the great transcontinental railroad was an epic task comprised of bold imagination, limitless resolve, and great heroism, as well as rampant political and financial corruption.

- Technology, in the form of the transcontinental railroad, did more than politics to bind East and West into a single nation.

Warpath (1862–1891)

The West was a land of many dreams, but what we seem to remember most vividly today are the nightmares. On the vast stage of prairie and mountain, the last act of a four-century tragedy was played out. The curtain had been raised by the crew of Christopher Columbus, who clashed in 1493 with the people they called Indians on an island they called Hispaniola. From then on, warfare between Native Americans and European Americans was chronic.

Read any standard history of the Civil War, and you will learn that this epic struggle was mainly an eastern conflict. In the West, battles were smaller and less frequent—yet often, they were even uglier.

Blue, Gray, and Red

The great fear of Union loyalists in the West was that Confederates would recruit Indian allies on the promise of securing for them land and other rights. To a limited extent, Confederates did drum up support from members of some eastern tribes, but both the North *and* South recruited troops from among tribes that had been "removed" west to Indian Territory: the Cherokees, Chickasaws, Choctaws, Creeks, and Seminoles. Among the *indigenous* western tribes, however, virtually no warriors served either the Union or the Confederacy. Nevertheless, they played a significant role in the war. To begin with, their presence drew off some Union troops who otherwise would have been used against Confederates. Far more important, however, were the demands of the Civil War, which meant that fewer troops were available to occupy the western posts. The absence of the army gave the Indians license to raid settlers with relative impunity.

The entire Southwest was seared by violence. The outbreak of the Civil War stripped the U.S. Army's western outposts of 313 officers—one third of the *entire* officer corps—who resigned their commissions to fight on the side of the Confederacy. Confederate lieutenant colonel John Robert Baylor exploited the Union's weakened position to take possession of Arizona Territory for the Confederacy. Baylor was able to roll over the greatly diminished Union presence, but he didn't count on the hostility of the Chiricahua and Mimbreño Apaches, who terrorized the region. Baylor hastily formed the Arizona Rangers in August 1861 and ordered them to "exterminate all hostile Indians."

In the meantime, hoping to retain New Mexico, Union General Edward R. S. Canby negotiated a treaty with the Navajos, pledging to distribute rations to them. At Fort Fauntleroy, designated site of the distribution, an ostensibly friendly series of horse races was run between Navajos and a regiment of New Mexico volunteers. The featured event was a race between a volunteer lieutenant and Chief Manuelito (ca. 1818–1894). Heavy wagers were laid, and from the beginning, it was apparent that Manuelito—an expert horseman—was not in control of his mount. After he came in a poor second, Manuelito protested that his bridle had been slashed, and he demanded a rematch. The soldiers refused, a fight broke out, and the troops began firing indiscriminately. Forty Indians were killed, and the Navajos retaliated. Through August and September, Kit Carson, leading the First New Mexico Volunteer Cavalry, relentlessly counterattacked the vengeance seekers.

The result was total defeat of the Navajos by the end of 1863, who were exiled to a desolate reservation called the Bosque Redondo. Eventually, 8,000 jammed the reservation, under conditions so intolerable that, after the Civil War—in an all-too-rare act of humanity—a U.S. peace commission granted Navajo pleas to return to their homelands.

Massacre in Minnesota

While the Southwest erupted, storm clouds also gathered far to the north. Unlike the Navajos, the Santee Sioux of Minnesota seemed willing to accept concentration on a reservation. But as increasing numbers of German and Scandinavian immigrants moved into the region, the Santees found themselves confined to a diminishingly narrow strip of land along the Minnesota River. Worse, provisions and annuity money guaranteed them by treaty were routinely withheld. In June of 1862, Chief Little Crow led the Santees to the Yellow Medicine Indian Agency to demand the pledged distribution of provisions and funds. When these items were not forthcoming by August, the Santee rose up and raided in and around the town of New Ulm. By the end of the month, 2,000 Minnesotans were refugees, and the Sioux had killed between 350 and 800 others.

Through the rest of August and most of September, fighting in Minnesota was brutal. On September 26, 2,000 Santee hostiles surrendered to General Henry Hopkins Sibley (not to be confused with Confederate General Henry Hastings Sibley), and the deadliest Indian uprising in the history of the West was at an end.

War for the Bozeman Trail

Throughout the Civil War, fighting with the Apaches continued. Wars also broke out with the Shoshonis, Bannocks, Utes, and Northern Paiutes—also called the Snakes—in parts of Wyoming, Nevada, Utah, and Idaho. Wars erupted with the Navajos in the Southwest and with the combined forces of the Cheyenne and Arapaho tribes in Colorado. All these wars ended badly for the Indians, although, as one officer observed, "Ten good soldiers are required to wage successful war against one Indian."

One of the few conflicts from which the Indians emerged unquestionably victorious broke out just after the end of the Civil War. Military authorities had anticipated that the collapse of the Confederacy would free up many troops for service in the West. What happened instead is that the Union army rushed to demobilize, and the post-Civil War army of the West shrank. A modest force under Colonel Henry B. Carrington was sent to protect the Bozeman Trail, a major route of western migration through Wyoming and Montana. The trail was being menaced by Oglala Sioux led by Red Cloud, who was determined to resist a white invasion of his people's land. Carrington was not popular with his officers, who felt that he devoted too much time to building forts and not enough to fighting Indians.

One subordinate, Captain William J. Fetterman, boasted that with just 80 men, he could ride through the entire Sioux nation. On December 21, 1866, Fetterman was given his chance to make good on the boast. Sent with a detachment of 80, his mission was to relieve a wood-hauling wagon train that was being harassed by Indians. Fetterman found himself up against 1,500 to 2,000 warriors led by Crazy Horse, and his command was wiped out in what came to be called the Fetterman Massacre.

Appalled by the Fetterman disaster, a peace commission concluded a treaty with Red Cloud on April 29, 1868, promising (among other things) to abandon the Bozeman Trail— which, in any case, the commissioners well knew, was about to be rendered obsolete by the transcontinental railroad.

A Plague of Pursuers

General William Tecumseh Sherman, in charge of western operations, decried the peace with Red Cloud as humiliating.

From April to July 1867, one of Sherman's best commanders, the Civil War hero Winfield Scott Hancock, fruitlessly pursued the Cheyenne and Sioux through Kansas. The following year, Sherman's most able lieutenant, another Civil War commander, General Philip Sheridan, conducted a harrowing winter campaign against the Sioux and Cheyenne. This campaign proved as punishing to the pursuers as to the pursued, all of whom suffered bitterly in relentless cold.

The colorful lieutenant colonel of the 7th Cavalry, George Armstrong Custer, laid claim to the biggest victory of "Sheridan's Campaign" when he attacked a peaceful Cheyenne camp on the Washita River. Among the 103 Indians he and his men killed were 93 women, old men, and children. Chief Black Kettle, though a leading advocate of peace, was slain along with his wife.

Struggle for the Black Hills

The futility and tragedy of Hancock's and Sheridan's campaigns were typical of the so-called Indian Wars. In 1873, the short but intense Modoc War broke out in California because a tiny tribe stubbornly refused to leave an utterly worthless volcanic wasteland, which the government coveted despite its manifest lack of value. In 1874, the Red River War was launched to punish the Comanches and Cheyennes for attacking a group of white hunters at Adobe Walls, Texas. At about the same time, an expedition led by Colonel George Armstrong Custer discovered gold in the Black Hills, the land most sacred to the Sioux. When government attempts to persuade the Indians to sell or lease the Black Hills failed, they were summarily ordered to vacate. The Sioux refused, and war erupted.

AMERICAN ECHO

Fortunately, genocidal phrases rarely enter folklore, but everybody knows the expression "The only good Indian is a dead Indian." It originated with General Philip Sheridan, when a Comanche named Tosawi came to him to sign a treaty after Custer's "victory" at Washita. "Tosawi, good Indian," said the Indian. Sheridan replied: "The only good Indians I ever saw were dead." The phrase was subsequently modified through repetition.

The Sioux were led by the charismatic Tatanka Iyotake, better known as Sitting Bull. On June 17, Sitting Bull mounted a pounding attack against General George Crook's column at the Rosebud Creek in southern Montana. This event made Custer more determined than ever to hunt down and destroy the "hostiles."

On the morning of June 22, 1876, to the strains of its jaunty regimental tune, "Garry Owen," the 7th Cavalry passed in review before Generals Alfred Terry and John Gibbon. They were embarking on what the commanders conceived as a final, coordinated pincers campaign against the Sioux. As Colonel Custer rode off to join his men, Gibbon called after him: "Now, Custer, don't be greedy, but wait for us."

Custer answered, "No, I will not."

REMEMBER THIS

Sitting Bull (Tatanka Iyotake, 1831–1890) made an early reputation as a warrior and was revered for his great bravery, strength, generosity, and wisdom. His fame and influence spread far beyond his own Hunkpapa Sioux people. With Chiefs Crazy Horse and Gall, Sitting Bull led resistance against the white invasion of the sacred Black Hills after gold was discovered there in 1874. Following Custer's annihilation at the Little Bighorn in 1876, Sitting Bull and his closest followers fled to Canada. Upon his return to the United States in 1881, Sitting Bull was imprisoned for two years and then sent to Standing Rock Reservation. In 1883, he traveled as a performer with Buffalo Bill Cody's Wild West Show. Buffalo Bill was perhaps the only white man Sitting Bull ever trusted.

In 1890, Sitting Bull was identified with the anti-white religious movement known as the Ghost Dance. He was killed during a scuffle when reservation police (who were Indians) attempted to arrest him on December 15, 1890.

Frustrated by long, futile pursuits, Custer—ever ambitious for martial glory—was determined to fight it out whenever and wherever he could. That is why, on June 25, 1876, when his scouts discovered a Sioux camp and warriors near the Little Bighorn River, Custer decided not to wait until the next day, when he was supposed to rendezvous with the others. Instead, he resolved to immediately attack. First, he sent Captain Frederick Benteen and 125 men south to make sure the Sioux had not moved to the upper valley of the Little Bighorn. Then he sent another 112 men under Major Marcus A. Reno in pursuit of a small body of warriors he had sighted. With his remaining troopers, Custer planned to charge the Sioux village. But it was soon apparent that Reno and his men were being overwhelmed, and Custer dispatched his bugler, Giovanni Martini, to recall Benteen. Custer then entered the fray, leading his men against the warriors. Almost immediately, they were engulfed by huge numbers of Sioux warriors, who killed Custer and 210 cavalrymen. Reno, joined by Benteen—368 officers and men total—held off a relentless siege for the next two days. U.S. Army casualties totaled about 268 killed and about 55 wounded. Sitting Bull reported 36 killed and some 168 warriors wounded. Red Horse put these numbers at 136 killed and 160 wounded.

"I Will Fight No More Forever"

The Battle of the Little Bighorn was the last major Indian victory of the Indian Wars. In subsequent engagements, the Sioux were defeated by the army's two most successful Indian fighters, Colonel Ranald S. Mackenzie and Colonel (later Lieutenant General) Nelson A. Miles. It was Miles who finally subdued the Nez Perces at the five-day Battle of Bear Paw Mountain in Montana (September 30 through October 5, 1877).

Led by Chief Joseph the Younger, a faction of the Nez Perces refused to leave their homeland in the Wallowa Valley of Oregon. Troops under the command of Major General Oliver O. Howard and Colonel Miles pursued and battled some 800 Indians over 1,700 miles of the most inhospitable terrain on the continent. When it was over, Joseph surrendered on October 5, 1877. "I am tired of fighting," he declared. "My people, some of them, have run away to the hills, and have no blankets, no food; no one knows where they are—perhaps freezing to death. I want to have time to look for my children and see how many of them I can find. Maybe I shall find them among the dead. Hear me, my chiefs! I am tired; my heart is sick and sad. From where the sun now stands I will fight no more forever."

After Geronimo

The pursuit of the Nez Perces involved a concerted military operation focused on a small band of fugitives. Down in the Mexican border region, an entire army task force was devoted to the pursuit of a *single* Indian. His Apache name was Goyathlay (One Who Yawns), but he was better known by the name the Mexicans gave him: Geronimo (1829–1909).

Since 1850, Geronimo had resisted Mexican and American settlers and military authorities. At last, in May 1882, Apache scouts working for the U.S. Army persuaded Geronimo and his followers to return to the reservation he had fled. But he fled again on May 17, 1885, with 35 warriors and 109 women and children. In January 1886, a small army unit, together with Apache scouts, penetrated deep into Mexico. They found Geronimo, who surrendered to General George Crook. Geronimo escaped one more time, but ultimately surrendered to Nelson Miles on September 4, 1886. Geronimo and some 450 other Apaches were sent to Florida for confinement in Forts Marion and Pickens. In 1894, the Apaches were removed to Fort Sill, Indian Territory (present-day Oklahoma), and Geronimo quietly lived out the rest of his life as a rancher.

A Place Called Wounded Knee

In 1886, when Geronimo surrendered to General Miles, 243,000 Native Americans were confined to 187 reservations. With Geronimo's last resistance extinguished, the Indian Wars were practically at an end.

Yet if the body of defiance was dead, its spirit lingered. Wovoka, the son of a Paiute shaman, began to preach to the reservation Indians, foretelling a new world in which only Indians dwelled, generations of slain braves came back to life, and the buffalo (nearly hunted to extinction during the first two-thirds of the nineteenth century) were again plentiful. To hasten this deliverance, Wovoka counseled, all Indians must dance the Ghost Dance and follow the paths of peace.

Among a people who had lost all hope, the Ghost Dance religion rapidly spread. At Pine Ridge, South Dakota, leaders among the Teton Sioux called not for peace but armed rebellion. The arrival of troops under Nelson A. Miles seemed only to make matters worse. As a precaution, Indian reservation police were sent on December 15, 1890, to arrest Sitting Bull, domiciled at Standing Rock Reservation. A scuffle broke out, and the most revered chief of the Plains tribes was slain.

In the meantime, Chief Big Foot of the Miniconjou Sioux was making his way to Pine Ridge. Miles assumed that his purpose was to bring to a boil the simmering rebellion, and he dispatched the 7th Cavalry to intercept him and his followers. The troops caught up with the Indians on December 28, 1890, at a place called Wounded Knee Creek, on the Pine Ridge Reservation.

Not only did Big Foot lack hostile intentions, he was, although desperately ill with pneumonia, traveling to Pine Ridge to try to persuade the rebellion leaders to surrender. Neither Miles nor Colonel James W. Forsyth, commander of the 7th Cavalry, were aware of the nature of Big Foot's mission. Forsyth quietly surrounded the chief's camp, deploying four 42 mm Hotchkiss guns (rapid-fire revolving cannons) on the surrounding hills. On December 29, the soldiers entered the camp and began to confiscate the Indians' weapons. A hand-to-hand fight developed, shots were fired—it is unclear whether these came from the Indians or the soldiers—and then the Hotchkiss guns opened up, firing almost a round a second at men, women, and children.

Nobody knows just how many died at Wounded Knee. The bodies of Big Foot and 153 other Miniconjous were found, but many more limped or crawled away. It is likely that some 300 of the 350 camped beside the creek ultimately lost their lives.

Another group of Indians ambushed the 7th Cavalry on December 30, but quickly withdrew. Two weeks later, on January 15, 1891, the entire Sioux nation formally surrendered to U.S. Army officials. It was a miserable end to 400 years of racial warfare on the American continent.

The Least You Need to Know

- ✪ Few Indians directly participated in the Civil War, but some did take advantage of a reduced military presence in the West to raid and plunder.

- ✪ The Indian Wars in the West, spanning the Civil War years to 1891, consisted mainly of long, exhausting pursuits and relatively few battles.

- ✪ To force the Indians onto reservations, the U.S. Army fought a total war, targeting women, children, and old men, as well as warriors.

- ✪ The massacre—some insist on calling it a battle—at Wounded Knee (December 29, 1890) ended the Indian Wars, but it has remained a shameful symbol of the long clash between the European Americans and Native Americans of North America.

Exploitation and Enterprise (1869–1908)

The phrase "Wild West" has become so worn with use that it's hard to say the second word *without* adding the first to it. The spirit that marked the West pervaded national life during the years following the Civil War. If the West had its cowboys and its outlaws, so did the world of big business and power politics in such eastern cities as New York and Washington, D.C. It seemed that fortunes were made and lost overnight. A wealth of new inventions suddenly materialized, accelerating American life to a pace some found frenzied. And if tycoons and inventors were pulling the strings, working men and women were often the ones being jerked around.

An Empire of Cows

The West equaled space, but the equation balanced out differently for different people. To the homesteader, space meant a place to live. To the cattleman, space meant grass and water to fuel the beef herds that made his fortune.

Before the U.S.–Mexican War, even *Texas* ranches were modest in size, but the war brought a tremendous demand for beef to feed the U.S. Army. Once the cattle industry geared up for this need, it never pulled back. Texans started to drive cattle beyond the confines of the ranch, pushing herds northward to fatten on the grass of public lands before being shipped east.

The range cattle industry didn't just make beef; it also created the single most beloved, celebrated, talked about, and sung about worker in American history. If generations of little boys and girls across the Atlantic grow up on tales of knights in shining armor, American children have long been raised on the lore of the noble riders of the range. Cowboys embody a powerful American myth of freedom and self-sufficiency. But from the cold, hard perspective of economic reality, "cowboy" was a job for desperate men: down-and-out ex-Confederates who had lost all they owned; liberated black slaves who, suddenly masterless, found themselves at loose ends; Indians who struggled at the bottom of the socioeconomic ladder; and Mexicans, who shared that bottom rung.

The most demanding labor was the trail drive, in which cowboys moved a herd of cattle to northern ranges for maturing or to market at railhead cattle towns like Abilene, Ellsworth, and Dodge City, Kansas; Pueblo and Denver, Colorado; and Cheyenne, Wyoming. Pay was about $100 for three or four months' work.

Law and Disorder

It was not unusual for a cowboy to blow his whole $100 stake during a few nights in the cattle town that lay at the end of the trail. The towns served as points of transfer from the trail to the rails. For the cowboy, a stay in town meant a bath, a shave, a woman (300 prostitutes plied their trade in the small town of Wichita), and plenty to drink (in many towns, saloons outnumbered *all* other buildings two to one). Gunfights were commonplace, but neither so frequent nor so violent as they are on the streets of some American cities today.

Arising from the mass of casually violent men were more than a few career criminals. Some have entered into American legend. During the Civil War, Jesse James and his older brother Frank joined the fierce Confederate guerrilla bands of William Quantrill and "Bloody Bill" Anderson. In the guise of carrying out military operations, these guerrillas were no better than vicious gangsters, and their units became the schools of a generation of accomplished criminals. Cole Younger and Arch Clement, who became principal members of the James Gang, were also Quantrill-Anderson alumni.

The gang robbed its first bank in February 1866 and continued to prey upon banks, stagecoaches, and trains until 1876. At that time, determined citizens ambushed and decimated the gang during a robbery attempt in Northfield, Minnesota. The James brothers escaped and formed a new gang, which included a recruit named Robert Ford. On April 3, 1882, eager to claim a bundle of reward money, the newcomer shot and killed Jesse, who was living in St. Joseph, Missouri, under the alias of Thomas Howard. In a popular ballad, Ford was reviled as the "dirty little coward who shot Mr. Howard and laid poor Jesse in his grave." Contemporary legend, dime novels, and movies and television transformed another outlaw into legend.

Markets and Monopolies

Jesse James and a host of lesser figures were unquestionably criminals. But who were their victims? As many Americans saw it, they never victimized innocent citizens but preyed upon big banks, big railroads, and big money—institutions that daily robbed the "common man." Victims? They were the American majority not born a Gould or a Rockefeller.

As for government, most people believed that lawmakers and cops could be counted on to go with the money. People who lived during the years following the Civil War took to calling their era the Gilded Age—after the title of a novel written in 1873 by Mark Twain and Charles Dudley Warner satirizing a society glittering with showy wealth but corrupt to the core.

Andrew Johnson, having narrowly escaped removal from office, was succeeded in the White House by Ulysses Simpson Grant in 1869. He proved one of the nation's greatest generals, but in two White House terms, Grant naïvely surrounded himself with scoundrels in thrall to big business. In the infamous 1883 phrase of railroad magnate William H. Vanderbilt, "The public be damned!"

Rockefeller's Oil

Following the Civil War, the nation ran on rails and was fueled by gold. Those who controlled either trains or finance drove the nation.

There was gold, and then there was *black* gold. In 1859, oil was struck in western Pennsylvania. This event gave a young Ohioan—his gaunt visage and thin lips lending him the air of an undertaker—an idea. John Davison Rockefeller (1839–1937) decided that oil would become a big business and that his hometown of Cleveland was ideally situated to refine and distribute it to the nation. Rockefeller built a refinery there in 1862 and put together the Standard Oil Trust, an amalgam of companies by which he came to control all phases of the oil industry: extraction, refining, distribution. Standard Oil was the first of many vertically integrated industrial trusts formed after the Civil War.

The Gospel of Wealth

The Gilded Age was an epoch of naked greed, the like of which would not be seen until the merger-crazy 1980s and the scandal-ridden opening decades of the twenty-first century.

Not that the era was entirely heartless. Andrew Carnegie (1835–1919) came to the United States with his impoverished family from Scotland in 1848. As a youth, he worked in a cotton factory, then in a telegraph office, and finally for the Pennsylvania Railroad, rising quickly through the executive ranks until he became head of the western division in 1859. In 1865, Carnegie formed the Keystone Bridge Company, the first in a series of iron and steel concerns he came to own. Consolidating his holdings in 1899 as the Carnegie Steel Company, he sold out to J. P. Morgan's United States Steel Company in 1901 for $492 million—roughly the equivalent of five billion of today's dollars. (And income tax wouldn't come into existence until ratification of the Sixteenth Amendment in 1913!)

Carnegie was as ruthless as any of his fellow robber barons, but in 1889, he published in the *North American Review* an essay titled "Wealth" but better known for what it preached, "The Gospel of Wealth." In this piece, Carnegie reeled out the familiar Social Darwinist line that wealth was essential for civilization and that the natural law of competition dictated that only a few would achieve wealth. But he added a twist. The rich, he wrote, had a moral responsibility to use their money for the benefit of society. "The man who dies rich," Carnegie proclaimed, "dies shamed."

As the Gilded Age drew to a close, from 1901 until his death, Carnegie dedicated himself to philanthropy, giving more than $350 million to many causes, focusing on ways to leverage his donations by endowing enterprises that educated or otherwise improved society. He founded more than 2,500 public libraries, and established the Carnegie Institute of Pittsburgh, the Carnegie Institution at Washington, the Carnegie Foundation for the Advancement of Teaching, the Carnegie Endowment for International Peace, and the Carnegie Corporation of New York. Many other robber barons took the Gospel of Wealth to heart. Rail magnate Leland Stanford founded and endowed Stanford University. Rockefeller endowed the University of Chicago, created the Rockefeller Institute of Medical Research, established the Rockefeller Foundation, and bought vast tracts of land that became national parks. The tradition continues to this day through the likes of Microsoft multibillionaire Bill Gates and super investor Warren Buffett.

An Age of Invention

If, blooming among the weeds of greed, the Gospel of Wealth seemed miraculous, so did the incredible series of inventions that burst forth during what might otherwise have been a dull Age of the Machine.

"Mr. Watson, Come Here!"

Alexander Graham Bell, a teacher of the deaf, became a professor of vocal physiology at Boston University. He began working on a device to record sound waves graphically to *show* his deaf students what they could not hear. Simultaneously, he tried to develop a "harmonic telegraph," a device capable of transmitting multiple telegraph messages simultaneously over a single line.

About 1874, speech and telegraphy merged in his mind. Bell wrote in his notebook that if he could "make a current of electricity vary in intensity precisely as the air varies in density during the production of sound," he could "transmit speech telegraphically."

The insight was staggering: convert one form of intelligible energy (sound) into another (modulated electric current). With his tireless assistant, Thomas Watson, Bell worked on the device for the next two frustrating years. One day, in 1876, while Watson maintained what he thought would be another fruitless vigil by the receiver unit in the next room, Bell (as he recorded in his laboratory notebook) "shouted into M [the mouthpiece] the following sentence: 'Mr. Watson—come here—I want to see you.' To my delight he came and declared that he had heard and understood what I said." It was the world's first telephone call.

The Bell Telephone Company, founded by Bell's father-in-law, Gardner G. Hubbard, transformed the invention into a utility of vast proportions and incalculable importance.

One Percent Inspiration

Born in Milan, Ohio, in 1847, Edison had little formal education. He did have an abundant passion for tinkering and a fascination with an invisible force called electricity. His first commercially successful invention was an electric stock ticker, which delivered stock quotations almost instantaneously. J. P. Morgan eagerly snatched it up, and Edison plowed his profits into building state-of-the-art laboratory/workshops first in Newark, then in Menlo Park, and later in West Orange, New Jersey. By the end of his long, creative life, Edison had more than 1,000 patents to his name.

Edison's greatest single invention was undoubtedly the incandescent electric lamp, which he publicly demonstrated on December 31, 1879, after many tedious months of trial and error. ("Genius," Edison once declared to a reporter, "is 1 percent inspiration and 99 percent perspiration.") By 1881, he built the world's first central generating plant, on Pearl Street in lower Manhattan. Within a very short time, electricity became a fixture not only of American life, but of life throughout the world.

Capturing Sound and Light

The incandescent lamp was Edison's most pervasive invention but not his personal favorite. Two years before he demonstrated his lamp, he sketched a simple machine, scrawled the directive "Build this" in the corner, and handed the sketch to one of his mechanic-technicians, John Kruesi.

Kruesi dutifully followed his employer's instructions, without any idea of what the device was supposed to do. A grooved metal cylinder was turned by a hand crank; a sheet of tinfoil was stretched over the cylinder; the point of a stylus rested against the tinfoil, and the other end of the stylus was affixed to a flexible diaphragm. Kruesi presented the finished model to Edison, who took it, turned the crank, and spoke into the diaphragm. Moving with the vibration of his voice, the stylus embossed the tinfoil. Edison stopped cranking and speaking, reapplied the stylus to the cylinder, and turned the crank. From the diaphragm, the machine recited "Mary Had a Little Lamb." Thomas Edison had invented the phonograph.

After recording sound and producing light, the Wizard of Menlo Park (as an enthralled press had dubbed the inventor) *recorded* light. Edison became interested in the photography of motion after he attended a lecture by Eadweard Muybridge (1830–1904) on his experiments with recording motion on film using multiple cameras. In 1882, a French scientist, E. J. Marey, invented a means of shooting multiple images with a single camera, and Edison patented his own motion picture camera in 1887. By the 1890s, he had a studio making short movies and in 1903 produced *The Great Train Robbery,* a 12-minute motion picture most historians consider the first feature film.

Bridge and Skyscraper, Kitty Hawk and Detroit

In 1857, a German immigrant named John Augustus Roebling (1806–1869), a master bridge builder who had constructed suspension bridges over the Monongahela River and at Niagara Falls, proposed a spectacular span over the East River to unite Manhattan and Brooklyn. Both were, at the time, separate cities. Roebling completed his plans in

1869, but suffered a severe leg injury at the construction site and died of tetanus. His son, Washington Augustus Roebling (1837–1926), took over the epic task. It very nearly killed him as well. He spent too much time in an underwater caisson, supervising the bridge-tower foundations' construction. Roebling developed a permanently crippling, excruciatingly painful case of "the bends," a disorder caused by nitrogen bubbles in the blood. The bridge, finally completed in 1883, was and remains a magnificent combination of timeless architecture and cutting-edge nineteenth-century technology.

If the Roeblings' masterpiece brought to its grandest expression the union of nineteenth-century art and science, the American skyscraper looked forward to the next century. William Le Baron Jenny's Home Insurance Company Building in Chicago (built 1883–1885) is generally considered the first skyscraper.

The very name "skyscraper" seemed to proclaim that nothing could keep the American spirit from taking wing. In 1903, two bicycle mechanics from Dayton, Ohio, transported to a beach at Kitty Hawk, North Carolina, a spindly, gossamer machine that resembled an oversized box kite. While his brother Wilbur (1867–1912) observed, Orville Wright (1871–1948) made history's first piloted, powered, sustained, and controlled flight in a heavier-than-air craft on December 17. Orville flew a distance of 120 feet over a span of 12 seconds. By 1909, the brothers were manufacturing and selling their airplanes.

Of course, in 1909, flight was still out of the reach of most "ordinary" people. But the year before, a farm boy from Dearborn, Michigan, gave the masses wings of a different sort. True, Henry Ford (1863–1947) did not lift his Model T purchasers off the ground, but he did give them unprecedented physical freedom.

VITAL STATISTICS

In 1908, Ford manufactured 10,607 cars retailing for $850 each. In 1916, he turned out 730,041 Model T cars at $360 each.

Ford did not invent the automobile but did make it practical and affordable. In 1908, he designed the simple, sturdy Model T and began to develop assembly line techniques to build it. The price of the car plummeted, and demand increased. With increased demand, Ford further perfected his assembly line, turning out more and more cars at lower and lower prices, which put them within reach of most Americans.

The Model T, a landmark achievement in mass production, transformed the way Americans lived. The car created a mobile society, and it created a skyrocketing demand for mass-produced consumer goods of all kinds. Even more than the transcontinental railroad had done in 1869, the automobile unified the United States, connecting city to city and village to village.

Yet for all this, there was a cost well beyond the $360 price tag of a 1916 Model T. It often seemed as if the automobile was an invader rather than a liberator. Worse, American labor lost a certain degree of humanity, compelled now to take its pace from the relentless rhythms of assembly line machinery. The gulf between management and labor, always wide, broadened into a bitter chasm. If the moneyed classes welcomed the technological revolution, they now had reason to fear a political one.

The Least You Need to Know

- ✪ The rise of the cattle industry in the West produced a colorful worker who, even in his own time, became an American icon: the cowboy.

- ✪ During the latter half of the nineteenth century, the kind of raw energy that animated the Wild West seemed to drive the rest of the country as well.

- ✪ After the Civil War, big business grew largely unchecked, even at the expense of the public welfare, creating a roller-coaster boom-and-bust economy.

Octopus and Jungle (1877–1906)

"The history of the world," said the nineteenth-century historian Thomas Carlyle, "is but the biography of great men." More recent historians believe such biographies relate only part of the story. History is also an account of the working men and women whose lives were influenced by the actions of politicians and (to use another phrase from Carlyle) the "captains of industry." While the moneyed elite fought one another for control of capital, the ordinary folk were tossed on the seas of economic tempest. For them, the waning nineteenth century were hard times.

The Golden Door

America is a nation of immigrants. During the sixteenth century, most Americans were Spanish. By the seventeenth century, many newcomers were French and even more English. By the eighteenth century, waves of German immigrants arrived, causing alarm among the English speakers, especially those who had been born on these shores.

AMERICAN ECHO

Give me your tired, your poor, Your huddled masses yearning to breathe free, The wretched refuse of your teeming shore, Send these, the homeless, tempest-tost, to me, I lift my lamp beside the golden door!

—Emma Lazarus, from "The New Colossus," verse inscription (composed in 1883) for the base of the Statue of Liberty (unveiled in 1886)

The next great wave of immigration began in 1841, when Ireland suffered a great potato famine, which caused untold hardship and even starvation. The influx of Irish-Catholics into what was principally an Anglo-Protestant nation prompted many to believe that "their" American culture had come under attack. Feared and despised, the Irish immigrants were subjected to abuse and prejudice, some of it even backed by local legislation.

Beginning around 1880, the clamoring demands of American industry began to drown out the anti-immigrant chorus. Immigrant labor was cheap labor, and employers needed unskilled and semiskilled workers to feed newly emerging assembly lines and do the heavy lifting required to build bridges and raise skyscrapers. American employers called not only on the German states and Ireland, but also encouraged the immigration of Italians, Greeks, Turks, Russians, and Slavs. For the first time, substantial numbers of Jews came to the United States, adding a new ingredient to the nation's blend of ethnic identities and religious faiths.

While the Eastern and Midwestern cities tended to readily assimilate the new immigrants, resistance to immigration remained strong in the rural and urban areas of the West and Southwest. By 1882, prejudice against Asians resulted in passage of the first of a series of Chinese Exclusion Acts, which blocked the importation of Chinese laborers.

By the second decade of the twentieth century, most Americans were eager to slam shut the golden door that opened onto their land. In 1917, would-be immigrants were required to pass a literacy test. And in 1924, Congress set a strict limit on immigration—154,000 persons annually. Congress also established special quotas aimed at reducing immigration from southern and eastern European countries.

How the Other Half Lived

At the end of the nineteenth century, most large American cities were deeply divided places. Established citizens lived in varying degrees of prosperity, decently clothed, fed, and housed. Many of the newer arrivals languished in overcrowded, dilapidated, and crime-plagued slums. The middle-class reaction to this "other half" of America was to ignore it—until immigrant journalist Jacob August Riis (1849–1914) published an eye-opening study in text and photographs of his city's slum life. *How the Other Half Lives* (1890), Theodore Roosevelt declared, came as "an enlightenment and an inspiration." The book heralded reform movements not only in New York, but across the nation.

Rush to New Land

To some, the United States seemed to be turning into a nation of teeming slums, but the dream of wide-open western spaces was not dead. At noon on April 22, 1889, government officials fired signal guns, sending hundreds of homesteaders racing across the border of Indian Territory to stake claims. It was the greatest mass settlement of the West since the Homestead Act of 1862, and the event kindled or rekindled the American Dream not just in those who rushed to new lands, but also in Americans who experienced the excitement only vicariously.

The kindling of one dream meant another was extinguished. The great land rush led to statehood for Indian Territory, which became Oklahoma on November 16, 1907. Tribal lands were drastically reduced in the process.

The Knights of Labor

The Indians, victimized by U.S. land policy, could do little but appeal, mostly in vain, to the white American conscience. The laboring man, victimized by big business operating in the absence of government regulation, fought back by organizing unions. The Knights of Labor was founded in 1878 as a national union of skilled and unskilled workers. The Knights agitated for the universal adoption of the eight-hour day. Targeting the railroads—the "octopus," as the reform-minded turn-of-the-century novelist Frank Norris labeled them—the union struck several lines in 1877. The strikes won certain concessions from the companies. In 1886, however, after a general strike failed in Chicago and the bloody Haymarket Riot ensued, the Knights of Labor dissolved.

Strike!

In 1892, workers struck the Carnegie Steel Company plant in Homestead, Pennsylvania, after company manager Henry Clay Frick slashed wages. On June 29, Frick hired some 300 Pinkerton "detectives" (they functioned more as hired thugs and scabs) to run the plant, and on July 6, an armed confrontation occurred, resulting in several deaths. The state militia was called in to protect nonunion laborers, who worked the mills from July 12 to November 20, at which point the strike collapsed.

In consequence of the Homestead Strike, the union movement suffered a setback, which was compounded two years later during the Pullman Strike of 1894. A violent confrontation between railroad workers and the Pullman Palace Car Company of Illinois tied up rail traffic across the United States from May to July. Workers, who lived in the company-owned town of Pullman (today a neighborhood on Chicago's South Side), were protesting wage cuts that had been made without corresponding reductions in company-levied rents and other employee charges.

American Railway Union head Eugene V. Debs (1855–1926) called a boycott of all Pullman cars, and company lawyers responded by using the newly enacted Sherman anti-trust legislation against the strikers. On July 2, a court injunction was issued to halt the strike, federal troops were dispatched to enforce it, and a deadly riot broke out. The strike was crushed by July 10.

The American Federation of Labor

Although the labor movement would not fully recover from these early blows until the 1930s, one enduring union did emerge in 1886. The American Federation of Labor (AFL) was led by former cigar maker Samuel Gompers (1850–1924). Recognizing that working people had certain common interests but also differing needs, the AFL existed as a coordinating group for separate trades. The union, which agitated for an eight-hour day, workmen's compensation, controls on immigrant labor, and protection from "technological unemployment" (losing your job to a machine), merged with the Congress of Industrial Organizations in 1955 and exists today as the AFL-CIO.

Wobblies

Although reasonably successful, the AFL did little to address the needs of unskilled labor. So, in 1905, the Industrial Workers of the World (IWW) was formed by the Western Federation of Miners and other labor organizations. Led by the charismatic William "Big Bill" Haywood (1869–1928), the IWW vowed permanent class warfare against employers and looked forward to a revolution that would replace capitalism with an "industrial democracy."

Day of the Bosses

Where unions fell short of looking after the needs, wishes, and demands of the masses, American city governments spawned *bosses* who operated political machines. The big-city boss was characteristically a demagogue, who presented himself as a common man looking out for the interests of common men. In truth, bosses were corrupt politicians, enriching themselves and their cronies at the expense of their constituents.

Typical was New York's William Marcy Tweed (1823–1878), who worked his way up through the city's political machine (known as Tammany Hall, after the name of a powerful Democratic club). Tweed amassed a fortune built on influence peddling and kickbacks from the sale of city contracts and franchises. He gathered about himself a band of cronies called the Tweed Ring, who collectively siphoned off anywhere from $40 million to $200 million in public funds. Convicted of fraud in 1873, Tweed jumped bail by fleeing to

Spain. He was ruthlessly caricatured by the great political cartoonist Thomas Nast (1840–1902), and in 1876, Tweed was recognized—in Spain—because of a Nast cartoon. He was arrested, extradited, and returned to New York, where he died after serving two years in prison.

The Age of the Machine soon gave rise to an Age of Reform in response to it. *The Shame of the Cities*, written in 1904 by freelance journalist Lincoln Steffens, exposed the corruption of St. Louis and showed that it was all too typical of big-city America. Public outrage flared, making way for such crusading politicians as New York's Theodore Roosevelt and Wisconsin's Senator Robert M. La Follette.

Chicago Meat

Talk of corruption and reform was all well and good, but to many, the subject remained abstract. It took a novel, *The Jungle,* written in 1906 by Upton Sinclair (1878–1968), to bring corruption to the gut level. Sinclair described the plight of one Jurgis Rudkus, a Lithuanian immigrant who worked in a Chicago meat-packing plant. Through the eyes of this downtrodden and exploited worker, Sinclair described in nauseating detail the horrors of modern meat packing. To fatten the bottom line, packers did not hesitate to use decayed meat, tubercular meat, assorted offal, and even rat meat in the manufacture of meat products. Comfortable middle-class Americans may or may not have cared about the exploitation of a blue-collar Lithuanian immigrant, but the idea of big business poisoning *them* and *their* families was downright sickening. "I aimed at the public's heart," Sinclair wrote of his novel, "and by accident I hit it in the stomach." As a result of the indignation stirred by *The Jungle,* Congress enacted the landmark Pure Food and Drug Act a mere six months after the novel was published. The federal government now directly intervened in free enterprise, taking upon itself the defense of the public welfare.

Muckrakers and Progressivism

Sinclair was one of a group of activists President Theodore Roosevelt, himself a progressive reformer, dubbed *muckrakers.* Sinclair, Lincoln Steffens, Ida Tarbell (author of an epoch-making exposé of the outrageous Standard Oil "trust"), and other writers reported on the exploitation rampant in Gilded Age America. The muckrakers exposed child labor practices, slum life, racial persecution, prostitution, sweatshop labor, and the general sins of big business and machine politics.

WHAT'S THE WORD?

Coined by Theodore Roosevelt, **muckraker** was a reference to *Pilgrim's Progress,* a Christian allegorical novel by the seventeenth-century British writer John Bunyan. One of Bunyan's allegorical characters used a "muckrake" to clean up the (moral) filth around him, even as he remained oblivious of the celestial beauty above.

The Government Takes a Hand

The muckrakers succeeded in galvanizing popular opinion and motivating government action. Under President Theodore Roosevelt, antitrust laws were used to break up certain monopolies or, as they were called at the time, "trusts."

Three years after Roosevelt left the White House, Robert M. La Follette, U.S. Senator from Wisconsin, led a faction of the most reform-minded Republicans to form a third party, the Progressive Party. The new party drafted an enthusiastic Roosevelt as its standard bearer in the 1912 presidential elections. The spirit of Progressive reform changed American government, bringing it more intimately into the everyday lives of everyday Americans.

The Least You Need to Know

- ✪ The late nineteenth century was the first great age of immigration into the United States—an era followed, early in the next century, by a backlash of immigration restrictions.

- ✪ The Oklahoma Land Rush of 1889, the greatest mass settlement of the West since the Homestead Act of 1862, usurped much land specifically set aside as a permanent homeland for Indians displaced by the Indian Removal Act of 1830.

- ✪ The greed and corruption rampant in the Gilded Age triggered the rise of Progressivism, a sweeping reform movement that encompassed politics, social justice, and general moral "uplift."

PART 6

World Power

A "splendid little war" is what Secretary of State John Hay called America's brief armed contest with Spain over Cuban independence. Although controversial at home, the Spanish-American War demonstrated to the world that the United States was a power to be reckoned with. The war was followed by a period of isolationist retreat, shattered by the United States' 1917 entry into World War I. Following the Armistice that ended the war, the nation was swept by simultaneous waves of a devil-may-care social morality and a contrasting mania for sobriety, resulting in an amendment to the Constitution outlawing liquor. Drunk or sober, the country spent money like mad, made unwise investments it couldn't cover, and went broke one dismal Tuesday in 1929. A Great Depression swept the nation and the world, bringing desperation and the rise of dictators to Europe, as well as a new leader, Franklin Delano Roosevelt, to the United States. Here is the story of some of the twentieth century's most frantic and frightening years.

Over There (1898–1918)

In his Farewell Address of 1797, George Washington cautioned his fellow Americans to avoid what has been paraphrased as "foreign entanglements." The outgoing president did not use that exact phrase in the speech, but Americans seem to have gotten the message. For *most* of the nineteenth century, the nation took advantage of the geographic insulation two oceans provided and basked in splendid isolation.

In 1823, President James Monroe promulgated what historians call the Monroe Doctrine, which declared the entire Western Hemisphere—North, Central, and South America—off-limits to European powers intending to create new colonies. The United States thus became the de facto major power of the hemisphere and, while other major powers built far-flung empires, America expanded only across its own vast continent.

Selling the News

By the end of the nineteenth century, the United States reached from "sea to shining sea." Some—"patriots," "imperialists," or *jingoes*—thought it should extend farther.

WHAT'S THE WORD?

In characteristically loud tones, Americans who voiced support for a warlike, imperialist foreign policy were called jingoes in the 1800s. The word **jingo** apparently came from "by jingo," an expression in the refrain of a bellicose nineteenth-century English music-hall song. "By jingo" also entered into American popular speech as a socially acceptable alternative expletive to "by Jesus."

As the nineteenth century came to a close, the *New York World*, owned by Joseph Pulitzer (1847–1911) and the *New York Journal*, published by William Randolph Hearst (1863–1951), were locked in a circulation war. Aiming to bag the "big story," both Hearst and Pulitzer dispatched reporters to cover a developing situation in Cuba, a colony of Spain that was a mere 90 miles off the Florida coast.

While a full-scale Cuban war of independence was slow to brew, the island had a long history of rebellion. In February 1896, Spain sent General Valeriano Weyler (whom Hearst dubbed "Butcher Weyler") as military governor. Weyler created global outrage by herding rebel sympathizers into "re-concentration camps." Like his predecessor, Grover Cleveland, President William McKinley resisted intervening in Cuba. But U.S. popular sentiment, whipped up by lurid atrocity tales published in Hearst's and Pulitzer's papers, moved him to order the battleship *Maine* into Havana Harbor to protect "American interests."

Remember the Maine!

The temperature of America's war fever was not raised by popular sentiment alone. U.S. companies had made major investments in the island, especially in sugar plantations. Not coincidentally, moguls like Hearst and Pulitzer had their own investments in such companies. Revolution threatened those companies and their shareholders. On the other hand, an "independent" puppet government in Cuba (or better yet, a Cuba annexed to the

United States) would be very good for business. On February 9, Hearst got a scoop by publishing a purloined private letter in which the Spanish minister (ambassador) to the United States personally insulted President McKinley. This propelled America to the brink of war.

On February 15, 1898, an explosion rocked Havana Harbor, and the USS *Maine* blew up, killing 266 crewmen (another eight later died of their injuries). The Hearst and Pulitzer papers vied with one another to affix blame on Spain, and cries of "Remember the *Maine* … to hell with Spain!" rang throughout the nation.

Reluctant to go to war, President McKinley convened a naval board of inquiry, which concluded that the ship had been destroyed by a mine but had no opinion as to whether it had been a Spanish attack or an attempt by Cuban revolutionaries to incite the United States to war against Spain. Despite the lack of verdict, McKinley was moved by popular political sentiment. In April, he asked Congress to authorize an invasion. Congress not only complied, but also gave the president something he hadn't asked for: a resolution recognizing Cuban independence from Spain. In response, Spain declared war on the United States on April 24.

The first action of the Spanish-American War took place not in Cuba, but in the Spanish-occupied Philippine Islands. U.S. admiral George Dewey (1837–1917) sailed the Asiatic Squadron from Hong Kong to Manila Bay, where, on May 1, he attacked the Spanish fleet, sinking all 10 ships in the bay. Following this action, 11,000 U.S. troops landed and, acting in concert with the guerrilla forces of Filipino rebel leader Emilio Aguinaldo, quickly defeated the Spanish army in the islands. In July, Spanish Guam also fell, and the United States gathered up previously unclaimed Wake Island as well. Most important, Congress passed a resolution annexing Hawaii.

REMEMBER THIS

All modern historians agree that the U.S. Navy board of inquiry investigating the explosion of the USS *Maine* erred in its conclusion that the ship made contact with a marine mine. Most believe that the devastating explosion was the result of spontaneous combustion in the battleship's powder magazine.

Combat in Cuba was equally swift and decisive. On May 29, the U.S. fleet blockaded the Spanish fleet at Santiago Harbor, and in June, 17,000 U.S. troops landed at Daiquiri and assaulted Santiago. The war's make-or-break land battle, at San Juan Hill (and adjacent Kettle Hill) on July 1, included a magnificent charge by the volunteer Rough Riders, led by Lieutenant Colonel Theodore Roosevelt. (These cavalrymen charged on foot because the army had failed to ship their horses to them.)

In the meantime, Spain's Admiral Pasqual Cervera sailed into the harbor of Santiago de Cuba, where he was blockaded by the U.S. fleet. On July 3, after the U.S. victory at San Juan Hill, Cervera decided to run the blockade in a bid to save his fleet. Within a four-hour battle, almost all of Cervera's ships were sunk, and on July 17, 24,000 Spanish troops surrendered. Nine days later, Madrid sued for peace. U.S. Secretary of State John Hay (1838–1905) summed it up by calling the 10-week conflict a "splendid little war."

Spain withdrew from Cuba and ceded to the United States Puerto Rico and Guam; it sold the Philippines to the United States for $20 million. The United States established a territorial government in Puerto Rico, but temporized on Cuba, first establishing a military government there and then allowing Cuba to draft its own constitution, albeit with certain provisos. These included the United States' right to establish military bases on the island and to intervene at will in Cuban affairs "in order to preserve [Cuban] independence."

Theodore Roosevelt assumed office after McKinley, shot by anarchist Leon Czolgosz on September 5, 1901, died on the 14th. Subsequently elected to a presidential term in his own right, Roosevelt promulgated the so-called "Roosevelt Corollary" to the Monroe Doctrine. In effect, this policy made the United States policeman of the Western Hemisphere, a step toward establishing the nation as a world power.

He Kept Us Out of War

After taking that step, however, Americans had second thoughts. Roosevelt anointed his friend William Howard Taft to succeed him as president, but Taft soon proved far more conservative than Roosevelt. Lacking Roosevelt's vigor, he failed to win reelection in 1912, finishing a poor third to Democrat Woodrow Wilson (1856–1924) and TR himself (who ran as a third-party Progressive—or as he called it, a "Bull Moose" candidate).

Wilson—former president of Princeton University and, afterward, reformist governor of New Jersey—was a vigorous Progressive. During his first term, the income tax was introduced with the Sixteenth Amendment, protective tariffs were lowered, the Federal Reserve Act (1913) reformed currency and banking laws, and antitrust legislation was strengthened in 1914 by the Federal Trade Commission Act and the Clayton Anti-Trust Act. Labor reform came with the Adamson Act, granting an eight-hour day to interstate railroad workers, and the Child Labor Act, curtailing children's working hours.

But Wilson faced staggering problems in foreign relations. He unsuccessfully attempted to negotiate a Pan-American pact to guarantee the Western Hemisphere's integrity. He also wrestled with Mexico, embroiled in revolution and even ordered the military occupation of Veracruz in 1914 in response to a purported attack on U.S. Navy sailors. In 1915 and 1916, Wilson sent troops to rebellion-racked Haiti and Santo Domingo, where he established U.S. protectorates. In 1916, he sent a "Punitive Expedition" deep into Mexico in pursuit of the revolutionary guerrilla leader Pancho Villa, who had sent raiders across the border to Columbus, New Mexico, where the men killed 14 U.S. soldiers as well as 10 town residents.

Despite these conflicts, most Americans were relieved that, under Wilson, the United States remained safely aloof from the "Great War," which broke out in Europe after June 28, 1914.

At first, it looked as if the war would be a short one. The German armies made a spectacular drive through France and Belgium, sweeping all resistance before them. Then, in a moment of strategic uncertainty, the Germans dug in along the Marne River, about 30 miles outside Paris. For the next four years, Europe was doomed to the fruitless horrors of trench warfare on the "Western Front": France, Britain, Russia, and lesser allies were on one side; Germany, Austria-Hungary, and their lesser allies on the other.

Lusitania Lost

Wilson adroitly managed to keep the American nation out of this charnel house. On May 7, 1915, a German U-boat torpedoed the British passenger liner *Lusitania*, killing 1,198 people, including 128 of the 139 U.S. nationals on board.

Many in the United States—among them Theodore Roosevelt—clamored for immediate entry into the war. Wilson demurred, but issued a strong protest to Germany, demanding reparations and the cessation of "unrestricted" submarine warfare—attacking civilian ships from underwater and without warning.

Although Germany protested that the *Lusitania* carried munitions (a truth vigorously denied by the British and largely ignored by almost every U.S. leader except for Secretary of State William Jennings Bryan), the Kaiser's diplomats were anxious to avoid facing yet another enemy. Germany ordered its U-boats to give civilian vessels warning before firing upon them so that passengers could abandon ship. Wilson's firmness with Germany, which appeared feeble to Roosevelt and other hawks, seemed overly warlike to Wilson's isolationist secretary of state, William Jennings Bryan, who resigned in protest. Most popular sentiment remained with Wilson, who won a second term by a slim majority driven by the slogan "He kept us out of war."

Telegram from Zimmermann

Although the Germans backed down on unrestricted submarine warfare, U.S.-German relations deteriorated. In February of 1917, Germany, stalled in the trenches and, wanting to tighten its stranglehold on British and French supply by sea, announced the resumption of unrestricted submarine warfare. On February 3, a U.S.-flagged civilian cargo ship, the *Housatonic,* was sunk. Although the U-boat captain warned the vessel's skipper and all hands abandoned ship without loss of life, President Wilson severed diplomatic relations with Germany.

The next month, on March 1, the American public learned of the "Zimmermann Telegram," a coded message, sent on January 19, 1917, from German Foreign Secretary Alfred Zimmermann to his nation's ambassador to Mexico. The telegram proposed a German-Mexican alliance against the United States: in return for a Mexican declaration of war against the United States, Germany would help Mexico get back what it had lost in the 1846–1848 U.S.–Mexican War. For good measure, the missive also instructed the ambassador to ask the Mexican president to "invite" Japan to declare war on the United States as well.

Provoked, on April 2, 1917, Wilson asked Congress for a declaration of war. Voted up on April 6, it was signed the same day.

Crusade for Democracy

In his war message delivered on April 2, Wilson told Congress that the "world must be made safe for democracy." With this statement, America's role as guardian of the Western Hemisphere expanded to cover the world.

The puny U.S. Army numbered fewer than 200,000 men and officers in 1917; by the end of the war, it would swell to four million. In May 1917, Wilson pushed through Congress a Selective Service bill, by authority of which 2.8 million men were drafted—and over a million more voluntarily enlisted. About half the army—some two million men—served in the American Expeditionary Force (AEF) led by General John J. Pershing. The navy sailed under the command of Admiral William S. Sims.

Pershing arrived in Paris on June 14, 1917, at a low point in the Allies' fortunes. Every French offensive had failed, and the demoralized French army was plagued by mutinies. The British had made a major push in Flanders, which resulted in a bloody stalemate. The Russians, fighting on the Eastern Front, had collapsed and were rushing headlong toward a revolution destined to end czarist rule and introduce communism into the world. The revolution brought a "separate peace" between Russia and Germany, freeing up masses of German troops for service on the Western Front.

Although the first AEF troops followed Pershing on June 26, it was October 21, 1917, before units were committed to battle and spring 1918 before American numbers were great enough to make a militarily significant impact. Ultimately, the Americans turned the tide.

VITAL STATISTICS

A total of 65 million men and women served in the armies and navies of combatant nations during World War I. Of this number, at least 10 million were killed and 20 million wounded. Of the two million U.S. troops who fought, 112,432 died and 230,074 were wounded. The filthy living conditions brought on by war contributed to the outbreak of an influenza epidemic that killed even more—some 21.64 million people worldwide, or 1 percent of the world's population.

Over the Top

Between June 6 and July 1, 1918, the "Yanks" recaptured for the Allies Vaux, Bouresches, and Belleau Wood, all key outposts on the road to Paris. The Americans also managed to hold the critically important Allied position at Cantigny against a great German offensive between June 9 and June 15.

Blooded at the Marne

Between July 18 and August 6, American troops broke the long war's seemingly endless deadlock by helping to crush Germany's last major offensive at the Second Battle of the Marne. Here, at last, was a battle that could be deemed a genuine turning point. The victory was followed by a series of Allied counteroffensives—at the Somme, Oise-Aisne, and Ypres-Lys—in August.

The Boys of St. Mihiel

Although Americans fought alongside the French and English in each of the major August offensives, they acted independently—and brilliantly—against the St. Mihiel salient from September 12 to September 16. This battle initiated the Meuse-Argonne Campaign, involving a huge number of U.S. troops—some 1.2 million of them—who pounded and then cut German supply lines between the Meuse River and the Argonne Forest. Fighting continued until the very day of armistice, November 11, 1918. For the Americans, it was triumphant but terribly costly. U.S. units suffered, on average, a casualty rate of 10 percent.

At the Eleventh Hour

It became apparent to Germany that American soldiers were not only willing and able to fight (a matter of doubt among overly optimistic German strategists the year before), but also inexhaustible in number, as was the American capacity for producing the hardware of war. Germany agreed to an armistice—a cessation of hostilities—to be concluded at the eleventh hour of the eleventh day of the eleventh month of 1918.

The Least You Need to Know

- ✪ The end of the nineteenth century saw the end of America's long tradition of isolation from world affairs.

- ✪ The Spanish-American War (1898) was in part a struggle against European tyranny and in part a symptom of U.S. imperialism.

- ✪ A zealous idealist, Woodrow Wilson devoted his first presidential term to sweeping domestic reform; this same idealism prompted him to lead the United States into World War I in 1917 "to make the world safe for democracy."

- ✪ The United States emerged from World War I, the most terrible war the world had seen up to that time, as the champion of world democracy.

Booze, Boom, Bust (1918–1929)

President Wilson told the American people that the "Great War" was a "war to end all wars," and he meant it. On January 8, 1918, almost a year before the Armistice, Wilson announced to Congress "Fourteen Points," which he called "the only possible program" for peace. After a complex web of treaty obligations had escalated an obscure Balkan conflict into a worldwide conflagration, Wilson hoped his Fourteen Points would create a single international alliance, making armed conflict among nations impossible. The alliance would be called the League of Nations.

Wilson's Dream

As vigorously as Wilson had worked to mobilize his nation for war, he now struggled to bring about a peace meant to make the future outbreak of wars unlikely if not impossible. Wilson personally headed the American delegation to the Paris Peace Conference, which was charged with creating a final treaty. Driven by his idealistic vision of an international league to promote a world of perpetual harmony, Wilson made the fatal political error of disdaining to develop bipartisan support at home for his peace plans. Worse, he made peace a partisan issue by appealing to voters to re-elect a Democratic Congress in 1918. This backfired, as the 1918 contest went to the Republicans, who won majorities in both houses. To many, this election seemed a no-confidence vote against Wilson and his internationalist crusade.

In Europe, Wilson was greeted with confidence in his leadership of the treaty-making process. But it soon became apparent that the other major Allied leaders—Georges Clemenceau of France, David Lloyd George of Great Britain, and Vittorio Orlando of Italy—wanted to conclude a settlement that punished Germany with the object of deindustrializing and bankrupting it, rendering it incapable of ever arming for war again.

Hampered by a climate of revenge, Wilson nevertheless hammered away at his Fourteen Points, ultimately seeing them embodied in the Treaty of Versailles, which, however, also imposed on Germany the ruinous terms the other Allied leaders advocated. Gratified that he had won inclusion of the League of Nations as part of the treaty, Wilson naïvely believed the League itself would, in the fullness of time, rectify the injustices presently imposed upon Germany.

Reds!

Even as Wilson was trying to engineer world harmony, popular American sentiment was already retreating into isolationism. The Russian Revolution of 1917 and the Bolshevik Revolution that followed it later in the year toppled the long regime of the Romanov czars and installed a short-lived republic followed by a Communist government. In the years following World War I, a "Red Scare" swept Western Europe and the United States.

REMEMBER THIS

Wilson addressed Congress on January 8, 1918, and promulgated his "Fourteen Points":

I. Open covenants of peace, openly arrived at ...

II. Absolute freedom of navigation upon the seas ...

III. The removal ... of [international] economic barriers ...

IV. Adequate guarantees ... that ... armaments will be reduced ...

V. ... impartial adjustment of all colonial claims ...

VI. The evacuation of all Russian territory ...

VII. Belgium ... must be evacuated and restored ...

VIII. All French territory should be freed and the invaded portions restored ...

IX. A readjustment of the frontiers of Italy should be effected along clearly recognizable lines of nationality.

X. The peoples of Austria-Hungary ... should be accorded the freest opportunity of autonomous development.

XI. Rumania, Serbia, and Montenegro should be evacuated ...

XII. The Turkish portions of the present Ottoman Empire should be assured a secure sovereignty ...

XIII. An independent Polish state should be erected ...

XIV. A general association [league] of nations must be formed ...

On the evening of January 2, 1919, U.S. Attorney General A. Mitchell Palmer launched simultaneous raids on the headquarters of radical organizations in 33 cities, indiscriminately rounding up 6,000 persons, U.S. citizens and noncitizens alike, *believed* to be "sympathetic to communism." Palmer and others lumped Communists together with the out-and-out anarchists who had mailed bombs to Palmer, John D. Rockefeller Sr., J. P. Morgan, and more than 30 other wealthy conservatives. Most of the bombs failed to reach their destinations—having been mailed with insufficient postage!

In a climate of intense fear, Palmer created the General Intelligence Division, headed by a zealous young Justice Department investigator named J. Edgar Hoover. Hoover directed the laborious compilation of a massive card index of 150,000 radical leaders, organizations, and publications. As all too often happened in American history, beginning with the Alien and Sedition Acts passed at the end of the eighteenth century, legislators took totalitarian measures in the name of defending American liberty.

Retreat into "Normalcy"

Fear of Communism was not the only thing that chipped away at Wilson's dream. The punitive terms of the Treaty of Versailles so destabilized Germany that it became ripe for the dark promises of Adolph Hitler, who came into prominence during the 1920s and 1930s. Instead of preventing another war, the Treaty of Versailles *guaranteed* one—a war that would prove even more devastating than the conflict of 1914–1918.

At home, Wilson's lapse of political savvy was taking its toll as Henry Cabot Lodge (1850–1924) led Senate Republican opposition to the U.S. commitment to the League of Nations. Wilson resolved to brook no compromise and decided to put pressure on the Senate by taking his case directly to the people. He embarked on a grueling 9,500-mile transcontinental whistle-stop speaking tour. On September 25, 1919, Wilson collapsed following a speech in Pueblo, Colorado. He was rushed back to Washington, but his condition deteriorated and, a week later, he suffered a devastating stroke that left him partially paralyzed. Ill, frustrated, and embittered, Wilson instructed his followers to accept no compromise on the League, even if that meant losing it entirely.

Without compromise, the Senate rejected the Treaty of Versailles, as well as the League of Nations. Wilson watched as the "war to end all wars" came to look more and more like just another war fought in vain. Warren G. Harding (1865–1923), the Republican who succeeded Wilson in the White House, called for a "return to normalcy." He told Congress that "we seek no part in directing the destinies of the world … [the League] is not for us."

A Generation Lost and Found

Woodrow Wilson was not the only embittered individual in postwar America. The war broke the spirit of some people; in others, it created a combination of boredom and thrill-seeking that earned the decade its nickname: the "Roaring Twenties." Some Americans found that they could not settle back into routine life at home after the war. A colony of expatriate artists and writers gathered in Paris. Many of these individuals congregated in the apartment of a remarkable medical school dropout named Gertrude Stein—writer, art collector, and cultivator of creative talent. One day, she repeated to one of these young people, Ernest Hemingway, something she had overheard a Parisian garage owner say to one of his young mechanics: "That's what you all are ... all of you young people who served in the war. You are all a lost generation." The phrase defined a generation unable to find new values to replace those they had lost in war.

Stein, Fitzgerald, Hemingway, and Co.

During the 1920s, a group of American writers made a stunning entrance onto the world stage. Among these was Francis Scott Key Fitzgerald (1896-1940), who burst onto the literary scene in 1920 with *This Side of Paradise,* a novel that ushered in the "Jazz Age" (Fitzgerald's own coinage) with a vivid portrait of Lost Generation youth. Two years later came *The Beautiful and Damned* and, in 1925, *The Great Gatsby.* This story of the enigmatic Jay Gatsby explored the American Dream in poetic, satirical, and ultimately tragic detail. The theme was plumbed again a decade later in *Tender Is the Night* (1934).

Women Get the Vote

The American woman emerged in the 1920s from long subjugation to straitlaced Victorian ideals of decorum and femininity. The most profound step toward the liberation of American women was the ratification of the Nineteenth Amendment to the U.S. Constitution, which gave women the right to vote.

Harlem Lights and Harlem Nights

There was growing liberation, too, for another long-oppressed group: African Americans. Slavery had ended with the Civil War, but black Americans hardly enjoyed the same opportunities and privileges as white Americans. They were discriminated against in education, employment, housing, and in just about every other phase of life. The French did not discriminate, and for some African American soldiers, service in World War I was an eye-opener. They returned to the States no longer willing to accept second-class citizenship.

AMERICAN ECHO

"The dark world is going to submit to its present treatment just as long as it must and not one moment longer."
—W. E. B. Du Bois, "Dark water," *The Souls of Black Folk,* 1920

The humble peanut helped to moderate the racism. In 1921, George Washington Carver, who had been born a Missouri slave in 1864, testified before Congress on behalf of the National Association of Peanut Growers to extol and explain the wonders of what had been a minor crop. Against all odds, Carver had worked his way through college, earning a Master's degree in agriculture in 1896 and accepting a teaching position at Tuskegee Institute. African American educator Booker T. Washington (1856–1915) founded Alabama's Tuskegee Institute as a source of practical vocational education for the black community. At Tuskegee, Carver concentrated on developing new products from crops—including the peanut and the sweet potato—that could replace cotton as the staple of southern farmers. Carver transformed peanuts and sweet potatoes into plastic materials, lubricants, dyes, drugs, inks, wood stains, cosmetics, tapioca, molasses, and most famously, peanut butter. His contribution to revitalizing the perpetually beleaguered agricultural economy of the South was significant; but even more, Carver showed both white and black America that an African American could accomplish great things.

Although oppression was still a fact of black life during the 1920s, white intellectuals became intensely interested in African American intellectual and artistic creations. Black artists and writers were drawn to New York City's Harlem neighborhood, where they produced works that commanded widespread attention and admiration. This literary and artistic movement was called the Harlem Renaissance and drew inspiration from the black political leader W. E. B. Du Bois (1868–1963). A sociologist, Du Bois had a Harvard doctorate (he was the first black PhD in the United States) and founded *The Crisis,* the magazine of the National Association for the Advancement of Colored People (NAACP), an important organization that Du Bois and a mostly white group of social activists created in 1909. In opposition to Booker T. Washington, who was willing to sacrifice or at least postpone social and political equality to achieve black economic progress, Du Bois argued that African Americans had to win social equality and their full political rights *as well as* economic self-sufficiency.

Some significant American writers associated with the movement Du Bois was instrumental in launching were poet Countee Cullen (1903–1946), novelist Rudolph Fisher (1897–1934), poet-essayist Langston Hughes (1902–1967), folklorist Zora Neale Hurston (1891–1960), poet James Weldon Johnson (1871–1938), and novelist Jean Toomer (1894–1967).

Harlem also became a popular spot for white night-clubbers seeking first-class jazz from great African American musicians like Fletcher Henderson (1898–1952), Louis Armstrong (1900–1971), and the young Duke Ellington (1899–1974).

America Goes Dry

The general moral liberalization that accompanied America's entry into World War I fueled a reactionary countermovement in the form of a drive toward temperance, which culminated in the Eighteenth Amendment to the Constitution, prohibiting the sale, importation, or consumption of alcoholic beverages anywhere in the United States. The Volstead Act, passed after ratification of the amendment, provided the federal police authority for the enforcement of Prohibition.

Prohibition was also an open invitation to crime. Otherwise law-abiding citizens made bathtub gin, brewed homemade beer, fermented wine in their cellars, and frequented "blind pigs" and "speakeasies"—covert saloons that served booze in coffee mugs and teacups. Police raids on such establishments were common occurrences, but mostly, officials looked the other way—especially if they were bribed to do so.

In this national atmosphere, mobsters thrived. By the end of the decade, a quasi-corporate entity called the Syndicate would be formed to "organize" crime.

Countdown to Black Tuesday

If morals, mores, and ideas were freewheeling in the 1920s, so was spending. For most— except farmers and unskilled laborers—the decade was prosperous. Americans speculated on stocks in unprecedented numbers, often overextending themselves by purchasing securities "on margin," putting down as little as 10 cents on the dollar in the hope that the stock would rise fast and far enough to cover what amounted to very substantial loans based on miniscule equity.

VITAL STATISTICS

Stocks lost an average of 40 points on Black Tuesday, October 29, 1929. In 1932, the Dow Jones Industrials hit an all-time low of 40.56 points, having fallen 89 percent from a September 1929 high of 386 points. In 1930, 1,300 banks failed. By 1933, another 3,700 would fail, and one in four workers would be jobless.

High Rollers

The fact was that so much stock had been bought on margin—backed by dimes on dollars—that much of it amounted to little more than paper. Even worse, although production in well-financed factories soared, the buying power of middle class consumers failed to keep pace. Industry was making more than people were buying. As inventories swelled, prices fell, and workers were laid off. People without jobs are not consumers. As more workers were laid off, the marketplace shrunk.

Ante Up

And so the cycle went. In the autumn of 1929, stock prices fluctuated wildly until, on October 24, the stock market was seized by a selling spree. Five days later, on October 29, "Black Tuesday," the bottom fell out. Many investors were wiped out in a day.

Herbert Hoover, elected president in 1928, now found himself nervously assuring his fearful fellow Americans that "prosperity was just around the corner." But as it so happened, that corner would not be turned for a full decade—and it would take a war to round it.

The Least You Need to Know

- ✪ The failure of the United States to join the League of Nations doomed that precursor of the United Nations to ultimate failure.

- ✪ The Eighteenth Amendment codified Prohibition and brought on the heyday of organized crime in America.

- ✪ The Nineteenth Amendment finally gave American women the right to vote.

- ✪ The climate of the 1920s, at once wildly creative, liberating, desperate, and reckless, was in large part the result of the aftereffects of World War I.

- ✪ The stock market crash of 1929 was the culmination of a cycle of careless, credit-based investments and increased industrial output in a shrinking industrial goods market.

A New Deal and a New War (1930–1941)

The son of a blacksmith, Herbert Clark Hoover was born on August 10, 1874, in West Branch, Iowa. Orphaned, Hoover was sent to live with an uncle in Oregon and enrolled in the mining engineering program at California's Stanford University, graduating in 1895. For some 20 years, Hoover traveled the world, earning a fortune as a mining engineer. During the United States' participation in the "Great War," Hoover served as food administrator, charged with promoting agricultural production and food conservation. At the end of the war, President Woodrow Wilson sent Hoover to Europe to direct the American Relief Administration. Hoover served as U.S. Secretary of Commerce in Warren G. Harding's and Calvin Coolidge's cabinets.

When Coolidge declined to seek a second term (privately observing that an economic disaster was on the way, and not wanting to be part of it), Hoover easily won election as the nation's thirty-first president. He ran on the optimistic platform that, if everyone would just put their heads together, poverty could be eliminated in America. The future looked bright. And who should know better than a man justly hailed as "the great humanitarian"?

Brother, Can You Spare a Dime?

After the 1929 Wall Street crash, Hoover proposed several relief programs but insisted that state and local governments take responsibility for funding them. In principle, this arrangement was prudent. Who better knew the needs of the people than their local governments? In practice, however, the policy was doomed: like just about everyone else, state and local governments had no cash.

Hoover refused to make federal aid directly available to individuals, believing this to be unconstitutional and fearing that federal intervention would compromise individual liberty and sap the gumption of the individual citizen.

In the meantime, shanty towns constructed of boxes and crates sprouted like weeds across the American landscape to house the homeless—"Hoovervilles" they were called. The great humanitarian's reputation was forever tarnished as blame for the Great Depression was laid mostly at the doorstep of the White House.

America had had its share of booms and busts before. But the Great Depression of the 1930s was unparalleled in magnitude, scope, and duration. Fifteen to 25 percent of the workforce was jobless in an era without government unemployment insurance and other elements of a social safety net.

The Age of Great Dictators

The Depression gripped the world, and despair bred revolution. First in Italy and then in Germany—and to a lesser extent, elsewhere in Europe—two major ideologies came into violent opposition: fascism and communism. To most Americans, both of these totalitarian ideologies seemed clearly repugnant to democracy.

But democracy was not putting beans on the table. Among American intellectuals and radical workers, communism appeared to offer a viable alternative to what seemed a failed political and economic system. Could the nation be on the precipice of revolution?

The Epoch of Franklin Delano Roosevelt

Born to substantial wealth in Hyde Park, New York, in 1882, Franklin Delano Roosevelt (FDR) never suffered poverty. The product of Groton School, Harvard College, and Columbia University Law School, young Roosevelt became a Wall Street lawyer. He devoted some of his time to serving the smaller clients of his white-shoe firm and thus came to sympathize with the cares and concerns of the so-called common man. FDR worked his way to prominence in Dutchess County (New York) politics and was appointed assistant secretary of the Navy in the Wilson administration. In 1920, he was running mate to James M. Cox, the democratic presidential hopeful who lost to Republican Warren G. Harding.

Then came FDR's darkest—and finest—hour. In the summer of 1921, while resident at his family's summer home on Campobello Island (New Brunswick, Canada), Roosevelt was stricken with a disease diagnosed at the time as polio. (Many recent medical scholars, however, believe it was more likely Guillain-Barré syndrome, an autoimmune disease that affects the peripheral nervous system with sometimes devastating effect, including significant paralysis.)

Roosevelt recovered but lost the use of his legs. His mother urged him to retire to Hyde Park. His wife, the remarkable Eleanor Roosevelt—FDR's fifth cousin once removed and the niece of Theodore Roosevelt—persuaded her husband to return to public life. With great personal courage, Roosevelt underwent intensive physical therapy, learning to stand using heavy iron leg braces and to walk with the aid of crutches. He ran for governor of New York and won, bringing to the state such progressive measures as the development of public power utilities, civil service reform, and social welfare programs.

He captured the 1932 Democratic nomination for president. "I pledge you, I pledge myself, to a new deal for the American people," he said in his acceptance speech. The phrase "New Deal" caught on in a way that transformed the federal government as well as people's attitudes about the role of government. Within the new administration's first three months—dubbed by the press with Napoleonic grandeur the "Hundred Days"—FDR introduced to Congress his program of relief legislation, which promised to stimulate industrial recovery, assist individual victims of the depression, guarantee minimum living standards, and help avert future crises.

AMERICAN ECHO

"The only thing we have to fear is fear itself."
—Franklin Delano Roosevelt, Inaugural Address, March 4, 1933

Most of the legislation of the Hundred Days was aimed at providing immediate aid and relief. The Federal Deposit Insurance Corporation (FDIC) was established to protect depositors from losing their savings in the event of bank failure. The measure did much to restore confidence in the nation's faltering banking system. The Federal Reserve Board, which regulates the nation's money supply, was strengthened. The Home Owners Loan Corporation was established to help beleaguered home owners avoid foreclosure. A Federal Securities Act reformed stock transaction regulations—an effort to avert the kind of wild speculation that contributed to the crash of 1929.

Next, the Civilian Conservation Corps (CCC) put thousands of unemployed young men to work on projects in national forests, parks, and public lands. The National Recovery Act (NRA), the most sweeping and controversial of the early New Deal legislation, established the Public Works Administration (PWA) and imposed upon industry a strict code of fair practice. The act set minimum wages and maximum working hours and gave employees the right to collective bargaining.

In May 1933, FDR called on Congress to create the Agricultural Adjustment Administration, a program of production limits and federal subsidies. Perhaps the single most visible manifestation of agricultural reform was the establishment of the Tennessee Valley Authority (TVA), which built roads, majestic dams, and massive hydroelectric plants in seven of the nation's poorest states.

More programs followed the Hundred Days. In 1935, the Works Progress Administration (WPA) was formed, which put 8.5 million people to work between 1935 and 1943—the year the program ended, but the most enduring program was Social Security, introduced in 1935, which created old-age and disability pension funds through payroll and wage taxes.

VITAL STATISTICS

Despite the New Deal, 9.5 million people remained unemployed by 1939.

None of the New Deal programs brought full economic recovery, but they helped restore confidence in the American government and propelled Roosevelt to a landslide second-term victory over Republican Alf Landon in 1936. A "Second New Deal" then went into effect, which concentrated on labor reforms.

Street Wars

In the end, it would take the approach of World War II, with its insatiable demand for the industrial materials of strife, to end the Great Depression.

Years before the United States entered World War II, another, different kind of combat was being waged on the nation's urban streets. Prohibition had spawned a gangster culture in the 1920s, which many Americans found colorful and almost romantic.

Then came St. Valentine's Day, 1929, the day Al Capone decided to "rub out" rival Chicago gangland leader "Bugs" Moran. Capone dispatched gunmen, disguised as policemen, who rounded up seven members of the Moran gang, stood them up against the wall of Moran's commercial garage, and executed them using Tommy guns.

Mobsters had been murdering one another for years, but the brazen butchery of the St. Valentine's Day Massacre hit a public nerve. Suddenly, Capone and other gangsters were no longer viewed as Robin Hoods, but as the cold-blooded killers they had been all along. Yet, as gangsters became more viciously violent, they also became increasingly organized.

In the same year as the St. Valentine's Day Massacre, Capone proposed to the gang leaders of New York and other cities that they meet to organize crime throughout the United States. The national crime "Syndicate" was born, consolidating gambling, prostitution, extortion, and liquor trafficking. After 1933, when the Eighteenth Amendment was repealed, thereby ending Prohibition, the Syndicate began to enter the narcotics trade.

Bloodlust

The Great Depression brought the United States to the brink of revolution, but a deeply ingrained tradition of democratic capitalism and FDR's inspired leadership averted a violent breakdown. In Europe, also hard hit by the depression, the people of Italy and Germany did not hunger for democracy. Rather, they turned to the strongman dictatorships promised by a political journalist named Benito Mussolini (1883–1945) and a failed artist, sometime house painter, and full-time political agitator named Adolf Hitler (1889–1945). In Germany and Italy, militaristic authoritarianism burst into iron blossom with promises of a return to national glory and national prosperity.

Lightning War

In Germany, Hitler and his Nazi Party won a popular following that propelled him to the position of chancellor under the aged and infirm President Paul von Hindenburg in 1933 and into absolute dictatorship after Hindenburg's death in 1934. Hitler took Germany out of the League of Nations in 1933 and, in defiance of the Treaty of Versailles, initiated a massive rearmament program.

Seeking an easy foreign conquest to solidify popular support, Benito Mussolini sent Italy's modern army into Africa against Ethiopians who were armed—if at all—with weapons from the last century. Ethiopia collapsed by 1936, and although the nation's emperor, Haile Salassie (1892–1975), appealed to the League of Nations for international aid, that world body proved impotent.

Hard on the heels of the Italian conquest of Ethiopia came the Spanish Civil War (1936–1939), a complex struggle between factions allied with the nation's liberal-leftist republican government, on one side, and the Fascist-sympathizing rightists led primarily by General Francisco Franco (1892–1975) on the other. Hitler and Mussolini eagerly sent military aid to Franco, and Hitler's Luftwaffe (air force) used Spanish towns as practice targets in preparation for the greater conflict looming on the dark horizon. Although Soviet dictator Joseph Stalin (1879–1953) gave military equipment to the Spanish republicans, the United States, Britain, and France—fearing the outbreak of a general war and unwilling to support a pro-communist regime—remained neutral.

While the former Allies waffled and waited, Germany and Italy forged the Rome-Berlin Axis in 1936. That same year, in Asia, the Empire of Japan concluded the Anti-Comintern Pact (an alliance against communism) with Germany; in 1937, Italy signed on to the pact as well. The following year, 1938, Hitler invaded Austria and annexed it to his Third Reich. The year 1938 also saw Hitler's demand for annexation of the Sudetenland—western Czechoslovakia, where many ethnic Germans lived. France and Britain were bound by treaty to defend the territorial integrity of Czechoslovakia, but they nevertheless yielded the Sudetenland to Germany, hoping to "appease" Hitler. British Prime Minister Neville Chamberlain told the world that the cession of the Sudetenland (by means of the 1938 Munich Agreement) ensured "peace for our time."

Chamberlain was wrong. In 1939, Hitler seized the rest of Czechoslovakia, then took a part of Lithuania and prepared to gobble up the so-called Polish Corridor, a narrow strip of land that, by the terms of the Treaty of Versailles, separated East Prussia from the rest of Germany. At this time, Mussolini's Italy annexed Albania. Finally, at four o'clock on the morning of September 1, 1939, Germany invaded—and quickly crushed—Poland. France and Britain could no longer stand by. World War II had begun.

Infamy at Pearl Harbor

While American eyes nervously focused on Europe, Asia was heating to the point of crisis. Japan invaded Manchuria in 1931 and transformed it into the puppet state of Manchukuo the following year. By 1937, Japan and China were engaged in a full-scale, if lopsided, war. On September 27, 1940, Japan signed the Tripartite Pact with Italy and Germany, thereby enlarging the Berlin-Rome Axis into the Berlin-Rome-Tokyo Axis.

Although it remained officially neutral, the United States edged steadily closer to war. The sale of military supplies to the Allies was authorized, and then, in March 1941, Congress passed the Lend-Lease Act, permitting the shipment of weapons and other war materials to nations (Great Britain and, later, China and the USSR) whose defense was considered vital to U.S. security. Cash payment was not required. In September 1940, the first peacetime conscription law in U.S. history had been passed, authorizing the Selective Service registration of 17 million men. In August and September 1941, U.S. merchant vessels were armed for self-defense.

The powder was packed in the keg. All it took was a flame for the war to explode upon America.

That came on December 7, 1941. At 7:50 on a quiet Sunday morning, Japanese aircraft struck with stunning surprise at Pearl Harbor, Hawaii, where some 75 major U.S. Navy ships were moored. By 10 A.M., the attack was over.

The next day, President Roosevelt asked Congress for a declaration of war, calling December 7, 1941, a "date which will live in infamy." Suddenly, the Great Depression dissolved in a headlong rush of young men into the armed forces and of others, women as well as men, into the nation's factories. Industries now tooled up to serve as the "arsenal of democracy."

The Least You Need to Know

- ✪ Although unjustly, Herbert Hoover is often blamed for having caused the depression; the federal government, however, did not take major steps to bring economic relief until Roosevelt assumed office.

- ✪ The massive programs of the New Deal probably averted social breakdown and revolution in the United States, but it was the economic demands of World War II that finally ended the Great Depression.

- ✪ U.S. policy was officially neutral at the outbreak of World War II in Europe, although President Roosevelt negotiated an aid program to England.

- ✪ The surprise Japanese attack on Pearl Harbor on December 7, 1941, immediately brought the United States into World War II.

Saving the World (1941-1945)

When America entered World War I, it rushed to mobilize forces for a *European* war. Now, even as Europe was being overrun by Nazi Germany, Japan had struck directly at United States territory (Hawaii did not become a state until August 21, 1959). Preparations for war were even more urgent in 1941 than they had been in 1917, and the blow at Pearl Harbor was just one of many Japanese assaults. The tiny U.S. garrison on Guam was overwhelmed and surrendered. On Wake Island, a small body of Marines and civilian defense contractors heroically repelled the first Japanese attack but yielded to a second assault by vastly superior forces. Britain's crown colony of Hong Kong collapsed, soon followed by Singapore (another British possession), and then the Dutch East Indies. Burma likewise fell, despite the efforts of Claire L. Chennault (1890–1958), a former U.S. Army Air Corps officer and then air advisor to China's Premier Chiang Kai-shek. Chennault led his American Volunteer Group—the famed "Flying Tigers," a small force of U.S.-made Curtiss P-40 fighter planes piloted by American civilian mercenaries—in surprisingly effective action against the enemy's far superior numbers of aircraft.

For the United States, as for the rest of the formerly "free" world, the opening years of World War II were humiliating, dismal, and terrifying.

"I Shall Return"

After Pearl Harbor, the severest blow in the Pacific came in the Philippines, at the time a U.S. commonwealth territory. General Douglas MacArthur (1880–1964), commanding 31,000 U.S. Army troops and 120,000 Filipinos, made a heroic stand on the Bataan Peninsula. But at last, in February 1942, President Roosevelt ordered MacArthur to evacuate to Australia to assume command of the Allied forces in the southwestern Pacific. Reluctantly, MacArthur left his soldiers to their fate. "I shall return," he pledged as soon as he arrived in Australia. But it would take until 1944 for the Allies to put him into a position to make good on that promise.

Under Lieutenant General Jonathan M. Wainwright, the Filipino-American forces held out until May 6, 1942, when they surrendered and were subject to unspeakable brutality at the hands of Japanese captors.

Desperate for a counterstrike against Japan, the U.S. Army Air Forces approved a mission led by Lieutenant Colonel James Doolittle (1896–1993). Flying at the front of 16 B-25s, launched from the aircraft carrier *Hornet* on April 18, 1942, Doolittle conducted a surprise bombing raid against Tokyo and other Japanese targets. Although the damage to Tokyo and other targets was minor, the attack shocked the Japanese, who were forced to tie up valuable fighter aircraft in home defense. As for the American home front, morale was given an incalculable boost.

Internment

On February 19, 1942, FDR signed Executive Order 9066, requiring all Japanese Americans living within 200 miles of the Pacific shores—citizens and resident aliens alike—to report for relocation in internment camps located in California, Idaho, Utah, Arizona, Wyoming, Colorado, and Arkansas. Government officials claimed fears of sabotage, but non-Japanese farmers in the region feared competition even more and were eager to get rid of their Japanese-American farming neighbors.

Trial, Error, and Triumph in North Africa

In 1941, North Africa was held by German Field Marshal Erwin Rommel (1891–1944), known as the "Desert Fox," whose Afrika Korps was seemingly invincible. The British and Americans agreed to conduct a North African campaign, to defeat the Germans and Italians there, and then to attack German-held southern Europe, what Britain's great wartime Prime Minister Winston Churchill called the "soft underbelly of the Axis." Forces under British General (later, Field Marshal) Bernard Law Montgomery and Americans General Dwight D. Eisenhower and General George S. Patton Jr. decisively defeated the Germans and Italians in North Africa by May of 1943.

Pacific Turning

While the Germans began to lose their grip on Africa, U.S. forces also started to turn the tide in the Pacific. Between May 3 and May 9, 1942, at the Battle of the Coral Sea, the Navy sank or disabled more than 25 Japanese ships, preventing Japan from projecting its forces to the south, where they could interdict supply lines to Australia. The Japanese soon resumed the offensive, however, by attacking the island of Midway, some 1,100 miles northwest of Hawaii. Mounting a task force of 200 ships and 600 planes, Japanese naval commanders counted on the element of surprise to achieve a rapid victory, which would finish off the American Pacific fleet that had already been badly battered at Pearl Harbor. Unknown to the Japanese, however, U.S. intelligence officers had broken the key Japanese naval codes, which gave U.S. Navy commanders advance warning of the task force's approach.

The battle commenced on June 3, 1942. American aircraft, launched from the *Hornet, Yorktown,* and *Enterprise,* sank four Japanese carriers. Reeling from this blow, the Imperial Navy withdrew its fleet, but the Americans gave chase, sinking or disabling two heavy cruisers and three destroyers, as well as shooting 322 planes out of the sky. Midway was one of history's great turning-point battles and set the United States on a victorious course in the Pacific war.

VITAL STATISTICS

Japanese soldiers and sailors characteristically fought to the death. Of the 5,000 Japanese troops defending Tarawa, for example, only 17 were taken prisoner when the island fell on November 26, 1943.

Island Hopping

After suffering defeat at Midway, the Japanese turned their attention to mounting a full-scale assault on Australia. They began by constructing an airstrip on Guadalcanal in the southern Solomon Islands. In response, on August 7, 1942, a U.S. task force landed Marines at Guadalcanal, where the Japanese resisted for six months. The battle on this island was the beginning of a U.S. strategy of "island hopping": a plan to take or retake Japanese-held islands by targeting some but "hopping" over others, which would be isolated and cut off from support.

The next step was to neutralize the major Japanese air and naval base at Rabaul, on the eastern tip of New Britain Island, just east of New Guinea. Under General MacArthur, U.S. and Australian troops attacked through the Solomons and New Guinea. When the Japanese rushed to reinforce their position on the islands of Lae and Salamaua, on March 3 and 4, 1943, U.S. B-24 Liberators and B-17 Flying Fortresses attacked troop transports and their naval escorts with devastating results. The Battle of the Bismarck Sea cost the Japanese 3,500 men; the Allies lost only five planes. The defeat was a severe blow to the Japanese presence in the southwest Pacific.

In the central Pacific, U.S. forces moved against Tarawa and Makin islands. Makin fell quickly, but Tarawa was defended by veteran Japanese jungle fighters, and the battle, begun on November 20, 1943, was extraordinarily costly to both sides.

On Mediterranean Shores

On July 9 and 10, 1943, British and American forces landed in Sicily, and the Italian army crumbled before them. German resistance was a different matter, however, and costly fighting ensued. The invasion of Sicily culminated in the capture of Messina by General Patton's Seventh U.S. Army on August 17, 1943.

By this time, Benito Mussolini had been overthrown by his own Fascist Council (July 25, 1943) and was saved from imprisonment or death by a daring German commando rescue mission. The Italian government, now under Marshal Pietro Badoglio (1871–1956), made secret peace overtures to the Allies while the Germans dug in on the Italian peninsula.

On September 3, 1943, British and U.S. forces left Messina and landed on the toe of the Italian boot. The Fifth Army (a combination of U.S. and British forces), under U.S. General Mark W. Clark (1896–1984), landed at Salerno, and within a month southern Italy fell to the Allies. The Germans evacuated Naples on October 1, but then, under Field Marshal Albert Kesselring, very effectively stiffened their resistance, struggling to hold Rome while exacting a terrible toll on Clark's Fifth Army. After Badoglio's government signed an armistice with the Allies and, on October 13, declared war against Germany, Hitler installed Mussolini as head of a puppet regime in northern Italy.

For the rest of 1943, the Italian front was deadlocked. On January 22, 1944, 50,000 U.S. troops landed at Anzio, just 33 miles south of Rome, but were pinned down by German forces. Not until June 4, 1944, did Rome fall to the Allies. From this point on, the Germans steadily retreated northward. On April 28, 1945, Italian anti-Fascists captured Mussolini and his mistress, Claretta Petacci, and then shot them to death, afterward transporting their bodies to Milan, where they were hung by the heels on an iron fence bordering a gas station near a public square.

The Longest Day

Although U.S. forces first entered Europe via Italy, combat on the main part of the continent was more widespread. The Soviets, devastated by a surprise German invasion begun on June 22, 1941, fought back with a vengeance across their vast homeland. The Battle of Stalingrad (present-day Volgograd), fought from July 17 to November 18, 1942, resulted in the loss of 750,000 Soviet troops but also 850,000 Nazis. It turned the tide of the war on the Eastern Front.

VITAL STATISTICS

Approximately 5,000 Allied ships, 11,000 Allied aircraft, and more than 150,000 troops participated in the June 6 D-Day landing.

In the meantime, British Royal Air Force (RAF) bombers and U.S. Army Air Forces bombers pummeled industrial targets throughout Germany. At sea, the Battle of the Atlantic had raged since early 1942. From January to June of that year, German U-boats sank 3 million tons of U.S. shipping. But the development of longer-range aircraft, capable of dropping underwater depth charges, and more advanced radar systems led to effective defenses against U-boats. By the spring of 1943, the U-boat threat had been greatly reduced.

With pressure applied from the South, from the East, from the air, and at sea, the time was at last right for the major Allied thrust from the West: a full-scale assault on what Hitler called *Festung Europa*—"Fortress Europe." For this offensive, the Allies mounted in Britain the largest and most powerful invasion force in history. Officially dubbed Operation Overlord, the Normandy invasion became popularly known by the military designation of the landing date: D-Day, June 6, 1944.

The Supreme Allied Commander in Europe, U.S. General Dwight David Eisenhower, was the single most powerful Allied military figure in World War II. German resistance was formidable at Normandy, but the Allies prevailed and, on August 15, 1944, launched a second invasion of France, this time in the South between Toulon and Cannes. On August 25, the Allies liberated France's beloved capital, which had been in German hands since 1940.

Blood for Liberty

From France, the Allies launched an invasion into the German homeland itself. By early September, British forces liberated Brussels, Belgium, and American troops crossed the German frontier at Eupen. On October 21, the First U.S. Army captured Aachen, the first German city to fall to the Allies. It was the Third U.S. Army, however, led by the war's single greatest field commander, Lieutenant General George S. Patton Jr. (1885–1945), that spearheaded the main breakout from Normandy, across France, and into Germany. In nine months, the Third U.S. Army moved faster and farther and destroyed or captured more of the enemy than any army had in World War II and, perhaps, in the history of warfare itself.

As 1944 came to a close, it was abundantly clear that the Germans had lost the war. Nevertheless, Adolf Hitler ordered his soldiers to fight to the last man. He reinforced his thinning lines with the *Volkssturm*, an army of underage boys and overage men.

On December 16, 1944, General Gerd von Rundstedt (1875–1953) led a desperate, entirely unexpected counteroffensive, driving a wedge into Allied lines through the thick forest lands of the Ardennes on the Franco-Belgian frontier. With German forces distending the Allied line westward, the ensuing combat was called the Battle of the Bulge. In the most desperate battle of the war in western Europe, the First and Third U.S. Armies pushed back the "bulge," which was wholly contained by January 1945. The last great German offensive, the battle had been Germany's final chance to stall the Allies' advance into its homeland.

During February 1945, U.S. forces advanced to the Rhine River and, after clearing the west bank, elements of the 9th Armored Division captured the bridge at Remagen, near Cologne, on March 7. Allied forces crossed this bridge as well as other points along the Rhine and were then poised to make a run for Berlin. Acting on orders from President

Roosevelt and Prime Minister Winston Churchill, Eisenhower, believing that Hitler would make his last stand in Bavaria, left the conquest of Berlin to the Soviet Red Army. It was a controversial decision with profound implications for postwar Europe.

While the British and Americans had been closing in from the West, the Soviets executed a massive assault on Germany's Eastern Front. By the end of January, the Red Army had pushed through Poland into Germany itself. The ruined German capital, Berlin, was fiercely defended and did not fall until April 16, 1945.

VITAL STATISTICS

Civilian deaths in World War II exceeded 25 million, of whom 6 million were Jews systematically murdered, for the most part in specially constructed death camps, by order of Adolf Hitler.

Indeed, Germans could have found few places of refuge in the spring of 1945, for the entire world was learning of war crimes committed on an unimaginably vast scale. In their drive toward Berlin, the Allies liberated one Nazi concentration camp after another—to which Jews, Gypsies, Slavs, homosexuals, and others deemed "undesirable" by the Reich had been sent for inhuman confinement, war-related slave labor, or outright extermination. The Nazis had not been content with conquest; they intended nothing less than genocide in what they called the "Final Solution to the Jewish Question" and the rest of the world, after the war, called "the Holocaust."

Westbound Soviet and eastbound American troops met at the river Elbe on April 25, 1945. Five days later, Adolf Hitler, holed up in a bunker beneath the shattered streets of Berlin, shot himself in the head while (it is believed) simultaneously biting down on a glass cyanide ampule in a double suicide with his long-time mistress, Eva Braun, whom he had married—in the bunker—the day before. On May 7, 1945, senior representatives of Germany's armed forces surrendered to the Allies at General Eisenhower's headquarters in Reims, France. Joseph Stalin insisted on a second surrender in Soviet-controlled territory, so another signing took place in Berlin on May 8. From the pages of American newspapers, headlines shouted the arrival of Victory in Europe Day, or V-E Day.

Fat Man and Little Boy

German scientists discovered the possibility of nuclear fission—a process whereby the tremendous energy of the atom might be liberated—in 1938. Fortunately for the world, Hitler's anti-Semitic reign of terror drove many of Germany's best thinkers out of the country, and the nation's efforts to exploit fission in a weapon came to nothing. Three Hungarian-born physicists who had fled to America—Leo Szilard, Eugene Wigner, and Edward Teller—were all intimately familiar with what a man like Hitler could do. They asked America's single most prestigious physicist, Albert Einstein (himself a fugitive from Nazi persecution), to write a letter to President Roosevelt, warning him of Germany's nuclear weapons research and urging that the United States begin research in the field.

Heeding Einstein's 1939 letter, along with two others written in 1940, FDR authorized research that, in 1942, became the Manhattan Project. The program grew into the greatest and most costly military enterprise in history to that point. The Manhattan Project employed the nation's foremost scientific minds and put at their disposal a virtually limitless industrial facility. A prototype atomic bomb was completed in the summer of 1945 and detonated near Alamogordo, New Mexico, on July 16, 1945.

VITAL STATISTICS

Dropped on Hiroshima, with a population of about 300,000, "Little Boy" killed 78,000 people instantly; 10,000 more were never found; more than 70,000 were injured; and many subsequently died of radiation-related causes. Nagasaki, with a population of 250,000, instantly lost some 40,000 people when "Fat Man" was dropped. Another 40,000 were wounded.

At this time, the Allies were planning the final invasion of Japan, which was expected to add a million more deaths to the Allied toll. Hoping to avoid the necessity of invasion, President Truman authorized the use of the terrible new weapon against Japan. On August 6, 1945, a lone B-29 bomber, named *Enola Gay* after pilot Paul Tibbets's mother, dropped "Little Boy" on Hiroshima, obliterating the city in three-fifths of a second. Three days later, "Fat Man" was dropped on Nagasaki, destroying about half the city.

On August 10, the day after the attack on Nagasaki, Japan sued for peace on condition that the emperor be allowed to remain as sovereign ruler. On August 11, the Allies replied that they and they alone would determine the future of Emperor Hirohito. But at last, on August 14, the emperor personally accepted the Allied terms. A cease-fire was declared on August 15, and on September 2, 1945, General MacArthur presided over the Japanese signing of the formal surrender document on the deck of the U.S. battleship *Missouri*, anchored in Tokyo Bay.

The Least You Need to Know

- Never before or since World War II have Americans fought with such unanimity and singleness of purpose.

- If ever a war was a contest of good versus evil, such was World War II, and America's role in achieving victory elevated the nation to superpower status in the postwar political order.

- The United States waged a war on two vast fronts, concentrating first against Germany in Europe and then against Japan in the Pacific.

- The war in Europe was ended by massive application of conventional weapons, while the war in the Pacific was brought to a terrible close by the dropping of two atomic bombs on the Japanese cities of Hiroshima and Nagasaki.

PART 7

Superpower

World War II was a contest between fascist, Nazi, and Japanese imperialist powers on one side and an alliance of democratic and communist powers on the other. Following the defeat of the fascist-Nazi-imperialist Axis, the alliance between the Western powers and the Soviet Union fell apart, setting up democracy and communism to square off against one another as the great opposing ideologies of the postwar world. The World War II alliance shattered into a long contest of diplomatic maneuvering and military posturing called the Cold War. This Cold War also spawned two bloody "proxy wars," one in Korea and one in Vietnam. In the meantime, the home front after World War II was both a booming and a turbulent place. The economy soared, the civil rights movement went into full swing beginning in the late 1950s, and the Vietnam War proved the catalyst for a general social protest movement during the 1960s. The chapters in this part cover what Anglo-American poet W. H. Auden aptly called "the Age of Anxiety."

War Served Cold—and Hot (1944–1954)

Rejoicing at the end of World War II was intense, but all too brief. The Union of Soviet Socialist Republics (USSR, or Soviet Union), portrayed by U.S. politicians and press alike as a valiant ally during the war, once again became an implacable ideological and political enemy. The Eastern and Central European nations occupied by the Red Army became less-than-willing USSR satellites, and the postwar world was divided between the Western democracies (led by the United States) and the "Soviet bloc." It seemed as if the seeds of World War III had been sown.

A Fight for Peace

It was clear to America's leaders that the Allies had won World War I, only later to "lose the peace." They were determined not to make the same mistake again.

The Nations Unite

During World War II, the powers aligned against the Axis called themselves the "United Nations." From August to October 1944, the United States, Great Britain, the USSR, and China met at Dumbarton Oaks, an estate in the Georgetown section of Washington, D.C., to sketch out plans for a new world body. The wartime allies—plus France—would constitute a peacekeeping ("security") council, while the other nations of the world, though represented, would play secondary roles. Later in the year, a formal United Nations Charter was drawn up and adopted by 50 nations at the San Francisco Conference. The charter became effective after a majority of the signatory nations ratified it on October 24, 1945.

The Germans Are Divided

Another element vital to winning the peace was the postwar treatment of Germany. American, British, and French leaders, mindful of how the punitive Treaty of Versailles had created the conditions that brought Hitler to power and plunged the world into the second great war of the century, did not clamor for revenge. The Soviet Union's Stalin, however, demanded the total subjugation of Germany. A compromise was reached, by which Germany was carved into four "zones of occupation," each under the control of a different ally: the United States, Britain, France, and the USSR.

AMERICAN ECHO

"The Marshall Plan will go down in history as one of America's greatest contributions to the peace of the world."

—Harry S. Truman, memoirs, 1955

Marshall Presents a Plan

On June 5, 1947, George C. Marshall proposed the single boldest step toward winning the peace. The former Army Chief of Staff, now Secretary of State in President Harry S. Truman's cabinet, concisely described in an address at Harvard University a plan whereby the nations of Europe would draw up a unified scheme for economic reconstruction to be funded by the United States. Sixteen Western European nations formed the Organization for European Economic Cooperation to coordinate the program formally known as the European Recovery Program, but familiarly called the Marshall Plan.

Having witnessed totalitarian regimes rush to fill the void of postwar economic catastrophe, Marshall and other U.S. leaders were eager to restore the war-ravaged economies of the West. Economic well-being, they felt, was the strongest ally of democracy.

Curtain of Iron

On March 5, 1946, Winston Churchill addressed little Westminster College in Fulton, Missouri. "From Stettin in the Baltic to Trieste in the Adriatic," he dramatically declared, "an iron curtain has descended across the continent." The term *Iron Curtain* was used for the next 50-plus years to describe the economic, social, and military barriers that Eastern Europe's Communist countries created against the West.

"Containing" Communism

In 1823, President James Monroe issued his famous "Monroe Doctrine," warning European powers that the United States would act to halt any new attempts to colonize the Americas. In 1947, President Harry S. Truman promulgated the "Truman Doctrine," warning the Soviet Union, which supported threatened Communist takeovers in Greece and Turkey, that the United States would act to halt the spread of communism wherever in the world it menaced democracy.

The Truman Doctrine proposed that the most effective way to combat communism was to contain it, confronting the Soviet Union—by economic and political means rather than military force, if possible—wherever it sought to expand its influence. The Cold War began in earnest, and the conflict prompted rapid passage of the National Security Act of 1947, which reorganized the War Department into the Department of Defense (under which the Armed Forces were unified), created the U.S. Air Force as an independent military arm, and established the Central Intelligence Agency (CIA).

A Second Battle of Berlin

Truman's containment policy prompted the United States and its Western allies to take a strong stand in Germany after the Soviet Union began detaining troop trains and other surface transport bound for West Berlin in March 1948. (Although Berlin was deep inside the Soviet sector of occupied Germany, the city, too, was divided into zones of Allied occupation.) In response, on June 7, the Western allies announced their intention to create the separate, permanent capitalist state of West Germany. Two weeks later, the Soviet Union blockaded West Berlin.

Would the West back down? Would this be the start of World War III?

Truman did not take armed action against the Soviets. Instead, he ordered an airlift, a spectacular chain of round-the-clock supply flights into West Berlin—277,569 flights over 321 days, carrying 1,325,500 tons of food and other supplies. The airlift was a political and logistical triumph, which caused the Soviet Union to lift the blockade after little less than a year. In April 1949, the airlift led to the creation of the North Atlantic Treaty Organization (NATO), a key defensive alliance of the Western nations against the Communist East.

Witch Hunts

While politicians and generals scrambled to "contain" communism abroad, some Americans looked homeward. Joseph R. McCarthy (1908–1957), a mediocre senator from Wisconsin, could not gain the political traction he sought until he made a provocative speech to the Women's Republican Club of Wheeling, West Virginia, on February 9, 1950.

Withdrawing from his coat pocket a piece of paper, he held it up, proclaiming that it was a list of 205 known Communists in the State Department.

The speech got on the Associated Press wire, and McCarthy suddenly became famous. During the next four years, he spearheaded a crusade to root out Communists in government and other positions of power. No one ever saw the list of names McCarthy held up, and only a few people were skeptical when the number of Communists was repeatedly—randomly—revised, finally getting pegged at 57.

AMERICAN ECHO

The crux of the North Atlantic Treaty, which created NATO, is Article 5: "The parties agree that an armed attack against one or more of them in Europe or North America shall be considered an attack against them all."

Crusade is the word McCarthy liked. Others called it a witch-hunt. McCarthy pointed fingers and leveled charges. Due process of law, the rules of evidence, and the presumption of innocence were discarded. A McCarthy accusation was enough to ruin a reputation and destroy a career. Presumed innocence became presumed guilt. Those called to testify before the committee were asked to "name names"—expose individuals with Communist affiliations. If witnesses refused, they were found in contempt of Congress and subject to imprisonment. If a witness exercised his Fifth Amendment right not to testify against himself, McCarthy presumed him guilty.

The McCarthy witch-hunts—and the parallel activity of the House Un-American Activities Committee (HUAAC) in the House of Representatives—were not born of fantasy. Many influential Americans had ties to Communist organizations, although most of these associations came and went with the 1930s, when intellectuals and liberals flocked to socialist and Communist groups to oppose fascism. The Cold War also spawned a legion of spies and moles, including those who communicated U.S. atomic secrets to the Soviets, thereby helping to enable the USSR to develop an atomic bomb in 1949 and a hydrogen bomb in 1954.

Like his HUAAC counterparts, McCarthy made no effort to separate fact from fantasy, and even after the Republican Party captured the White House in 1952, he continued his strident attacks. In 1954, he accused Secretary of the Army Robert T. Stevens and others of deliberately hampering the investigation of Communist infiltration of the U.S. military. This accusation was sufficient to provoke President Eisenhower to encourage Congress to form a committee to investigate McCarthy's attempts to coerce army brass into granting preferential treatment for a former McCarthy aide, Private G. David Schine.

From April to June 1954, the "Army-McCarthy Hearings" were broadcast on an infant medium called television. Joseph McCarthy was exposed as a reckless, self-serving demagogue. Censured by action of the Senate later that year, he was overtaken by the alcoholism that had long dogged him. McCarthy died in 1957, at age 49.

"Police Action" in Korea

The Cold War was not just a contest of rattling sabers and strong language. As Eastern Europe had fallen behind an "Iron Curtain," so China, the world's most populous nation, became the Communist-controlled People's Republic of China in 1949. Elsewhere in Asia, Communist factions positioned themselves to take power. After World War II, Korea was divided along the 38th parallel between a Soviet occupation zone in the north and a U.S. zone in the south. In November 1947, the United Nations resolved to create a unified independent Korea, but the Communists barred free elections in the north. Only in the U.S. southern zone were elections held, and on August 15, 1948, the Republic of Korea was born. In North Korea, the Communists created the Democratic People's Republic of Korea in September 1948.

Invasion, Counterstrike, Invasion

On June 25, 1950, Communist-backed forces from the North invaded South Korea. The United States secured a United Nations sanction against the invasion and contributed the lion's share of troops to repel it. World War II hero of the Pacific Douglas MacArthur was put in command of the UN forces.

The North Korean troops, trained and equipped by the Soviets and the Chinese, pushed the South Koreans back toward the southern tip of the Korean peninsula. MacArthur struggled to hold the critical southern port of Pusan to buy time until reinforcements arrived. He executed an extremely risky landing at Inchon, on the west coast of Korea, behind North Korean lines. The landing was a stunning success, and by October 1, 1950, the North Koreans had been forced out of South Korea in a long, disorderly retreat. UN forces were now arrayed along the 38th parallel.

Within the Truman administration, debate raged over whether to cross the 38th parallel and invade North Korea. To do so might trigger World War III by drawing the Communist Chinese and the Soviets into the conflict. To do less might mean the loss of all Korea to the Communist camp. President Truman compromised, authorizing the crossing, but taking steps to avoid directly provoking the Chinese and the Soviets. On October 7, the UN General Assembly called for the unification of Korea and authorized MacArthur to invade. On October 19, the North Korean capital of Pyongnang fell, and the North Korean armies were pushed far north, to the Yalu River, the nation's border with Manchuria, China.

The war seemed to be over. But between October 14 and November 1, some 180,000 Communist "volunteers" crossed the Yalu from China. MacArthur launched an offensive on November 24, only to be beaten back by massive Chinese resistance, which forced UN troops back across the 38th parallel. The South Korean capital of Seoul fell to the Communists in January 1951.

Meatgrinder

Halting their retreat south of Seoul, U.S. and other allied troops began probing northward once again in an offensive that front-line soldiers dubbed the "meatgrinder." By March 1951, UN forces had returned to the 38th parallel and had established a strong defensive position.

Old Soldiers ...

In light of the Chinese intervention, General MacArthur demanded permission to retaliate against the Chinese by bombing Manchuria. President Truman and the United Nations turned down MacArthur's request, fearing that direct aggression against China would trigger nuclear war with the Soviets. On March 25, 1951, just after Truman had completed preparation of a cease-fire proposal, MacArthur broadcast an unauthorized ultimatum to the enemy commander, preempting the president's proposal, which had to be shelved. MacArthur also sent a letter to Republican House minority leader Joe Martin, criticizing Truman's war policy. Martin read the letter into the Congressional Record. In response to this final act of insubordination, Truman relieved MacArthur of command in Korea on April 11, 1951.

VITAL STATISTICS

Just how many Chinese and North Korean troops were killed in the Korean War is unknown, but estimates range between 1.5 and 2 million, in addition to at least a million civilians. The UN command lost 88,000, of whom 23,300 were American. Many more were wounded. South Korean civilian casualties probably equaled those of North Korea.

Thrust, Counterthrust, and Stalemate

The highly capable Lieutenant General Matthew B. Ridgway assumed command of UN and U.S. forces, and Lieutenant General James A. Van Fleet led the Eighth U.S. Army northward. But on April 22, nearly half a million Chinese troops drove the Eighth Army to within 5 miles of Seoul. On May 10, the Chinese launched a second offensive, concentrating on the eastern portion of the UN line; however, Van Fleet counterattacked in the West, north of Seoul, taking the Communists by surprise. In full retreat, the Communists suffered their heaviest casualties of the war and withdrew into North Korea. By the beginning of summer 1951, the war was stalemated at the 38th parallel.

Talking Peace and Talking Some More

Armistice negotiations had begun at the instigation of the Soviets in June 1951 and dragged on for those two years of guerrilla combat. At last, during April 1953, the seemingly insoluble POW issue was settled with a compromise permitting freed prisoners to choose sides.

The Unhappiest Ally

The only individual who remained thoroughly displeased was Syngman Rhee (1875–1965), president of South Korea. Nevertheless, an armistice was signed on July 27, 1953—but did not include South Korea.

The Korean War succeeded in containing communism to North Korea, but this costly conflict was otherwise inconclusive, the Korean War has never officially ended, and today the world faces the threat of a nuclear-armed North.

The Least You Need to Know

- ✪ Jubilation at the end of World War II was short lived, as the Western capitalist nations and the Eastern European and Asian Communist nations squared off for a Cold War.

- ✪ The Marshall Plan was a humanitarian and political triumph for the forces of democracy.

- ✪ A policy of "containing" communism and a fear of touching off a nuclear World War III dominated American foreign policy in the postwar years.

- ✪ The Korean War demonstrated the horrible dilemma of fighting worldwide communism: defeat an enemy without touching off a new—atomic—world war.

CHAPTER 30

From the Back of the Bus to the Great Society (1947–1968)

With the ruins of war-ravaged Europe and Asia still smoldering, much of the planet's population was hungry, politically oppressed, or both as the first half of the twentieth century came to an end. But Americans basked in the blessings of liberty and had much to be proud of. The postwar world was scary, with nuclear incineration seemingly a push of a button away, but the 1950s would find America complacent and prosperous, spawning a web of verdant suburbs interconnected by new highways built under the National Interstate and Defense Highways Act of 1956.

Postwar suburbia was an expression of the long-held American Dream: a house of one's own, a little plot of land, and a clean and decent place to live. But if suburban lawns were green, the suburbanites were white. Most African Americans were excluded from the dream.

Executive Order 9981

On July 26, 1948, President Harry S. Truman (1884–1972) issued Executive Order 9981, which mandated "equality of treatment and opportunity to all persons in the Armed Services without regard to race." African Americans had served in the military since the American Revolution, but, beginning in the mid-nineteenth century, always in racially segregated units under white officers. Truman's order ended that policy.

The Dream Deferred

Truman's order was a start, but racial prejudice was ingrained in American life. In the South, it was the law. "Jim Crow" legislation passed during the bitter years following Reconstruction remained on the books. In its 1896 decision in the case of *Plessy* v. *Ferguson,* the United States Supreme Court upheld the segregation of public services and facilities, such as schools, provided that such services and facilities were "separate but equal."

During and following both world wars, African Americans migrated in large numbers from the rural South to the industrial cities of the North. Northern industry welcomed their cheap labor, but many whites—fearing they would lose their jobs to the newcomers—met them with hostility. Blacks typically found themselves restricted to menial labor and compelled to live in slum districts that became known as ghettos.

The entire American nation, not just the South, was both separate *and* unequal.

Rosa Parks Boards a Bus

On Thursday, December 1, 1955, Rosa Parks, an African American department store tailor and seamstress, boarded a Montgomery, Alabama, city bus at the end of the workday. She walked past seats marked "Whites Only" and sat with three other blacks in the fifth row, the first row that a city ordinance permitted them to occupy—provided that no white person who wanted to sit was left standing. After a few more stops, the front four rows filled with whites. One white man was left standing. The same ordinance that barred African

Americans from the first four rows of the bus seats also forbade blacks and whites from occupying the same row. Accordingly, the bus driver directed all four of the passengers seated in the fifth row to move.

Three moved. Parks refused. When the driver told her that he would call the police and have her arrested, she replied calmly, "You may do that."

Park's arrest launched a well-organized boycott of city buses and downtown businesses. In the end, the year-long boycott not only succeeded in desegregating Montgomery buses, it suddenly focused the attention of the entire nation—black and white—on civil rights.

REMEMBER THIS

The year before Rosa Parks's bus ride, the United States Supreme Court effectively declared segregation illegal when, on May 17, 1954, it handed down a decision in the case of *Brown* v. *Board of Education of Topeka, Kansas.* The decision was the culmination of a long series of lawsuits that the National Association for the Advancement of Colored People (NAACP) first brought against segregated school districts in the 1930s. Repeatedly, the Supreme Court consistently ruled with its 1896 decision in *Plessy* v. *Ferguson* that found "separate but equal" accommodations for black people constitutional as long as all *tangible* aspects of the accommodations were, indeed, equal. But in 1954, Thurgood Marshall (1908–1993) and other NAACP lawyers demonstrated that segregated school systems were inherently unequal because of *intangible* social factors. The high court agreed. Desegregation of the nation's schools became the law of the land. In some places, the process of integration proceeded without incident; in others, it was accompanied by violent resistance that required the intervention of federal marshals and even federal troops. (In 1967, President Lyndon Baines Johnson appointed Thurgood Marshall to the Supreme Court; he was the first African American to serve.)

A Preacher from Atlanta

The Reverend Martin Luther King Jr., pastor of the Dexter Avenue Baptist Church in Montgomery, entered the national spotlight during the Montgomery boycott and used his sudden growing prominence to infuse the national Civil Rights Movement with what he had learned from the example of India's great leader, Mahatma Gandhi. Gandhi taught the Hindu-inspired principle of *satyagrapha*, "holding to the truth" by nonviolent civil disobedience, steadfastly refusing to cooperate with unjust laws.

King became president of the Southern Christian Leadership Conference (SCLC), leading voter registration drives, marches, and other campaigns. In August 1963, he organized a massive March on Washington, where he delivered one of the great speeches in American history, "I Have a Dream."

AMERICAN ECHO

"… I have a dream that one day on the red hills of Georgia sons of former slaves and the sons of former slave-owners will be able to sit down together at the table of brother-hood …. I have a dream that one day down in Alabama, with its vicious racists, with its governor having his lips dripping with the words of interposition and nullification, one day right there in Alabama little black boys and black girls will be able to join hands with little white boys and white girls as sisters and brothers."

—Martin Luther King Jr., speech of August 28, 1963

In 1964, King was recognized with the Nobel Peace Prize and went on to conduct deseg-regation efforts in St. Augustine, Florida. He organized a voter-registration drive in Selma, Alabama, leading a march from Selma to Montgomery in March 1965. At Selma, on the Edmund Pettis Bridge, King and the other marchers were met by a phalanx of club-wielding state troopers. King responded by asking the marchers to kneel in prayer, and then he turned back with them. Some—especially younger black civil rights activists—fell away from commitment to nonviolence. From 1965 on, the civil rights movement developed an increasingly strident and outraged militant wing.

After 1965, King expanded the movement into the North and attacked not just social injustice, but economic inequality, seeking to unite the poor of all races and ethnicities.

While planning a multiracial "poor people's march" on Washington in 1968, King flew to Memphis, Tennessee, to support striking sanitation workers. In that city, on April 4, he fell to a sniper's bullet.

Or Does It Explode?

The assassination of Dr. King, a compelling apostle of nonviolent social change, sparked urban riots across the country. More than 100 cities erupted.

The racial violence of the 1960s was dramatic evidence of the pent-up frustration and outrage long simmering within black America. But it was not until the emergence of Malcolm X in the early 1960s that African American militancy was given compelling and eloquent direction. Malcolm X was born Malcolm Little in Omaha, Nebraska, in 1925. He turned bitter and rebellious after his father, an activist preacher, was murdered by white racists in 1931, presumably for advocating the black empowerment ideas of the charismatic Marcus Garvey.

Malcolm Little moved to Cambridge, Massachusetts, and then to New York's Harlem. He plied a criminal career until, convicted of burglary, he was imprisoned from 1946 to 1952. In prison, he became a follower of Elijah Muhammad (1897–1975), leader of the Lost–Found Nation of Islam, popularly called the Black Muslims. Rejecting his surname as a "slave name," Malcolm Little became Malcolm X and, upon his release, emerged as a leading spokesman for the Black Muslim movement.

AMERICAN ECHO

The great African American poet Langston Hughes (1902–1967) asked in a poem called "Harlem" …

"What happens to a dream deferred? Does it dry up like a raisin in the sun? … *Or does it explode?*"

Malcolm X electrified many in the black community, giving young black men in particular a sense of pride, purpose, and potential, even as his rhetoric intimidated and outraged many white people. Yet Malcolm X evolved ideas that were not only quite different from those of Martin Luther King, but also from the others identified as "militants."

Initially advocating the separation of blacks and whites, Malcolm X became increasingly committed to Islam and, during a *hajj,* or pilgrimage to Mecca, in 1964, he worshiped with whites as well as blacks.

Breaking with the Black Muslims, he founded the Organization of Afro-American Unity in June 1964 and advocated a socialist solution to the corruption of American society that had led to racial hatred. His original message of racial separation became a religiously inspired quest for racial equality.

The evolution of Malcolm X was cut short on February 21, 1965, when he was gunned down by three Black Muslims during a speech at Harlem's Audubon Auditorium.

The journey of black America, like the life of Malcolm X, remained incomplete during the 1960s and remains incomplete to this day. Even on January 20, 2009, as Barack Obama placed his hand on Abraham Lincoln's Bible and took the oath of office as the first African American president of the United States, most black citizens were still living less affluently, amid more crime and with less opportunity than most white Americans.

AMERICAN ECHO

"If you are born in America with a black skin, you're born in prison."

—Malcolm X, interview, 1963

Sputnik and the New Frontier

Despite growing racial disharmony, the United States was a fairly self-satisfied place in the 1950s—at least until October 4, 1957, when the world learned that the Soviet Union had successfully launched a 184-pound satellite into Earth orbit, *Sputnik I.* Suddenly, the USSR, our adversary in the postwar world, the embodiment of "godless communism," had demonstrated to the world its technological superiority. The launching of *Sputnik* began a "Space Race" in which the United States came in dead second during all the early laps. The Soviets put a man, "cosmonaut" Yuri Gagarin, into orbit four years after *Sputnik* and almost a month before American "astronaut" Alan B. Shepard was launched on a lesser 15-minute suborbital flight on May 5, 1961.

Sputnik shook Americans out of complacency. In the 1960 presidential race, between Eisenhower's vice president, Richard M. Nixon, and a dashing, youthful senator from Massachusetts, John F. Kennedy, voters chose the candidate who embodied new energy and embraced challenge.

"The Torch Has Been Passed ..."

At 43, John F. Kennedy (JFK) was the youngest elected president in American history. (Vice President Theodore Roosevelt was 42 when he assumed office in 1901 after the assassination of President William McKinley.) Kennedy's administration established the Peace Corps (an organization of young volunteers assigned to work in developing nations), created the Alliance for Progress (which strengthened relations with Latin America), and set a national goal of landing an American on the moon before the end of the 1960s.

Intelligent, handsome, idealistic, and a war hero, Kennedy declared in his inaugural address that the "torch has been passed to a new generation"—of which he was clearly the embodiment.

From the Bay of Pigs to the Edge of Armageddon

Adored by many, Kennedy never succeeded in winning substantial Congressional support. Even though both houses held Democratic majorities, Southern Democrats were conservative on foreign policy and vehemently resistant to Kennedy's domestic initiatives, especially those furthering civil rights.

Early in Kennedy's administration, the nation suffered the tragic humiliation of a bungled attempt to invade Cuba, which had been under the Communist rule of Fidel Castro (b. 1926) since 1959. In March 1960, President Eisenhower approved a CIA plan to train anti-Castro Cuban exiles for an invasion intended to ignite a popular coup d'etat against the Cuban leader. Kennedy allowed the preparations to proceed, and some 1,500 exiles landed on April 17, 1961, at Bay of Pigs on the island's southwestern coast.

The result was an unmitigated military disaster. By April 19, the invasion had been crushed and 1,200 survivors were captured. (They were released in December 1962, in exchange for $53 million worth of U.S. medicines and provisions.)

Soviet Premier Nikita Khrushchev saw the failure of the Bay of Pigs as a sign of the new administration's vulnerability. He moved to exploit this flaw by covertly sending nuclear-armed missiles to Cuba along with the technical and military personnel to install and operate them. An American U-2 spy plane photographed the missile bases under construction. On October 22, 1962, President Kennedy addressed the nation in an urgent television broadcast, announcing a naval blockade (officially called a "quarantine" to avoid committing an overt act of war) of the island. Kennedy demanded that the Soviets withdraw the missiles, and by October 24, the blockade was in place.

For the next four days, Americans braced themselves for Armageddon, but on October 28, Khrushchev offered to remove the missiles under UN supervision. For his part, President Kennedy pledged never again to attempt to invade Cuba, and he also secretly promised to remove U.S. missiles from Turkish bases near the Soviet border. On October 29, the blockade was lifted, and JFK had scored a signal victory in Cold War brinkmanship.

Motorcade in Dallas

On November 22, 1963, President Kennedy visited Texas to bolster his popularity as he geared up for the reelection campaign. As the motorcade passed by the Texas School Book Depository in downtown Dallas, three shots rang out, the second of which ripped into the president's head, fatally wounding him. Texas's Governor John Connally, riding in the limo's jump seat in front and slightly below the president, was seriously wounded, but recovered.

The accused assassin, captured later in the day (although not before gunning down Dallas police officer J. D. Tippett), was Lee Harvey Oswald, a misfit who had lived for a period in the Soviet Union, having renounced his U.S. citizenship. As he was being transferred from the city lock-up to the county jail, Oswald himself was murdered on November 24 by Dallas nightclub owner and small-time mobster Jack Ruby.

Lyndon Baines Johnson

John Fitzgerald Kennedy was pronounced dead at Dallas's Parkland Hospital at 1 P.M. local time. Lyndon Baines Johnson (1908–1973), or LBJ, the popular Texas senator tapped by Kennedy as vice president to improve his standing in the South and West, took the oath of office inside Air Force One at 2:39 P.M.

One of Johnson's first acts was to appoint a commission, headed by Supreme Court Chief Justice Earl Warren, to investigate the assassination. Despite the Warren Commission's finding that Oswald had acted alone, conspiracy theories proliferated. A 1976 congressional investigation reached conclusions (based on a now-discredited analysis of an audio recording purported to reveal more than the three shots reported by the Warren Commission) that gave these added weight. Speculation persists to this day.

The Great Society

JFK's sudden martyrdom cast an unassailable aura of enchantment over Kennedy and his unfinished legacy. President Johnson refashioned the JFK social programs that had struggled in Congress and, in the name of the slain president, oversaw their passage into law. When Johnson ran for president in his own right in 1964, he called upon America to build a "Great Society," one that "rests on abundance and liberty for all."

Like Franklin Delano Roosevelt's "New Deal," the phrase "Great Society" became the label for an ambitious, idealistic package of social welfare legislation, including Medicare, which helped finance medical care for Americans over 65; Medicaid, which provided health care for the poor of all ages; elementary, secondary, and higher education acts to enhance education and provide financial aid to college students; and legislation relating to what Johnson called a "War on Poverty."

An Act of Civil Rights

Of all the creations of the Great Society, none has had more lasting or profound impact than the Civil Rights Act of 1964, banning segregation and discrimination in public accommodations and barring employers from discriminatory hiring practices based on race.

The Civil Rights Act of 1964 was followed by the Voting Rights Act of 1965, which tore down the last vestiges of state and local legislation intended to prevent or discourage African Americans from voting. (In its controversial decision in *Shelby County v. Holder* [2013], the Supreme Court struck down a portion of the act that provided for federal supervision of local governments with a history of discriminatory voting ordinances.)

By the end of the Johnson years, equality in America was not a fact of life, but neither was it a condition of law anywhere in the United States.

The Least You Need to Know

- The modern Civil Rights Movement began with the integration of the armed forces in 1947 and developed through a nonviolent program of civil disobedience led by Dr. Martin Luther King Jr. and others.

- The Kennedy administration's record is ambiguous, but the young president became and remains a potent symbol of the great potential of American democracy.

- Although John F. Kennedy attempted to create an ambitious program of civil rights and social legislation, it was Lyndon Baines Johnson's administration that secured passage of legislation creating the "Great Society."

- The landmark Civil Rights Act of 1964 extended civil rights protection into the nongovernmental sector by banning segregation and discrimination in public accommodations such as restaurants, theaters, and hotels, and barring employers from discriminatory hiring practices based on race.

Nam (1946–1975)

In 1964, the beacon of the Great Society shone brightly. Motivated by the memory of John F. Kennedy and energized by the moral passion of Lyndon Johnson, the social reform program, even more ambitious than FDR's New Deal, seemed unstoppable.

Then, on August 2 of that year, the American destroyer *Maddox,* conducting electronic espionage in what U.S. authorities claimed to be international waters, was reported as under attack by North Vietnamese torpedo boats. Undamaged, *Maddox* was joined by a second destroyer, the *C. Turner Joy.* Two days later, both ships reported coming under fire.

Published in 1971, *The Pentagon Papers* (Chapter 32) revealed that the first attack did not occur in international waters and the second did not occur at all. But at the time, Johnson ordered retaliatory air strikes against North Vietnam. At his request, on August 7, the U.S. Senate passed the Tonkin Gulf Resolution, giving the president almost unlimited authority to escalate American involvement in a war destined to wreck the Great Society, nearly tear the United States apart, spawn an idealistic youth counterculture, and cost the lives of more than 58,000 young Americans.

A Long Story

During World War II, France effectively lost its colonies in Southeast Asia as Japan seized control but did not succeed in crushing local nationalist movements, the most powerful of which, in Vietnam, was that of the communist-aligned Viet Minh led by Ho Chi Minh (1890–1969).

When the war ended, Nationalist Chinese troops (under Chiang Kai-shek) occupied northern Vietnam, and the British secured southern Vietnam for the re-entry of the French. The Viet Minh launched a guerrilla war. Chiang Kai-shek withdrew from northern Vietnam and turned the territory over to the French, assuming they were better able to resist the communist insurgency than he.

The March to Dien Bien Phu

In the early Cold War, U.S. leaders feared communist expansion in Southeast Asia and supplied the French with funding, military equipment, and—on August 3, 1950—the first contingent of U.S. military "advisors."

France launched a blow against the communists on the strategically located plain of Dien Bien Phu, near Laos. President Eisenhower stepped up military aid, but Dien Bien Phu fell to Ho Chi Minh's forces on May 7, 1954. A string of Viet Minh victories followed, the French and the Viet Minh concluded a cease-fire and agreed to divide Vietnam along the 17th parallel, much as Korea had been divided along the 38th.

Domino Theory

During the thick of the Dien Bien Phu campaign, on April 7, 1954, President Eisenhower presented reporters with his rationale for aiding a foreign colonial power in its fight against communism in Vietnam, a remote country. "You have a row of dominoes set up," he explained, "you knock over the first one, and what will happen to the last one is the certainty it will go over very quickly." This clumsily expressed metaphor was christened the Domino Theory. It became the basis for an escalating American involvement in Vietnam.

American Advice

As a condition of the armistice agreement between Ho Chi Minh and French representatives, divided Vietnam was to hold elections within two years with the object of
reunification. South Vietnam's President Ngo Dinh Diem refused to hold the promised
elections. The United States, more concerned with blocking communism than with
practicing democracy in Vietnam, backed Diem's position. Under John F. Kennedy,
who succeeded Eisenhower in 1961, the number of military "advisors" sent to Vietnam
rose.

A Monk on Fire and the Fall of a "Friend"

Anxious to stop the toppling dominoes, Kennedy turned a blind eye on the unpopularity
and corruption of the Diem regime. The world was soon horrified by a series of extreme
protest demonstrations, including the self-immolation of a Buddhist monk, Thích Quang
Dúc, on a busy Saigon intersection on June 11, 1963.

By mid-1963, the Kennedy administration determined that Diem was no longer "viable."
JFK acquiesced to a CIA-sponsored plot to murder Diem in a U.S.-backed military coup
d'etat on November 1, 1963. Diem's death unleashed additional coups, which encouraged
the communists to escalate the war.

American Thunder Rolls

After the Kennedy assassination, Lyndon B. Johnson named General William
Westmoreland to head the Military Assistance Command, Vietnam (MACV) and
increased the number of military "advisors" to 23,000. Johnson found the Domino Theory
persuasive, even as the conflict began to look increasingly hopeless.

On February 7, the Viet Cong (which included but largely supplanted the earlier Viet
Minh) attacked U.S. forces, killing 9 Americans and wounding 108. The Americans retaliated, provoking a Viet Cong counterstrike on February 10 against a U.S. barracks at

Qui Nhon. The next day, U.S. forces struck back with a program of air strikes deep into the North. Code named "Rolling Thunder," the operation began on March 2, 1965, and marked the start of escalation as 50,000 new ground troops were sent to Vietnam, ostensibly to protect U.S. air bases.

VITAL STATISTICS

In 1965, 75,000 Americans were fighting in Vietnam. The number jumped to 375,000 in 1966, and to half a million by 1968.

"Escalation" and "Vietnamization"

Johnson's strategy was gradual escalation, bombing military targets in a war of attrition intended to wear down the North Vietnamese without provoking overt intervention from China or the USSR.

While American leaders saw the war in Vietnam as a phase of the Cold War struggle between communism and democracy, the North Vietnamese regarded it as a fight for nationhood. North Vietnamese political cadres won widespread grassroots support from the rural populace of the South. With this support, the Viet Cong enjoyed great mobility throughout the country, often fighting from a complex network of tunnels that were all but invisible. The growing numbers of U.S. troops were successful in clearing enemy territory, but, once cleared, battle zones were soon overrun again.

Believing that the war would not be won by U.S. intervention, LBJ embarked on "Vietnamization," giving the Army of the Republic of Vietnam (ARVN) the tools and training to take over the fighting.

Hearts and Minds

In the early stages of the war, President Kennedy spoke of the need to win the "hearts and minds" of the Vietnamese people. But American war policy was not only failing to win the hearts and minds of the Vietnamese, it was also losing its hold over the hearts and minds of U.S. citizens. President Johnson increasingly relied on the Selective Service System—the draft—to supply troops, although most combat soldiers were, in fact, volunteer enlistees. Middle class young men could avoid conscription through student deferments (college enrollment skyrocketed during the war) and by other means, including—at the most extreme—fleeing to sanctuary in Canada and other countries. The options of minority youth were more limited, a fact that stirred resentment and unrest, especially in the African American community.

VITAL STATISTICS

Popular perceptions aside, two thirds of U.S. soldiers who served in Vietnam were voluntary enlistees; most draftees served State-side duty or assignments in other noncombat regions. Eighty-six percent of the U.S. troops who were killed in Vietnam were white, 12.5 percent were black, and 1.2 percent were members of other races—percentages that accurately reflected the racial makeup of the general civilian population.

Antiwar sentiment rapidly evolved into a full-blown antiwar movement, beginning with leftist college students and peace activists. As more Americans came home maimed or in body bags, the movement spread into the mainstream.

Antiwar protest widened what was popularly called the "generation gap," pitting young people against "anyone over 30." The antiwar movement became associated with a general counterculture movement, which featured young people in long hair (for both sexes) and wearing what to their elders seemed bizarre gypsy-hobo outfits. Such youngsters called themselves "hippies" and ostentatiously indulged in "recreational" drugs (such as marijuana and the hallucinogenic LSD) and "recreational" sex. Government officials assumed that the entire peace movement was backed by communists and used the FBI as well as the CIA (illegally, because this agency was forbidden by law to conduct domestic espionage or counterespionage) to infiltrate antiwar organizations.

The Endless Tunnel

By the end of 1967, it was clear that the Vietnam War was gruesomely deadlocked. President Johnson repeatedly went before the nation, assuring television viewers that there was "light at the end of the tunnel," but the increasing number of U.S. casualties created what media-savvy politicians dubbed a "credibility gap" between what the administration claimed and what the public believed.

Tet

In this period of growing doubt, the North Vietnamese staged a series of massive offensives, beginning with attacks against the U.S. base at Khe Sanh, then against South Vietnamese provincial capitals and principal cities beginning on January 30, 1968, a traditional Vietnamese lunar holiday called Tet. The offensive, which included an assault on the U.S. Embassy in Saigon, was costly to U.S. and ARVN forces, but it was far costlier to the Viet Cong. Militarily, the United States and its ally prevailed, but the three-week campaign came across as a devastating psychological victory for the communists, persuading many Americans that the war was unwinnable.

A President Opts Out

On March 31, President Johnson made two surprise television announcements. He declared that he would restrict bombing above the 20th parallel—that is, refrain from bombing most of the North Vietnamese homeland—thereby opening the door to a negotiated peace, and he announced that he would not seek another term as president. Johnson recognized that his advocacy of the war was tearing the nation apart.

Cease-fire negotiations began in May, only to stall over Hanoi's demands for a complete bombing halt and National Liberation Front (NLF) representation at the peace table. Johnson agreed to these terms in November. Despite the boost this move gave the sagging presidential campaign of Democrat Hubert Humphrey, Richard M. Nixon emerged victorious in the presidential contest.

Nixon's War

Richard Milhous Nixon (1913–1994) was a man who believed in winning at any cost. To ensure victory in the 1968 election, he made repeated—although vague—promises that he had a plan to end the war. Once elected, he expanded the war into neighboring Laos and Cambodia. Nixon had evolved a grand strategy with his foreign policy advisor, Henry Kissinger (b. 1923), calling improving relations with the Soviets (mainly through trade and an arms-limitation agreement) to disengage Moscow from Hanoi, and for normalizing U.S. relations with China. After the USSR and China cut the North Vietnamese loose, Nixon and Kissinger reasoned, the United States could negotiate "peace with honor" in Vietnam.

The strategy failed. The peace talks stalled.

Paris, Cambodia, and Laos

As negotiators spun their wheels in Paris, Nixon accelerated Vietnamization, turning more responsibility for the war over to ARVN forces, which continued to perform poorly. Despite the discouraging results, Nixon commenced and then accelerated withdrawal of U.S. ground troops.

Hoping to force the North to negotiate favorable peace terms, Nixon invaded Vietnam's neighbor Cambodia to attack communist supply and staging areas there. This incursion, made without consulting Congress, triggered angry protests at home, including a campus takeover by students at Kent State University in Ohio on May 4, 1970. The event resulted in the killing of four unarmed students and the wounding of nine more when inexperienced National Guardsmen fired on them. Subsequently, 100,000 demonstrators marched on Washington, and Congress registered its own protest by rescinding the Tonkin Gulf Resolution. Nixon withdrew troops from Cambodia but stepped up bombing raids. When communist infiltration continued unabated, the United States supplied air support for an ARVN invasion of Laos in February 1971.

Death for Easter

In March 1972, the communists launched a new invasion, initially routing ARVN troops until President Nixon retaliated by redoubling air attacks, mining Haiphong harbor, and establishing a naval blockade of the North. Following the communist "Easter Offensive," Henry Kissinger and North Vietnamese representative Le Duc Tho finally formulated a peace agreement. The terms called for the withdrawal of U.S. troops, the return of all POWs, and the laying of a foundation for political settlement through establishment of a special reconciliation council. South Vietnamese president Nguyen Van Thieu rejected the peace terms because they permitted Viet Cong forces to remain in place in the South.

Bombs for Christmas

The fact that Nixon's negotiator, Henry Kissinger, had been able to announce that "peace is at hand" ensured the president's re-election in 1972. Once in office, however, Nixon supported Thieu, repudiating the peace terms Kissinger had negotiated. Nixon ordered massive B-52 bombing raids north of the 20th parallel, which forced the North Vietnamese back to the negotiating table.

The agreement reached after the bombing was not materially different from what Kissinger had originally negotiated. This time, President Thieu and his renewed objections were ignored.

Hard Lessons

On January 31, 1973, the United States and North Vietnam signed the Paris Peace Accords, which brought U.S. withdrawal and the return of the POWs, some of whom had been languishing in North Vietnamese prisons for nearly a decade.

Both the North and South freely violated the accords. To pressure the North into abiding by them, the United States resumed bombing Cambodia. But in November a war-weary Congress passed the War Powers Act, which required the president to inform Congress within 48 hours of deployment of U.S. military forces abroad; the act also mandated the forces' withdrawal within 60 days if Congress did not approve. U.S. aid to South Vietnam was slashed.

What hopes Thieu continued to hold were dashed when the American president, facing certain impeachment, resigned in August 1974. Beginning in early 1975, the dispirited South suffered one military defeat after another. Thieu resigned his office, leaving his nation's leadership to Tran Van Huong, who promptly resigned, turning over power to General Duong Van Minh. Minh's single official act was to unconditionally surrender to the North on April 30, 1975. A frenzied evacuation of Americans remaining in Vietnam followed. At a cost of more than $150 billion and more than 58,000 Americans killed, the Vietnam War had ended in defeat for South Vietnam and (as many saw it) for the United States.

The Least You Need to Know

○ U.S. involvement in the Vietnam War was an extreme result of the Cold War policy of the "containment" of communism.

○ The Vietnam War was the most unpopular and divisive war in American history, wrecking Lyndon B. Johnson's grand social programs and badly undermining popular faith in the federal government and the nation's leaders.

○ Taking over the war from President Johnson, President Richard Nixon attempted to do more with fewer U.S. troops, simultaneously expanding the war while withdrawing from it.

○ President Nixon sought "peace with honor" in Vietnam, but the war ended in the total defeat of ostensibly democratic South Vietnam after the United States completed its total disengagement from the country in 1975.

PART 8

Identity Crisis

By the late 1960s, a deep division opened up between a rebellious under-30 generation and their elders, with youngsters developing a colorful separate culture compounded of psychedelic art and music, as well as mind-altering, mind-expanding, and mind-numbing drugs. The nation reached a great technological and human pinnacle in the successful lunar mission of Apollo 11, and the Cold War began to thaw. Yet Americans were stunned by the revelation of democracy's failings in *The Pentagon Papers* and by the Watergate scandal that forced President Nixon to resign from office in 1974.

Rooted in the suffrage movement and accelerated by a so-called sexual revolution, the women's liberation movement was finally taken seriously. But if men were now compelled to readjust their attitudes and egos, the nation as a whole found itself facing demands from beyond its borders. It was taken hostage by the "oil sheiks" of the petroleum-rich Middle East and by the new moguls of an economically ascendant Japan as the American economy bogged down in a phenomenon called "stagflation." Compounding these woes was a power change in Iran, which brought to leadership the Ayatollah Khomeini, who, in the name of religious fundamentalism, quite literally took America hostage. Iranian revolutionaries abducted most of the diplomatic staff of the U.S. Embassy in Tehran. This part recalls a most unquiet period in American history.

Of Love, the Moon, and Dirty Tricks (1968–1974)

Who were the victims of the Vietnam War? Two, perhaps three million Indochinese died, and more than 58,000 American lives were lost. Many thousands more were wounded, some disabled for life. U.S. Vietnam veterans were not welcomed home with parades but regarded with suspicion. Some Americans saw veterans as "baby killers"; others deemed them "damaged goods"—young men who may have escaped physical wounds, but who bore psychological scars that made productive adjustment to civilian life impossible. (This popular perception is not supported by fact. Vietnam veterans did not suffer from psychological illness at any higher rate than the general population.) The fact is that all of America was a victim of the war, which had created a rift between citizens and government. Vietnam killed people, and it killed trust.

Turn On, Tune In, Drop Out

Since the early twentieth century, illegal drug abuse had been associated with the fringes of society, with desperate and disturbed individuals, and to some extent, with urban African Americans. This all changed by the mid-1960s. A new generation of white middle-class youth became passionately dedicated to forms of music and other types of popular art that expressed a turning away from much that had been accepted as the American Dream: material prosperity and a house surrounded by a white picket fence. Youngsters craved the experience of new music (a metamorphosis of the prior decade's rock 'n' roll) and new clothing—colorful, wild, casual, sometimes evoking the bygone world of British Edwardian extravagance, and sometimes suggesting the realm of the ultimate thorn in the American Dream's side, the hobo. As they looked with distrust on their elders (defined as "anyone over 30"), 1960s youth indulged in so-called recreational drugs.

Marijuana was one form of protest. The decade also spawned a series of spiritual leaders, or *gurus,* including one who exhorted his followers to "expand" their minds with a hallucinogenic drug called *LSD,* which offered users a universe of "psychedelic" experience. "My advice to people today is as follows," proclaimed Harvard psychologist and LSD advocate Timothy Leary (1920–1996) in 1966: "If you take the game of life seriously, if you take your nervous system seriously, if you take your sense organs seriously, if you take the energy process seriously, you must turn on, tune in, and drop out."

Peace and Love

Americans who had turned on, tuned in, and dropped out called themselves *hippies* (derived from *hip,* slang for being attuned to the latest social trends). The hippie movement placed emphasis on kindness, affection, looking out for one's fellow being, caring for the natural environment, social justice, freedom of expression, tolerance, fostering creativity, general peaceful coexistence, and other life-affirming values.

The Eagle Has Landed

As much as the counterculture wanted to believe it, the Establishment did not fail in all it put its hand to. On July 20, 1969, at 4:17 P.M. (Eastern Daylight Time), the people of a world shaken by a multitude of fears watched live television pictures of two American astronauts setting foot on the lunar surface, some quarter-million miles from Earth.

AMERICAN ECHO

"Houston, Tranquility Base here. The *Eagle* has landed."
—Neil A. Armstrong, radio message from *Apollo 11*, July 20, 1969

"That's one small step for [a] man," Neil Armstrong declared as he hopped down off the ladder of the lunar excursion module (LEM) *Eagle*, "and one giant leap for mankind." *Apollo 11*'s successful mission was a national—and human—triumph in a time of bitterness, pain, doubt, and rejection of long-cherished values.

Pentagon Secrets

Unfortunately, the government that put men on the moon was about to reveal that it was also capable of moral lapses as deep as its lunar aspirations were lofty. During June 1971, *The New York Times, Washington Post*, and other papers published a series of articles on a secret government study popularly called *The Pentagon Papers*. The 47-volume document, which Defense Department analysts had compiled between 1967 and 1969, meticulously revealed how the federal government had systematically deceived the American people about its policies and practices in Southeast Asia. Among many other things, the study showed how the CIA had conspired to overthrow and assassinate South Vietnam president Diem, and it revealed that the Tonkin Gulf Resolution was drafted months in advance of the purported attacks on the destroyers *Maddox* and *C. Turner Joy*, the events that supposedly prompted the resolution.

The revelations marked a low point of popular faith in the American government and the continued prosecution of the Vietnam War.

Thawing the Cold War

President Richard M. Nixon, who had risen to power in Congress through his virulent and often opportunistic stance against communism, now worked with his advisor Henry Kissinger to engineer "détente" with the Soviets and "normalization of relations" with the communist Chinese. The consummate "cold warrior," Nixon initiated the long thaw that ultimately led to the end of the Cold War.

Strategic Arms Limitation Talks

In 1968, the United Nations sponsored the Nuclear Non-Proliferation Treaty, which sought to limit the spread of nuclear weapons by persuading nations without nuclear arsenals to renounce their acquisition in return for a pledge from the nuclear powers that they would reduce the size of their arsenals. The following year, the United States began negotiations with the Soviet Union to limit strategic (that is, nuclear-armed) forces. These Strategic Arms Limitation Talks (SALT) produced a pair of important arms-control agreements in 1972. Then, from 1972 to 1979, the SALT II talks were conducted, extending provisions formulated in 1972. Although the U.S. Senate never ratified SALT II (President Jimmy Carter asked that ratification be suspended after the Soviets invaded Afghanistan in 1980), the two nations generally abided by its arms-limitation and arms-reduction provisions.

Ping Pong Peace

Perhaps even more remarkable than détente and SALT was President Nixon's February 1972 journey to China, where he was received in Beijing by Chairman Mao Zedong, the very incarnation of the communism Nixon had spent his life opposing. In a single stroke of diplomacy, Nixon reversed the long-standing U.S. policy of refusing to recognize China's communist government. By January 1979 (under President Jimmy Carter), full diplomatic relations were established between the nations.

Committee to Re-Elect the President

As the 1972 elections approached, there was little doubt that President Nixon would be re-elected. Yet the prevailing optimism was insufficient for Nixon. He directed his re-election organization, the Committee to Re-Elect the President—known (incredibly enough) by the acronym CREEP—to stack the deck. The committee engaged in a campaign of espionage against the Democratic Party and a program of what CREEP insiders referred to as "dirty tricks" aimed at smearing and otherwise sabotaging Democratic challengers.

Plumbers at Work

On June 17, 1972, early in the re-election campaign, five burglars were arrested in the Democratic National Committee (DNC) headquarters at the Watergate office building in Washington, D.C. The men were "Plumbers"—covert White House operatives whose original mission had been to plug leaks (security breaches) in the aftermath of *The Pentagon Papers.* The Plumbers became a kind of palace guard for the administration, given jobs that lay both outside the chief executive's constitutional mandate and the law. One such job was planting bugs (listening devices) at the DNC.

The Plumbers included anti-Castro Cuban veterans of the ill-fated Bay of Pigs invasion, and James McCord Jr., former CIA agent and now "security" officer for CREEP. In a slapstick security faux pas, one of the burglars carried in his pocket an address book with the name of E. Howard Hunt. A former CIA agent (he'd been in charge of the Bay of Pigs operation) and pulpy spy novel writer, Hunt was assistant to Charles Colson, special counsel to President Nixon. Hunt's address? "The White House." It said so in the burglar's address book.

The Watergate burglary pointed to conspiracy at the very highest levels of government, which began to unravel due to the investigative journalism of two young *Washington Post* reporters, Bob Woodward and Carl Bernstein. Guided in part by a super-secret government source they dubbed "Deep Throat"—revealed in 2005 as Mark Felt, the deputy director of the FBI—Woodward and Bernstein peeled back the layers of a vastly illegal covert White House operation.

All the President's Men

President Nixon, running against an obscure senator from South Dakota, George McGovern, won re-election despite the arrests and early Watergate revelations. Soon after Nixon began his second term, however, each of the "president's men" gave testimony to federal authorities, and the noose tightened. In February 1973, the Senate created an investigative committee headed by North Carolina Senator Sam Ervin Jr. The Watergate Hearings riveted Americans to their television sets. Patiently, persistently, and with the cunning of a country lawyer educated at Harvard, the drawling Ervin elicited testimony revealing crimes and corruption far beyond Watergate.

In the midst of the turmoil, Vice President Spiro T. Agnew was indicted for federal income tax fraud and for bribes taken when he had served as Maryland's governor. Pleading no contest to charges of tax evasion and money laundering, he resigned as vice president in October 1973 and was replaced by Congressman Gerald Ford of Michigan.

Finally, it was revealed that President Nixon had covertly taped White House conversations; the tapes were subpoenaed, but the president claimed "executive privilege" and withheld them. Nixon ordered Elliot L. Richardson (who had replaced John Mitchell as attorney general when Mitchell resigned that post to head up CREEP) to fire special Watergate prosecutor Archibald Cox. On October 20, 1973, Richardson refused and resigned in protest; his deputy, William Ruckelshaus, likewise refused and also stepped down. The duty to discharge Cox fell to Nixon's solicitor general, Robert H. Bork, who did not scruple to comply. This so-called "Saturday night massacre" served only to suggest that Nixon had more to hide. Much more.

At length, the president released transcripts of some of the White House tapes (containing a highly suspicious 18½ minutes of gaps). On July 27 through 30, the House Judiciary Committee recommended that Nixon be impeached. Nixon released the remaining tapes on August 5, 1974. They included what the press called "the smoking gun," a revelation that the President had taken steps to block the FBI's inquiry into the Watergate burglary. On August 9, 1974, Richard Milhous Nixon became the first president in U.S. history to resign from office.

The Least You Need to Know

○ As World War I had produced a lost generation in America, so Vietnam spawned a youth counterculture movement, founded on idealism, rock music, sexual freedom, and "recreational" drugs.

○ Through a deviousness that was characteristic of his style, President Nixon simultaneously withdrew U.S. troops from Vietnam, even as he (sometimes illegally) intensified the war by ordering massive air strikes.

○ Perhaps the most disturbingly complex leader the United States has ever had, Richard Nixon was both a ruthless "cold warrior" and the president who opened the door to sane relations with the Soviets and the Chinese.

○ The turbulent Nixon years saw men land on the moon and the Cold War begin to thaw, but the era ended in the gravest national crisis since the Civil War.

CHAPTER 33

Women Rise, the Nation Drifts, and Reagan Rallies (1963–1980)

The 1960s marked a period of self-examination in the United States, an era of sometimes liberating reflection and sometimes debilitating self-doubt. During the decade, women joined African Americans and other minorities in calling for equal rights and equal opportunity. In the course of the following decade, all Americans were forced to rethink attitudes and assumptions about limitless economic growth, unrestrained spending, and the natural environment as the vulnerability of the nation's energy sources was dramatically exposed. Then, in 1980, after 20 years of often painful introspection, Americans elected a president whose message to the nation was to greet what his best-remembered TV campaign ad called "morning in America."

A Woman's Place

The sweet land of liberty was largely a man's world until 1920, when ratification of the Nineteenth Amendment gave women the constitutional right to vote. The first presidential election in which women had a voice brought Warren G. Harding (1865–1923) into office, mediocre product of the GOP's "old boy" consensus. No, it would take a second world war to bring even temporary change to American gender roles.

From Rosie the Riveter to *The Feminine Mystique*

The national war effort, spurred into action by the December 7, 1941, surprise attack on Pearl Harbor, required maximum military force and all-out industrial production. With the men off fighting the war, women invaded all the traditionally male workplaces. An iconic poster exhorting workers to give their all for war production depicted a woman in denim overalls and a bandanna flexing her muscular bicep. She was Rosie the Riveter, radical symbol of American womanhood during World War II.

But when the war ended, most women quit their jobs and settled into lives as homemakers. Few openly questioned their role until, in 1963, Betty Friedan wrote *The Feminine Mystique*. Its data-backed thesis was that American women were often the unhappy victims of the "feminine mystique," a myth that the female of the species could gain satisfaction only through marriage and childbearing. The blockbuster book prompted many women to re-examine the roles in which society had cast them.

Pill Power

In May 1960, just a few years before Friedan's book appeared, the U.S. Food and Drug Administration (FDA) approved Enovid, the world's first effective oral contraceptive. The birth control pill—which many called simply "The Pill"—brought radical change to the nation's sexual mores, enabling the "sexual revolution" of the 1960s. It also "liberated" women, allowing them to delay having children (or to choose not to have them at all) and use the time to establish a career.

NOW and Ms.

In 1966, Friedan helped found the National Organization for Women (NOW) and served as NOW's first president. A "Women's Liberation" movement crystallized around NOW, which advocated for equality in society and the workplace, liberalized abortion laws, and passage of the Equal Rights Amendment (ERA), a proposed constitutional amendment declaring that "equality of rights under the law shall not be denied or abridged by the United States nor by any State on account of sex." The ERA had been drafted years earlier by radical feminist Alice Paul (1885–1977), founder of the National Woman's Party, and had been introduced in Congress in 1923, where it was essentially ignored until NOW revived it in 1970.

AMERICAN ECHO

"A liberated woman is one who has sex before marriage and a job after."
—Gloria Steinem, quoted in *Newsweek,* March 28, 1960

In 1972, feminist journalist Gloria Steinem started *Ms.* magazine, a popular vehicle for the feminist message. Its masthead title came from the new form of female address that had been gaining ground since the 1960s: both "Miss" and "Mrs." linked a woman's identity to her marital status, as if she had no social legitimacy apart from her relationship to a man. *Ms.* was proposed as the equal counterpart of *Mr.* in that it defined a self without reference to a spouse.

Feminist activism made an impact on American life. As of 2017, more than 47 percent of the U.S. workforce was female and 70 percent of mothers with children under 18 participate in the workforce. According to the Bureau of Labor Statistics, in 2016 women were still being paid at a lower average rate than men, earning 83 percent what men are paid for equivalent work.

REMEMBER THIS

In 1973, the Supreme Court ruled in the case of *Roe* v. *Wade*, which had its origin in a suit brought by a woman against the state of Texas for having denied her the right to an abortion. In a seven-to-one vote, the high court determined that women have a constitutional right to abortion during the first three months of pregnancy.

Abortion is the most controversial right women have asserted, and the *Roe* v. *Wade* decision gave rise to a so-called Right to Life anti-abortion movement. Usually motivated by religious conviction, Right to Life advocates have campaigned for a constitutional amendment banning abortion (except in cases of rape, incest, or threat to the mother's life).

ERA Collapse

Thanks to NOW, the ERA was passed by the House of Representatives in 1971 and by the Senate in 1972. The amendment was then sent to the states for ratification. When the necessary three-fourths majority of states failed to ratify it by the original March 1979 deadline, a new June 30, 1982, deadline was fixed. Yet, by this date, ratification was still three states short of the 38 needed. Reintroduced in Congress on July 14, 1982, ERA failed to gain approval and was dead as of November 15, 1983, although it has been repeatedly reintroduced.

Oil Almighty

U.S. citizens, men and women, have always cherished their liberty. After 1908, when Henry Ford introduced his Model T, they have increasingly identified a part of that liberty with the mobility automobiles provide. With just 6 percent of the world's population, the United States consumes little more than a third of the world's energy—much of it in the form of petroleum. In 1970, the Organization of Petroleum Exporting Countries (OPEC), consisting of the Middle Eastern nations and Venezuela, pressed for oil price hikes. On October 17, 1973, OPEC temporarily embargoed oil exports to punish nations that had supported Israel in its recent war with Egypt. Chief among the embargo's targets was the United States.

The effects of the OPEC embargo were stunning. Prices shot up from 38.5 cents per gallon in 1973 to 55.1 cents by June 1974, and gasoline shortages were severe. Americans found themselves idled in gas lines stretching from the pumps and snaking around the block.

Cruising full speed ahead since the end of World War II, Americans were forced to come to grips with an energy crisis. In a modest way, they learned to do without, and oil consumption was reduced by more than 7 percent—enough to prompt some OPEC price rollbacks by the early 1980s.

Stagflation

The energy crisis came on top of an economic crisis, characterized by a combination of inflation and recession christened *stagflation* ("stagnant growth" coupled with "inflation"). To use a phrase popular during the period, the economy was "in the toilet." And so, it seemed, was the American spirit. Accustomed to being preeminent manufacturer to the world, Americans found their industries losing ground to those of other nations.

Scary Cities, Crumbling Bridges

The post–World War II building boom had developed suburban America, and throughout the 1950s, many middle-class families left the old cities for the new suburbs. The pace of this exodus accelerated following the racial violence that plagued many urban centers during the 1960s. Social commentators began to speak of "white flight"—although, in fact, the abandonment of inner city for suburb was as much a matter of economics as it was of race. The result was cities that rotted at their cores.

The American infrastructure was also in need of repair. The very roads that had carried the middle class out of the inner city were eaten away with potholes. A growing proportion of the nation's bridges were failing inspection.

The Verge of Meltdown

The single most terrifying event that suddenly and dramatically forced Americans to question their faith in U.S. technology, big business, and government regulation occurred on March 28, 1979. Through a combination of mechanical failure and human error, a nuclear reactor at the Three Mile Island electric generating plant, near the Pennsylvania capital of Harrisburg, lost coolant water, briefly allowing an uncontrolled nuclear chain reaction, which caused a partial meltdown of the reactor's radioactive core.

During the late 1950s and early 1960s, the peaceful use of the atom was seen as the key to supplying cheap, virtually limitless energy to the nation. But by the 1970s, environmentalists and others were questioning the safety of atomic power. By the end of the decade, a beleaguered nuclear power industry was on the defensive.

AMERICAN ECHO

"A normal aberration."
—Metropolitan Edison Company Vice President Jack Herbein's description of the Three Mile Island incident, quoted in *Time* magazine, April 9, 1979

Subsequent inquiries showed that, despite human error, automatic backup safety features built into the Three Mile Island plant prevented a major disaster. Nevertheless, the incident seemed to many people just one more in a long string of American technological failures and lapses of corporate accountability.

The Fanatics

The year 1979 brought a shock of a different kind to national pride. A revolution in Iran, led by the Ayatollah Ruhollah Khomeini (1900–1989), toppled longtime U.S. ally Muhammad Reza Shah Pahlavi, the Shah of Iran, who fled into exile in January 1979. In October, terminally ill with cancer, the Shah was granted permission to come to the United States for medical treatment. Angered by this gesture, 500 Iranians stormed the U.S. Embassy in Tehran on November 4, 1979, and took 90 hostages, including 65 U.S.

nationals. Non-Americans and 13 American women and black hostages were released during November 19–20, leaving 52 in captivity. Their captors demanded the Shah's return.

Although President Carter refused to yield to this demand, the Shah voluntarily left the United States in early December. Still, the hostages remained in captivity. President Carter authorized an elite army Delta Force unit to attempt a rescue on April 24, 1980, but a combination of mechanical and human errors caused the mission to be aborted. The failure did not result in harm to the hostages, but came as yet another humiliating defeat for a battered superpower.

Not until November 1980 did the Iranian parliament propose definitive conditions for the hostages' liberation. An agreement was signed early in January 1981, but the Ayatollah Khomeini deliberately delayed the hostages' release until January 20, the day Jimmy Carter left office and Ronald Reagan was inaugurated.

The Great Communicator

The hostage release was widely regarded as a miracle performed by the incoming president. Depressed and downcast, many Americans looked to smiling, unflappable Reagan for even more miracles.

Born above a grocery store in the central Illinois town of Tampico in 1911, Reagan worked his way through college, and became a sportscaster and then an actor. A Democrat during his on-screen years, Reagan left acting to enter Republican politics with a strong stop-communism and end-big-government message. In 1966, he handily defeated incumbent Democrat Pat Brown for the governor's office in California and served two terms, during which he made a national reputation as a tax cutter. Delivering a feel-good message to the nation and promising large tax cuts, a vast reduction in the size of government ("getting government off our backs," he called it), and a return to American pride and greatness, Reagan defeated the incumbent Carter by a wide margin in 1980: 42,797,153 to 34,434,100. Even those who opposed what they saw as his shallow conservatism admitted that Reagan deserved the title of *The Great Communicator*.

The Least You Need to Know

○ The 1960s and 1970s saw Americans re-examining themselves and struggling to redefine their nation in an effort to renew the American Dream.

○ The U.S. economy suffered a severe recession, which also dragged down American morale.

○ The unshakable American faith in technology was severely shaken by a faltering auto industry, decaying infrastructure, and a near nuclear meltdown at the Three Mile Island reactor in Pennsylvania.

○ Ronald Reagan took his sweeping victory over Jimmy Carter in 1980 as a mandate for a rebirth of patriotism and a revolution in economics.

PART 9

America, Disrupted

A beleaguered America was highly receptive to the tax-cutting promises, minimalist government, federal deregulation, and patriotic feel-good message of Ronald Reagan. Although the 1990s saw the end of the Cold War in the breakup of the Soviet Union, which left the United States as the world's only superpower, the decade also was marked by profound dissatisfaction with domestic "politics as usual" and by a sinister undercurrent of political rage that exploded into incidents of "homegrown" terrorism.

At the turn of a new century, the American democracy passed through the crucible of scandal, a tortured presidential election, and an attack by ruthless Middle Eastern terrorists, followed by highly divisive wars in Afghanistan and Iraq with no end in sight. As the second term of President George W. Bush drew to a close, the nation was submerged in a financial crisis for which the only historical precedent was the Great Depression of the 1930s. Against the roiling background of an unpopular war and economic meltdown, Americans voted in record-breaking numbers in 2008 to elect the nation's first African American president and then followed in 2016 by sending to the White House perhaps its most unlikely occupant ever, celebrity real estate mogul Donald Trump.

CHAPTER 34

A New Economy, a Fallen Wall, and a Desert in Flames (1980-1991)

The phrase often applied—if not very accurately—to the presidency of James Monroe (1817–1825), the "era of good feelings," might also serve to describe the widely perceived sense of national well-being that prevailed during at least the first term of Ronald Reagan. Where President Carter took a stern moral tone with the nation, admonishing his fellow Americans to conserve energy, save money, and generally do with a little less of everything, President Reagan congratulated his countrymen on simply being Americans and assured them that all was well—or *would* be well, just as soon as he got "big government off our backs."

For a time, business boomed during the Reagan years, which also saw the beginning of the end of the Cold War and the disintegration of the Soviet Union. Yet, the national debt also rose from a staggering $1 trillion to a then stupefying $4.2 trillion (adjusted for inflation).

The Trickle-Down Solution

Following his inauguration, President Reagan lost no time in launching an economic program formulated by his conservative economic advisors.

The Reagan revolution turned on three major policies: a reduction in government regulation; aggressive budget cutting; and aggressive tax cutting—principally for wealthy individuals and businesses. Reducing the tax burden on the rich and on corporations, Reagan and Reaganites claimed, would free up more money for investment and employment, the benefits of which would "trickle down" to the less affluent in the form of more and better jobs.

If *trickle down* was a hard concept for many to swallow, Reagan's insistence that a *reduction* in tax rates would actually *increase* government revenues seemed downright bizarre to some. When Ronald Reagan and the man who would be his vice president, George H. W. Bush, were battling one another in the Republican primaries, Bush branded the notion "voodoo economics."

Plausible or not, a majority of the American people were prepared to take the leap with their new president. In 1981, a major tax cut, a staggering $43 billion reduction in the budget for domestic programs, and broad cutbacks in environmental and business regulation were hurried through Congress. The "Great Communicator" parried all resistance. When catastrophe struck on March 30, 1981, in the form of would-be assassin John Hinckley Jr., the 70-year-old president's calm and heroic response to his having been shot in the lung with a .22-caliber Devastator bullet drew even more support for his programs.

REMEMBER THIS

President Reagan had been in office only two months when he exited the Washington Hilton Hotel on March 30, 1981, after delivering a speech. Six shots rang out, fired from a .22-caliber revolver loaded with explosive "Devastator" bullets. Secret Service agent Timothy J. McCarthy and Washington police officer James Delahanty were hit, as was White House press secretary James S. Brady, who suffered a severe head wound.

The shooter, 25-year-old John Warnock Hinckley Jr., was obsessed with screen actress Jodie Foster, who had made a sensation as a teenage prostitute in *Taxi Driver,* a 1976 film dealing in part with political assassination. Hinckley decided to kill the president to impress Foster. He was found not guilty by reason of insanity.

Greed Is Good

Much of the new wealth of the Reagan years was generated by a frenzied crescendo of corporate acquisitions and mergers. Unemployment, generated by the high-level financial manipulations of the 1980s, was hard on the man and woman in the street, but the movement of massive wealth benefited those who could afford to invest in the right companies at the right time. In the words of Gordon Gecko, a fictional tycoon played by Michael Douglas in the popular movie *Wall Street* (directed by Oliver Stone in 1987), "Greed is good."

AMERICAN LIFE

The words put into Gordon Gecko's mouth were paraphrased from a real-life Wall Street manipulator, Ivan Boesky, who told the graduating class of the School of Business Administration at the University of California, Berkeley, on May 18, 1986: "Greed is all right, by the way … I think greed is healthy. You can be greedy and still feel good about yourself."

Early confidence in Reaganomics faltered when the recession of the Nixon-Ford-Carter years deepened further. Inflation did roll back, though interest rates remained high, as did unemployment. By 1983, however, acquisitions and mergers made the stock market a very active place. This change, combined with relatively low inflation (at last), rising production, and slowly decreasing unemployment, portended recovery.

VITAL STATISTICS

On "Black Monday," October 19, 1987, $870 billion in equity simply evaporated as the market dropped from a Dow of 2,246.73 to 1,738.41 points.

What hopeful observers tended to ignore was the prodigiously growing national debt and the often-corrupt sources of the profits being turned on Wall Street. Beginning in 1985, Wall Street was rocked by a series of massive insider trading scandals.

To finance company buyouts, traders turned to junk bonds, high-risk investments (usually issued by a company without an established earnings history or the burden of poor credit) acquired cheaply but with high interest rates. Such transactions, called leveraged buyouts, were pioneered in the 1970s by Wall Street firm Kohlberg Kravis Roberts (KKR) and were brought to a point of frenzy by Michael R. Milken.

Black Monday

The junk being bought and sold hit the fan on October 19, 1987, when the Dow Jones Industrial Average (key measure of stock market performance) plunged 508 points— a far steeper fall than that of the 1929 crash, which brought on the Great Depression. Fortunately, the market gradually recovered, but the high-flying era of Reaganomics had careened to a gut-wrenching end.

A Suicide Bombing and a Feel-Good War

Defense spending was dramatically stepped up during the Reagan years, dwarfing domestic budget cuts in welfare and other programs. The president acted aggressively to meet perceived military threats throughout the world, sending U.S. Marines in the summer of 1982 to Lebanon as a peacekeeping force.

On October 23, 1983, 241 marines were killed in their sleep, and another 70 wounded, when an Islamist suicide bomber drove a truck laden with 25,000 pounds of TNT into the marines' Beirut headquarters building.

Reagan immediately withdrew the marines from Lebanon but just two days later ordered an invasion of Grenada, a Caribbean island nation. Cuban troops had been sent to the tiny country (population 110,100) at the behest of its anti-American dictatorship, and the president expressed his absolute determination to protect the approximately 1,100 U.S. citizens there, mostly students at a medical school.

It is widely believed that the president saw Grenada's liberation as "feel-good" compensation for the marines' deaths in Beirut, and while his saber-rattling was indeed gratifying to some Americans, others were distressed by the deadlock of U.S.–Soviet arms-control talks as a fresh deployment of U.S. nuclear missiles began in Europe in November 1983.

A War Without Bullets

During 1983, President Reagan announced the most spectacular, ambitious, elaborate, and expensive military project in world history. It was called the Strategic Defense Initiative (SDI), but the popular press dubbed the system *Star Wars,* after the popular George Lucas science-fiction movie of 1977. Using an orbiting weapons system, the idea was to create a shield against intercontinental ballistic missile (ICBM) attack by destroying incoming ICBMs before they could begin their descent. The weaponry was so far beyond even the foreseeable cutting edge as to be fanciful. Critics claimed that the system could never be made to work, and others protested that the staggering cost of the program—$100 to $200 billion—would permanently cripple the nation.

Yet presidents Reagan and George H. W. Bush pursued Star Wars to the tune of $30 billion, even though the program produced few demonstrable results. Years later, Caspar Weinberger, who had served as President Reagan's secretary of defense, claimed that Star Wars had been an elaborate decoy designed primarily to dupe the Soviet Union into bankrupting itself on a Star Wars program of its own—a concept U.S. scientists already knew was unworkable.

The gargantuan Reagan defense budget contributed to the quadrupling of the national debt, but may well have ended the Cold War without a shot. The Soviet Union government was first liberalized and then fell apart, the nation's economy in tatters and the people clamoring for democratic capitalist reforms. Even though Mikhail Gorbachev (b. 1931), General Secretary of the Soviet Communist Party (1985–1991) and president of the USSR (1988–1991), introduced unheard of liberal reforms—under the banners of perestroika (social restructuring) and glasnost (openness)—President Reagan prodded him to go even further. In 1987, standing near the Berlin Wall—brick, stone, and razor-wire symbol of a half-century of communist oppression—the president made a stirring speech calling out to the Soviet leader: "Mr. Gorbachev, open this gate! Mr. Gorbachev, tear down this wall!" Two years later, ordinary Berliners, in the West and in the East, began chipping away at the wall, tearing it down piece by piece, as a liberalized Soviet Union merely looked on, offering no resistance.

Communist hardliners staged an unsuccessful coup against Gorbachev in 1991, after which Gorbachev disbanded the Communist Party and stepped down as leader of the Soviet Union. Boris Yeltsin (1931–2007), reformist president of the Russian Republic, assumed leadership not of the Union of Soviet Socialist Republics, which ceased to exist, but of a commonwealth of former Soviet states.

Ollie, Iran, and the Contras

In November 1986, President Reagan confirmed reports that the United States had secretly sold arms to Iran, an implacable enemy since the hostage crisis of the Carter years. The president at first denied rumors and media leaks that the purpose of the sale had been to obtain the release of U.S. hostages held by terrorists in perpetually war-torn Lebanon, but he later admitted to the existence of an arms-for-hostages swap. Then the plot thickened—shockingly—when Attorney General Edwin Meese learned that a portion of the arms profits had been diverted to finance so-called Contra rebels fighting against Nicaragua's leftist Sandinista government. As part of the ongoing U.S. Cold War policy of containing communism, the Reagan administration supported a right-wing rebellion in Nicaragua. But Congress, not wanting to become mired in a Central American version of the Vietnam War, specifically prohibited material aid to the Contras. The secret diversion of the secret arms profits was blatantly unconstitutional.

As was the case with Watergate during the 1970s, investigation and testimony implicated officials on successively lofty rungs of the White House ladder—through national security advisors John Poindexter and Robert McFarlane, CIA Director William J. Casey, and Defense Secretary Caspar Weinberger. Few people believed that President Reagan had been ignorant of the scheme.

In the end, Marine Lieutenant Colonel Oliver North, mastermind of the Iran-Contra scheme, was convicted on 3 of 12 criminal counts against him, but the convictions were subsequently set aside on appeal. Poindexter, CIA administrator Clair E. George, and Caspar Weinberger were pardoned by President Reagan's successor, George H. W. Bush. Although the 1994 report of special prosecutor Lawrence E. Walsh harshly criticized both Reagan and George H. W. Bush, neither was charged with criminal wrongdoing.

Weighing the Reagan Years

President Reagan's second term, marred by the Iran-Contra affair, a bumbling performance at the 1986 summit with Mikhail Gorbachev, and the 1987 stock market crash, nevertheless saw the so-called "Teflon president" (against whom nothing seemed to stick) emerge personally unscathed. In fact, no president since FDR put his personal stamp on the nation's character more deeply than Ronald Wilson Reagan.

Desert Shield and Desert Storm

Vice President George H. W. Bush sailed to easy victory in the presidential race of 1988. Where the "Great Communicator" Reagan had been charismatic, however, Bush was widely perceived as aloof. With the economy again faltering (the principal issue was high unemployment), his popularity rapidly slipped in the polls. Bush seemed doomed to a one-term presidency.

A Line in the Sand

Then, on August 2, 1990, Iraqi's President Saddam Hussein, a dictator whose florid mustache recalled Joseph Stalin and whose ruthlessly irrational actions summoned to mind Adolf Hitler, ordered an invasion of the small, oil-rich Arab state of Kuwait. It was the beginning of a tense and dramatic crisis, but it was also President Bush's finest hour. His administration brilliantly used the United Nations (UN) to sanction action against Iraq, and with masterful diplomacy, the president assembled an unprecedented coalition of 31 nations to oppose the invasion. As to the U.S. commitment, it was the largest since Vietnam: more than a half-million troops, 1,800 aircraft, and some 100 ships.

Called Operation Desert Shield, this was a massive, orderly buildup of U.S. forces. In January 1991, the U.S. Congress voted to support military operations against Iraq in accordance with a UN Security Council resolution, which set a deadline of January 15, 1991, for the withdrawal of Iraqi forces from Kuwait. When Saddam Hussein failed to heed the deadline, President Bush declared that the "line in the sand" had been crossed, and Operation Desert Shield became Operation Desert Storm, a meticulously coordinated lightning campaign against Iraq from the air, the sea, and on land. After continuous air attack beginning January 17, the ground war was launched at 8 P.M. on February 23 and lasted exactly 100 hours before Iraqi resistance collapsed, and Kuwait was liberated.

VITAL STATISTICS

Combined U.S. and coalition forces in the Gulf War amounted to 530,000 troops as opposed to 545,000 Iraqis. U.S. and coalition losses were 149 killed, 238 wounded, 81 missing, and 13 taken prisoner (they were subsequently released). Iraqi losses have been estimated in excess of 80,000 men killed or wounded, with overwhelming loss of materiel.

Victory Constrained

Bush enjoyed overwhelming popular approval in the wake of the Persian Gulf War's successful outcome. Although some administration critics complained that the president had foolishly stopped the war short of toppling Saddam Hussein from power, the overall military success in the Gulf seemed to exorcise the demons of failure born in the Vietnam War. This, combined with the liberalization and ultimate collapse of the Soviet Union, made most Americans feel that their nation was in the vanguard of what President Bush called a "new world order."

The Least You Need to Know

- ✪ President Reagan started a conservative revolution in America, introducing supply-side economics and undoing much of the welfare state that had begun with FDR.

- ✪ President Reagan's second term was marked by economic decline and the Iran-Contra scandal, neither of which seemed greatly to damage Reagan's unassailable popularity.

- ✪ The Reagan-Bush years saw victory in the 50-year Cold War (as well as victory in the brief but dangerous Persian Gulf War), but at the cost of quadrupling an already staggering national debt.

- ✪ President George H. W. Bush, his popularity declining in a listless American economy, realized his finest hour as commander in chief during massive military operations against Iraq's Saddam Hussein.

E Pluribus Unum (1991–1999)

In 1980 and again in 1984, the American electorate voted Ronald Reagan into office with gusto. In 1988, Americans had relatively little enthusiasm for either Democrat Michael Dukakis, governor of Massachusetts, or Republican George H. W. Bush, vice president of the United States. Nor was there much enthusiasm in 1992, when the youthful governor of Arkansas, Bill Clinton, opposed Bush. During the Bush administration, however, the American Dream seemed somehow to have slipped further away. True, from an American perspective, the world certainly seemed a safer place than it had been at any time since the end of World War II. Yet the electorate felt that President Bush neglected domestic issues, especially the state of the economy, to focus almost exclusively on foreign affairs. Candidate Bill Clinton's acerbic campaign manager, James Carville, put it bluntly, advising Governor Clinton to write himself a reminder lest he forget the issue on which the election would be won or lost: "It's the economy, stupid."

The Economy, Stupid

It was not that America teetered on the edge of another depression in 1992, but a general sense existed among the middle class that this generation was not "doing as well as" the previous generation. Bill Clinton, promising a return to the domestic agenda, entered the White House by a comfortable margin.

But if voters had rejected Bush, a sizable minority also turned away from Clinton. For the first time since Theodore Roosevelt ran as a Progressive (Bull Moose) Party candidate in 1912, a third-party contender made a significant impact at the polls. Billionaire Texas businessman H. Ross Perot (b. 1930) told Americans that they were the "owners" of the nation and that it was about time they derived real benefit from what they owned.

VITAL STATISTICS

Even though third-party candidate H. Ross Perot dropped out of the race for a time (stunning his many supporters), he won 19,237,247 votes, an astounding 19 percent of the popular vote total.

The New Right

The Perot candidacy was not the only evidence of widespread discontent with politics as usual. A conservative movement gained increasing strength. Its values rested on the family as traditionally constituted (father, mother, kids), a strong sense of law and order, reliance on organized (Christian) religion, a belief in the work ethic (and a corresponding disdain for the welfare state), and a Reaganesque desire for minimal government.

Right to Life

Many who identified themselves with the "New Right" held passionately to a belief that abortion is murder. The self-styled Right to Life movement spawned a fanatic fringe, whose members bombed abortion clinics and even murdered physicians who perform abortions.

The mainstream relied on legal means to effect social change, with the ultimate object of obtaining a constitutional amendment banning abortion. The Right to Life movement became so powerful a political lobby that the Republican Party adopted a stance against abortion as part of its 1992 platform.

Christian Right

In 2001, a powerful lobbying group called the Christian Coalition of America boasted a membership of nearly two million in 1,500 local chapters in all 50 U.S. states. The organization claimed responsibility for the Republican sweep of Congress during the 1994 midterm elections. In 1995, the Coalition spent more than a million dollars mobilizing its "born-again" evangelical "values voters" (voters who support religiously oriented so-called "family values") behind the conservative "Contract with America" promulgated by Republican Speaker of the House Newt Gingrich. While many welcomed what they saw as a return of morality to American political life, others viewed the Christian Right as narrow, coercive, and intolerant.

The Age of Rage

The dominant voice in 1990s politics was neither liberal nor conservative. It was angry. Most of the time, it was part of the background: endless staccato of sound bites from the television, a jagged litany that issued endlessly from talk radio, and the remarkable volume of violence that was played out across movie screens. And sometimes the rage exploded, front and center in all too real life.

Waco and Oklahoma City

April 19, 1993, saw the fiery culmination of a long standoff between members of a fundamentalist religious cult called the Branch Davidians and federal law officers. Followers of David Koresh (his real name was Vernon Howell), holed up in a fortified compound outside of Waco, Texas, had been holding off agents of the U.S. Treasury Department's Alcohol, Tobacco, and Firearms (ATF) unit. The agents were investigating reports of an illegal arms stockpile, as well as allegations of child abuse in the compound. When ATF officers initially moved on the compound on February 28, the cultists opened fire, killing four agents. Koresh was wounded in the exchange, and at least two of his followers were killed. The FBI was called in, and for the next 51 days, the FBI and ATF laid siege to the Branch Davidians, until April 19, when agents commenced an assault with tear gas volleys. The Branch Davidians responded (according to law-enforcement officials) by setting fire to their own compound, a blaze that killed more than 80 cultists, including 24 children. Millions witnessed both the February 28 shoot-out and the April 19 inferno on television.

Millions also saw the bloody aftermath of the bombing of the Alfred P. Murrah Federal Office Building in Oklahoma City on April 19, 1995, which killed 168 persons, including children at play in the building's daycare center. Timothy McVeigh and Terry Nichols, two disaffected U.S. Army veterans, were tried in connection with the bombing. In June 1997, Timothy McVeigh was found guilty on 11 counts of murder and sentenced to death. He was executed at the Federal Penitentiary in Terre Haute, Indiana, on June 11, 2001—the first federal execution since 1963. On December 23, 1997, a federal jury found Nichols guilty of eight counts of involuntary manslaughter and conspiring with McVeigh. Nichols was sentenced to life imprisonment. Subsequently, the state of Oklahoma charged him with capital murder. Convicted of 161 counts of first-degree murder on August 9, 2004, he was given additional life sentences.

McVeigh and Nichols were loosely associated with what was widely called in the 1990s the "militia movement," a phrase that described militant groups organized in several states after the Waco raid and a 1992 government assault on extreme conservative and white supremacist Randy Weaver and his family in Ruby Ridge, Idaho.

And It Was Still the Economy ...

Bill Clinton had run his first presidential campaign largely on issues of the sluggish economy. When he stood for reelection in 1996, the economy, lackluster during the second term of Ronald Reagan and even duller during the only term of George H. W. Bush, had at last taken fire and Wall Street was now aflame.

"Ordinary people" were now investing—and doing quite well at it. There was no need to talk about Reagan's "trickle down." For many people, the money came, if not in a torrent, at least on tap. Bill Clinton sailed into a second term, handily defeating the caustic and much older Robert Dole, Republican senator from Kansas, who was in the unenviable position of having to argue with success.

To Fight for Peace

President Clinton had been re-elected on the strength of his domestic performance at a time when most of the public gave little thought to the international scene. The president was soon faced with a series of international crises.

Shortly before Clinton took office at the start of his first term, American soldiers arrived in Somalia, on the East Coast of Africa, pursuant to a pledge of military and humanitarian aid made by President George H. W. Bush. The Somali people, dying from famine and civil war, were at the mercy of competing warlords. The name of the UN mission in which U.S. troops participated suggested its humanitarian purpose: Operation Restore Hope. American soldiers were to function as peacekeepers.

Clinton soon discovered the futility of being a cop in a place without law. Among all the warlords, the most powerful was Mohamed Farah Aideed, gangster leader of a large "militia" force. At 3:40 P.M. on October 3, 1993, an elite cadre of U.S. Army Delta Force commandos swooped down on Somalia's capital, Mogadishu, in Black Hawk helicopters, disembarked, then swept through the Olympic Hotel in search of Aideed and his top officers. Aideed was not present, but the operation netted several of his lieutenants. After 15 minutes, the commandos and their prisoners made for the Black Hawks.

That is when the unit came under heavy attack from Aideed's militia in a gruesome street battle that lasted for 15 bloody hours. In the end, 18 American soldiers were killed, and American television screens beamed an image of the body of one soldier being dragged triumphantly through the streets of Mogadishu by militiamen.

The grim image stuck painfully in the American imagination. On March 31, 1994, Clinton withdrew all U.S. forces from Somalia. Operation Restore Hope came to an end.

Nightmare in the Balkans

The post-Soviet "new world order" George H. W. Bush had spoken of following the collapse of communism had a very dark side.

Yugoslavia was a twentieth-century invention, cobbled together from the fragments of the old Austro-Hungarian Empire, which had been broken up by the Treaty of Versailles after World War I. Political and ethnic fragments do not make a nation, however, and until World War II, Yugoslavia was a collection of strongly nationalistic, ethnically diverse, and largely irreconcilable factions united only in their opposition to German Nazi and Italian fascist invasion.

Following World War II, strongman Josip Broz Tito continued to hold Yugoslavia together until his death in 1980. After that, the nation began to break apart.

A civil war developed, which soon ceased to be a political struggle and became tribal warfare among Serbs, Croats, and Moslems in what had been Yugoslavia.

In January 1992, the United Nations imposed a truce on all factions in the region, but it proved short-lived when Bosnia seceded from Yugoslavia in March 1992. The Serb population of Bosnia rebelled, and the breakaway republic was reduced to bloody anarchy using modern weapons to fight age-old ethnic feuds.

Beginning in August 1995, the Clinton administration helped to bring about a peace settlement among the warring factions in Bosnia. On November 21, 1995, after protracted negotiations, a comprehensive agreement called the "Dayton Accord" was initialed at Wright-Patterson Air Force Base near Dayton, Ohio. The agreement was formally signed in Paris the following month, and President Clinton joined the ranks of such chief executives as Theodore Roosevelt and Jimmy Carter in having brokered peace in an apparently intractable foreign conflict.

Kosovo Crisis

Bosnia was not the only hot spot in what commentators clumsily referred to as "the former Yugoslavia." In the breakup of that nation, a place called Kosovo was accorded the ambiguous status of an "autonomous province" within Serbia. This arrangement was bound to create trouble; ethnic Albanians—mostly Muslims—made up 90 percent of

Kosovo's population, with Serbs accounting for the other 10 percent. The Albanian majority protested Serbia's control of the Kosovar administration, and in 1992, Kosovo voted to secede from Serbia as well as from Yugoslavia, with the intention of merging with Islamic Albania. Slobodan Milosevic at first responded by tightening his control on Kosovo. When this failed, he waged all-out war against the Albanian majority in Kosovo.

Kosovo was caught between the violent passion of Serbia and the political opposition of other European powers, which feared that Kosovar independence would trigger a wider war in the Balkans, one that might engulf the whole of Europe as had happened in 1914.

President Clinton brought the prestige of the United States to bear in proposing a solution: wider autonomy for Kosovo, but autonomy well short of independence. The ethnic Albanians accepted the compromise plan, but Milosevic rejected it. Beginning in February 1998, he launched an offensive against the Kosovo Liberation Army (KLA). In response, NATO, with the United States leading, launched massive airstrikes against Serbian forces.

The United States, NATO, and the United Nations attempted to broker peace, but talks in Rambouillet, France, dissolved early in March 1999. On March 24, again spearheaded by the United States, NATO launched air strikes on Serbian Yugoslavia. After weeks of unremitting attacks, on June 10, 1999, the Milosevic government agreed to a military withdrawal from Kosovo, which may be counted as a victory of American diplomacy.

The Least You Need to Know

- ⊛ The 1990s were characterized by discontent, political extremism, and rage that threatened democracy, but also by a renewed passion to gather and share information and ideas, the very elements that keep democracy strong.

- ⊛ During this period, the Christian conservatism, or the Christian right, emerged as an increasingly powerful force in American politics.

- ⊛ Despite continued political and racial divisions in America, unprecedented economic prosperity buoyed the nation's confidence during much of the 1990s.

- ⊛ The United States closed the century by intervening in civil wars in Africa and Eastern Europe.

CHAPTER 36

Democracy at the Turn of the Millennium (1991–2004)

American democracy had a bumpy ride at the threshold of the new millennium, beginning with the impeachment of a president and ending with an election in hot dispute.

High Crimes and Misdemeanors?

On September 11, 1998, the Republican-controlled U.S. Congress published on the internet the full text of a report written under the direction of Kenneth Starr, an "independent counsel" appointed to investigate allegations of possibly impeachable offenses committed by President Bill Clinton. Millions of Americans were free to read laboriously detailed accounts of the president's liaison with a 21-year-old White House intern, Monica Lewinsky.

The Starr Report was the culmination of a four-year, $40 million investigation into questionable aspects of Clinton's conduct. It began as an inquiry into the President's and First Lady's involvement in a shady real-estate undertaking known as Whitewater and other possible financial improprieties. When Starr failed to find evidence of wrongdoing in these areas, he focused instead on the president's sexual behavior.

Bill Clinton was no stranger to sexual scandal. In 1992, Gennifer Flowers—an aspiring rock 'n' roll singer and, later, a Little Rock, Arkansas, TV news reporter—announced that she had had a 12-year sexual affair with Clinton, had become pregnant by him in 1977 (she aborted the baby), and had smoked marijuana and used cocaine with him. The affair, according to Flowers, did not end until 1989.

Candidate Clinton coolly and earnestly denied the accusations, his candidacy survived the scandal, and the Arkansas governor went on to spoil George H. W. Bush's bid for a second term.

The Starr Report appeared when the president was midway through his second term. The lurid details of the report notwithstanding, Starr and the others involved in the investigation insisted that sex was not the issue in question. The issue, they claimed, was that the president had violated his oath of office by lying about the affair in a sworn deposition he had given in a sexual harassment civil lawsuit brought against him by a former Arkansas state employee, Paula Jones. It was alleged that the president had also lied about the affair to a grand jury.

AMERICAN ECHO

"I did not have sexual relations with that woman—Miss Lewinsky."
　　　　　　　　—President Bill Clinton, televised press conference, January 26, 1998

Based on the Starr Report, the House of Representatives voted, along strict party lines, to *impeach* President Clinton. For the first time since Andrew Johnson was impeached in 1868, the U.S. Senate was the scene of an impeachment trial.

WHAT'S THE WORD?

To **impeach** is to charge an office holder with offenses that, if proven, warrant removal from office. Impeachment is not synonymous with such removal.

Although Republicans held a simple majority of Senate seats, a president's removal from office requires more: a two-thirds Senate vote. Although most people deplored President Clinton's unbecoming personal behavior, they also overwhelmingly approved of his performance as a chief executive presiding over a booming economy.

Heedless of popular sentiment, the Republican-controlled Senate pressed on with what members solemnly called their "constitutional duty." Nevertheless, on February 12, 1999, to no one's surprise, the Senate acquitted the president.

Paper Money

Americans who had come of age in the economically troubled 1970s and the economically volatile 1980s could hardly believe the bounty of the 1990s. With each passing year, the optimism became a little less cautious. The Dow Jones Industrial Average shattered one record after another. The new information-technology industries, centered on computers, digital communications (including cellphones), and the internet, spawned major new companies seemingly every day, creating what was touted as the "dot.com economy."

Investors rushed to fund each new venture, sending internet and other computer-related stocks soaring, in turn propelling the equity markets to ever greater heights. More and more people made more and more money. At least on paper.

Dot.Com and Dot.Bomb

The explosive growth of technology and internet companies, whose perceived value changes minute by minute, made for sharp, sudden rises and falls in the stock market. In the late 1990s, high-tech stocks had the potential to rise or fall by 5 to 10 percent in a day, so buying 1,000 shares of a major computer chip maker at $63\frac{7}{8}$ on August 5, 1999, and selling them at $68\frac{5}{8}$ at the end of the day would yield $4,750, a 7.6 percent return in a single day. Of course, if the numbers happened to go the other way—$68\frac{5}{8}$ in the morning and $63\frac{7}{8}$ that afternoon—the *loss* was that same $4,750.

The digital technology explosion during the last decade of the twentieth century did not refashion human nature or remodel the American Dream, but it did enable instant access to information that had once been the privileged domain of a relatively few professionals. And of even greater consequence, it provided a means of instantly and perhaps impulsively acting on much of that information.

Greedy to get in on the ground floor of an initial public offering (IPO), investors wildly bid up dot.com stocks. Then, as the bubbles started to burst one by one—costs soared, markets proved ephemeral, a promised technology failed to materialize, and profits were nil—they just as precipitously let the stocks fall. For example, more than 117 dot.coms imploded between September 1999 and October 2000.

Pillars of the Community

They were dubbed "dot.bombs," and they precipitated a slump in the stock market. The Dow, which had ascended into what was then the stratosphere of the 11,000-point range before the end of the 1990s, receded into the four figures.

Cooked Books

The "Gilded Age" of the post–Civil War years reveled in unregulated capitalism, the excesses of which promoted the reforms introduced by the "trust-busting" Theodore Roosevelt and other Progressives as the nineteenth century gave way to the twentieth. And so it went for much of the century, with business under the watchful eye of government regulators, until the election of pro-business governments under Presidents Ronald Reagan and George H. W. Bush, who promoted the "deregulation" of business across the board. It all seemed to work remarkably well. As a Democrat, President Clinton might have been expected to try to reintroduce more government regulation, but he had no wish to interfere with an economic recovery that was becoming an economic boom.

Many firms flourished in the climate of deregulation. One, a company called Enron, emerged during the 1990s as the veritable poster boy of deregulation.

The company began in 1985 as nothing more than an oil pipeline enterprise in Houston. During the heady years of Reaganomics, which lifted the lid on American energy policy, and in the long economic expansion under Bill Clinton, Enron morphed from running pipes to trading electricity and other energy-related commodities. It became a new kind of business: an energy broker.

By the start of the twenty-first century, Enron had gone even beyond that role. A broker brings buyers and sellers together. Enron, as the *Washington Post* pointed out, "entered the contract with the seller and signed a contract with the buyer, making money on the difference between the selling price and the buying price." Moreover, by processing—camouflaging, really—transactions through incredibly complex bookkeeping and a maze of partnerships and subsidiaries, Enron became the only party privy to all sides of its baroquely complex contracts. This allowed the company to post losses as apparent profits by passing expenses off to one of its many "partners." Moreover, the greatly loosened federal laws under which the firm operated actually permitted it to show *projected* profits as *realized* profits, without distinguishing between the two.

No wonder that, from the outside, Enron looked like one terrific company—a no-brainer investment if there ever was one.

On October 16, 2001, the company sent a shockwave through the financial markets by posting a devastating $638 million loss for the third quarter. That same day, Wall Street reduced the value of stockholders' equity by $1.2 billion. On November 8, company officials admitted having overstated earnings for the past four years—by some $586 million. Worse—if anything could be worse—Enron also owned up to liabilities of some $3 billion in obligations to various partnerships.

After Enron's lenders downgraded the company's debt to junk-bond status in November, a much-hoped-for merger with chief rival Dynegy, representing a life-giving $23 billion infusion of funds, was unceremoniously withdrawn.

Enron's stock value plummeted to pennies, and the company began proceedings to consummate the biggest bankruptcy in American corporate history (nevertheless destined to be dwarfed in September 2008 when the venerable Lehman Brothers investment bank went belly up in the mortgage and credit "meltdown" that heralded a major recession), whereupon Congress opened a round of investigations and hearings. Politicians rushed to the rostrum to express their outrage, rarely if ever alluding to the fact that, during the 2000 elections, Enron had spent $2.4 million in individual, political action committee, and soft-money contributions to federal candidates and parties.

There was more to come. Amid a slipping stock market and the shriveling of retirement funds nationwide, the talk of political reform and "new" government regulation grew in volume, even as other major firms—communications giants Global Crossing and WorldCom among them—came under investigation for "accounting irregularities."

The New Ethics?

The new century saw top Enron, WorldCom, and other executives facing indictment, trial, and, in many cases, conviction for various shades of fraud and other financial malfeasance. Some in Congress clamored for a reversal of the deregulation trend, but nothing of the kind happened.

Too Close to Call

If the ethical failings of American business were especially troubling because capitalism and democracy go hand in hand, even more urgently distressing was a convulsion at democracy's very core: the institution and process of electing national leaders. In 2000, the entire procedure fell under a shadow.

Democrat Al Gore, Bill Clinton's vice president, ran against Republican George W. Bush, son of Clinton's predecessor, George H. W. Bush. The two ran campaigns that failed to generate enthusiasm and that resulted in a neck-and-neck election too close to call. The first complete tally gave Gore 50,996,116 votes against Bush's 50,456,169. It is the Electoral College, however, not the popular vote, that puts a candidate into the White House, and it is on this point that democracy seemed to falter.

In Florida, governed by candidate Bush's younger brother, Jeb, the popular vote was almost a dead heat. Initial counts gave Bush a razor-thin lead of 1,784 votes over Gore, which would deliver to Bush the state's 25 electoral votes and, with them, the presidency. Florida law, however, mandated an automatic recount when results were this close. After the recount on November 9, the Bush lead was narrowed to 327 votes.

The notion that a choice made by 327 Floridians would determine who would become the most powerful political leader on the planet was stupefying to contemplate. But this was just the beginning.

Unsatisfied with an automatic recount, Democrats demanded a recount by hand in four counties where they had reason to believe significant numbers of Gore votes had not been counted. The basis of this assumption was Florida's reliance on an antiquated punch-card ballot, on which voters indicated their choices by pushing a stylus through a card. If a voter failed to push the stylus all the way through, the resulting hole might be blocked by a tiny rectangular fragment of cardboard—called a "chad"—which prevented the tabulating machine from registering the vote.

Acting in accordance with Florida law, which required election officials to evaluate disputed ballots in a way that attempts to "determine the intention" of the voter, Democrats called for each ballot to be inspected for "hanging chad." Where such was found, the vote was to be counted. Now it seemed that the future of the nation and, perhaps, the world depended not just on 327 Floridians, but on a few tiny fragments of scrap cardboard, each smaller than a piece of confetti.

On November 11, the Bush camp filed suit to stop the ongoing manual recounts, even as Katherine Harris, Florida's secretary of state, declared that she was prepared to certify Bush as winner on the legal deadline for certification, November 14. Democracy in action? Harris, the state's top election official, was not only a Republican, but also had served as a Bush delegate to the Republican National Convention and was one of eight co-chairs of the Bush campaign in Florida.

Over the next several days, recounts stopped and started and stopped again in several Florida counties, and the Democrats and Republicans battled in court. The dispute escalated to the United States Supreme Court, which on December 12, by a five-to-four vote, overturned a decision by the Florida Supreme Court and barred all further manual recounts. Defeated in the courts and the Electoral College, though not in the popular vote, Al Gore conceded the election to George W. Bush on December 13. Bush had carried Florida, it was decided, by 537 votes.

Later unofficial recounts sponsored by the *Miami Herald, USA Today,* and others came to ambiguous conclusions. Some suggested that, even if a full manual recount had been completed in the counties where Democrats demanded recounts, Bush would have prevailed. Others, however, concluded that if manual recounts had been conducted throughout Florida, Gore would have won, although only by 393 votes.

However one looked at it, the first election of the new century stood as a disturbing testament to voter apathy and to a certain randomness uncomfortably close to the very heart of the democratic system.

The Least You Need to Know

- ✪ Around Bill Clinton revolved two of the most important trials of the closing decade of the twentieth century.

- ✪ As the century ended, the internet emerged as a great force in our economy, our culture, and our lives.

- ✪ Political and corporate ethics was a hot-button issue during this period, which saw the trials of high-profile corporate moguls in spectacular financial collapses.

- ✪ George W. Bush defeated Democratic candidate Al Gore in a disputed election, which was ultimately arbitrated by the Supreme Court. The nation emerged from the 2000 presidential contest deeply divided.

Asymmetric Threats (2001–2008)

Were Florida's voting machines flawed? Absolutely. Was the United States Supreme Court flawed? Perhaps. Was democracy itself flawed? As it turned out, not fatally. The people and the candidates accepted the rule of law, and George W. Bush entered the White House on the day appointed by that law and without violence.

9/11

Nine months after the resolution of the disputed election, at 8:45 A.M. (EDT) on the morning of September 11, 2001, a Boeing 767 passenger jetliner (later identified as American Airlines Flight 11 out of Boston) crashed into the north tower of the World Trade Center in lower Manhattan. The usual morning television shows were interrupted by live coverage of the disaster, cameras focused on the thick black smoke that billowed from the wound torn in the gleaming silver skin of the 110-story skyscraper.

Stunned

Television news pictures of the burning World Trade Center began to be broadcast just three minutes after the impact, and so much of America—and the world—bore witness to the horrific impact of a *second* 767 (United Airlines Flight 175) at 9:03 A.M., this time into the World Trade Center's south tower.

During the attacks, President Bush was visiting a Sarasota, Florida, classroom reading *The Pet Goat* with second graders. The president's chief of staff, Andrew Card, was also in a nearby room when he heard the news. He waited until there was a pause in the reading drill to walk into the classroom and whisper in Bush's ear. Reports vary as to whether this moment came at 9:05 A.M. or 9:07 A.M.

It was 9:30 A.M. before President Bush appeared on television to announce that the nation had suffered "an apparent terrorist attack."

AMERICAN ECHO

"Clandestine, foreign government, and media reports indicate bin Laden since 1997 has wanted to conduct terrorist attacks in the U.S. Bin Laden implied in U.S. television interviews in 1997 and 1998 that his followers would follow the example of [1993] World Trade Center bomber Ramzi Yousef and 'bring the fighting to America.'"

—from a Presidential Daily Briefing (PDB) dated August 6, 2001, entitled "Bin Laden Determined to Strike in U.S."

More Attacks

Thirteen minutes after the president's announcement, at 9:43 A.M., a Boeing 757 (American Airlines Flight 77) sliced into the Pentagon, headquarters of the U.S. military. Back in New York, at 10:05 A.M., the south tower of the World Trade Center collapsed, swallowing up 110 stories of steel, concrete, and humanity. At 10:10 A.M., the peace of rural Somerset County, Pennsylvania, was shattered when another 757, United Airlines Flight 93, blasted a crater into the dark earth. Eighteen minutes after this, the north tower of the World Trade Center collapsed.

The Terrorists

Before the day was over, the media reported that the airplane downed in Pennsylvania had been headed for the White House or the United States Capitol. It was quickly learned that all four planes had been hijacked by terrorists willing to sacrifice themselves to take the lives of untold thousands by using the giant jets—loaded with thousands of pounds of jet fuel—as guided missiles.

The terrorists had been members of al-Qaeda (Arabic for "The Base"), an Islamist guerrilla organization of perhaps 10,000 men (at the time) dedicated to fighting a *jihad*—a holy war—against Israel, the West, and the United States. The organization was led by Osama bin Laden, a Saudi multimillionaire sponsor of terrorism living under the protection of the radical Islamic Taliban government in Afghanistan.

Days after the attacks, the nation learned that cell phone calls made by crew members and passengers on the doomed planes described how the terrorists had commandeered the aircraft using weapons no more sophisticated than box cutters. The first three planes hit their targets, but by the time the fourth plane had been seized, passengers who surreptitiously phoned loved ones were told of the attack on the World Trade Center. Apparently understanding that this hijacking was part of a larger attack against the nation, a group of Flight 93 passengers resolved to try to regain control of the plane. They apparently stormed the cockpit and rushed the hijackers. In the struggle, the plane crashed—but it did so in rural Pennsylvania, and not into the White House or the Capitol.

First War of the Twenty-First Century

In the hours and days following the attacks, officials did move quickly to identify the perpetrators. They were 19 Middle Eastern terrorists, trained and financed by bin Laden's al-Qaeda; they had (for the most part) quite easily entered the United States illegally and had, for months before the attacks, lived in American motels and apartment complexes. The attackers paid cash to train in small American flight schools, hardened their bodies in American gyms, and banked at American banks.

On September 12, President Bush remarked, "We have just seen the first war of the twenty-first century." Eight days later, he issued a warning in an address to a special joint session of Congress on September 20, announcing that the United States would attack the Taliban in Afghanistan unless it surrendered "all the leaders of al-Qaeda who hide in your land."

The Taliban replied with defiance, and the United States unleashed an air war followed by a limited ground war that made extensive use of local warlords, which toppled the Taliban—for a time. Osama bin Laden was neither captured nor killed. That would not happen until U.S. Navy SEALs breached his refuge in Pakistan on May 2, 2011. As for the "limited" war in Afghanistan, as of 2018 it was about to enter its seventeenth year, easily making it the longest war in U.S. history.

The Toll of Terror

While the war was being fought in Afghanistan, crews completed months of hazardous and heartbreaking clean-up operations at the World Trade Center. The death toll there was fixed at 2,893—added to 189 killed at the Pentagon, including the 64 passengers and crew of Flight 77.

In the Pennsylvania crash, all 44 passengers on the plane died. Among those killed at the World Trade Center were 23 New York City police officers, 37 Port Authority police officers, and 343 New York City firefighters. They had begun September 11, 2001, as ordinary people. Before the morning was over, they were the heroic defenders of a democracy under attack.

VITAL STATISTICS

While the Taliban government in Afghanistan quickly collapsed and was replaced by a provisional regime friendly to the United States, fighting continued, the Taliban repeatedly reemerged, and, as of summer 2018, 43,362 "coalition" troops (2,271 U.S.) and 51,000-67,000 Taliban and other "insurgent" fighters had been killed. An estimated 31,000 Afghan civilians died in the war between 2001 and 2016.

PATRIOT Act

While the United States backed the installation of democracy in distant Afghanistan, many began to feel that democracy at home was under siege. Of several laws rushed through Congress to expand the investigative powers of U.S. law enforcement agencies, the most important was the USA PATRIOT Act, which was passed by the Senate on October 11, 2001, and the next day by the House. The act provided an array of anti-terrorist measures, including extensive provisions for federal wiretaps and surveillance programs, including so called "Sneak-and-Peek" surreptitious search warrants and seizures. Despite lawsuits and protests, the controversial act was renewed by Congress in 2006 and portions renewed again in 2010 and 2011.

Operation Iraqi Freedom

Throughout the summer of 2002, there was much debate about where the "war on terrorism" should be taken next. A clique of so-called neoconservatives—"neocons"— in the Bush administration, foremost among them Vice President Cheney, Secretary of Defense Donald Rumsfeld, and Deputy Secretary of Defense Paul Wolfowitz, persuaded the president to invade Iraq, which they said was the linchpin of the Middle East. Transform it into a democracy, and the entire region would become friendly to U.S. interests, which included access to Middle Eastern oil. Other political leaders questioned the wisdom, justice, and feasibility of invading Iraq, which, unlike Taliban-controlled Afghanistan, had no direct link to 9/11.

No matter. On September 12, 2002, President Bush addressed the United Nations General Assembly, declaring that Iraq presented a threat to the United States and other nations. On October 11, the president secured congressional resolutions authorizing the use of military force against Iraq. On November 8, the United Nations approved U.S.-sponsored Resolution 1441, obliging Iraq to prove that it had divested itself of all weapons of mass destruction.

Pursuant to the resolution, UN inspectors were sent to Iraq. They found nothing, but the Bush administration persisted in its claim that Iraq possessed weapons of mass destruction (WMDs). On February 5, 2003, U.S. Secretary of State Colin Powell (b. 1937) took the administration's case to the UN Security Council.

Despite Powell's presentation, most of the international community withheld support for a war. But while international and domestic debate over the prospective war was underway, President Bush suddenly shifted his reason for going to war. No longer were the putative WMDs the sole issue. On March 16, 2003, the president issued an ultimatum to Saddam Hussein, demanding that he and his immediate cohorts (including his sons, Uday [1964–2003] and Qusay [1966–2003]) permanently leave Iraq within 48 hours. When this deadline passed, on March 19, President Bush authorized an aerial attack on a bunker in Baghdad believed to shelter Saddam. This attack, from which Saddam emerged uninjured, was the commencement of the undeclared war called Operation Iraqi Freedom.

After more attacks by air- and ship-launched "smart bombs" and guided missiles, the war's ground phase commenced on March 20, as U.S. Army troops and Marines captured strategically vital oil fields. The invasion of Iraq progressed with lightning speed and resulted in very few U.S. or British casualties.

On April 6, U.S. and British troops began encircling Baghdad, the Iraqi capital. On the 7th, U.S. forces advanced into the city itself. Attempts were made to capture or kill Saddam

Hussein. These failed, but by April 14, 2003, the Pentagon announced that the "major combat phase" of Operation Iraqi Freedom had ended.

"Mission Accomplished"

On April 20, the U.S. Marines left Baghdad, turning it over to U.S. Army occupying forces. Lieutenant General Jay Garner (b. 1938) arrived in the capital to lead U.S. reconstruction efforts in Iraq and to arrange for an interim civil authority in Baghdad. Chaos reigned throughout the unpoliced country as looters raided everything from stores to government arsenals, from which they carried off weapons and ammunition. Secretary of Defense Rumsfeld dismissed the civil disorder in an April 12 press conference with an off-handed "Stuff happens."

On May 2, 2003, President Bush dramatically landed in an S-3 Viking aircraft on the deck of the aircraft carrier *Abraham Lincoln* anchored off its San Diego base. Emerging from the jet in full flight suit, the smiling president waved to the crew, went below, and changed into a suit and tie. A short time later, he stood before a huge banner emblazoned with the phrase "Mission Accomplished" to deliver a speech affirming victory in the invasion of Iraq.

True, Saddam Hussein and his sons were still at large; the two young men would be killed in a July 22 raid, however, and Saddam Hussein himself was discovered on December 14, 2003, hiding in a hole on a remote farm.

Yet even after Hussein's capture, the fighting continued at an intense level. Soon, the United States found itself in the middle of a civil war. As U.S. casualties mounted month after month and then year after year, the phrase "Mission Accomplished" entered the American popular lexicon as a bitter punchline applied to any fiasco.

There was worse to come. On April 25, 2005, the CIA issued a final report on the WMD question, concluding that there were none and presumably never had been any located in Iraq.

The Iraq War's increasing unpopularity did not dissuade Americans from re-electing President Bush in 2004 over Democratic challenger John Kerry, a liberal senator from Massachusetts.

A Hundred Years War?

During its second term, the Bush administration belatedly discovered that it had ordered the invasion of Iraq with a force large enough to achieve a military victory against regular Iraqi forces but far too small to impose civil order. After defending his secretary of defense, Donald Rumsfeld, for some three years against charges of having mismanaged the war, President Bush "accepted" his resignation on December 18, 2006. Rumsfeld was replaced by Robert Gates, under whom troop strength was temporarily increased in a "surge," which proved effective in reducing the general level of violence.

Unclear, however, was how and when the United States would begin withdrawing combat forces from a war that, as of October 2008, had cost 4,190 American lives and required a *monthly* expenditure of $10 billion to prosecute. In January 2008, during the Republican presidential primaries, Senator John McCain answered a voter's question about a statement President Bush had made that U.S. troops might stay in Iraq for 50 years. "Maybe 100," McCain off-handedly replied.

In fact, President Barack Obama withdrew U.S. forces on December 18, 2011. From June 15, 2014, to December 22, 2017, a U.S.-led coalition of air and ground forces intervened in a civil war and an insurgency instigated by the Islamic State of Iraq and the Levant (ISIL—also known as ISIS). More than 5,000 U.S. troops remained in Iraq as of summer 2018.

No Shelter from the Storm

Beginning in 2001, terrorism had unleashed a storm of human creation upon the United States and the world. On August 24, 2005, the National Hurricane Center warned of a new threat to America, and on the next day, Hurricane Katrina struck Florida. The storm cut across the state and headed for the Gulf of Mexico. By August 28, as it pounded toward New Orleans, Katrina was a Category 5 storm, winds reaching 160 miles per hour. Mayor Ray Nagin ordered an evacuation, but 30 percent of New Orleans lived below the national poverty line. Many people, especially in African American neighborhoods, had no means of leaving the city and nowhere to go. For those unable to leave, 10 shelters were set up, including one at the aging Superdome stadium and another at the city's convention center.

Despite dire warnings, President Bush vacationed at his ranch in Crawford, Texas, leaving management of the approaching hurricane to the recently created Department of Homeland Security (DHS), of which the Federal Emergency Management Agency (FEMA) was now a part. FEMA's funding and authority had been reduced after its move to DHS. As for FEMA's director, Michael Brown, longtime Bush aide Joseph Allbaugh had recruited him from his job as commissioner of the International Arabian Horse Association. He had no experience in disaster management.

At 6:10 A.M. local time, on August 29, Katrina made landfall near Buras, Louisiana, rather than over New Orleans. It looked as if the "Big Easy" had dodged a bullet.

But then the rains came, two New Orleans flood walls gave way, and 80 percent of the city was inundated, in some areas to a depth of 20 feet. With that, the city and much of the Alabama and Mississippi Gulf Coast descended into chaos. A handful of Coast Guard helicopters managed to lift a few survivors from the rooftops of buildings in which flood-waters had risen to the second or even the third floor, but no FEMA workers, Army troops, or National Guardsmen were in sight. There were television images of bodies floating in rivers and floodwaters. There were television images of some 10,000 persons huddled in the squalor of the Superdome and, later, another 20,000 packed into even worse conditions at the convention center. There were images and reports of looting that had risen to the point of civil insurrection. On September 1, Mayor Nagin broadcast over the radio a "desperate SOS" for evacuation buses and the promised federal aid.

On September 2, after Congress voted for $10.5 billion in emergency funds, President Bush appeared on television to acknowledge the failure of government efforts, and National Guardsmen began arriving with food, water, and their weapons.

VITAL STATISTICS

Katrina's toll has been set at 1,833 killed.

Americans, many of whom had voted for George W. Bush because he promised to reduce "big government," now expressed outrage that the government had failed to serve and protect them.

AMERICAN ECHO

"Brownie, you're doing a heck of a job."
—President George W. Bush to FEMA director Michael D. Brown, September 2, 2005

The Least You Need to Know

- ✪ The terrorist attacks on September 11, 2001, motivated the United States to topple the terrorist-supporting Taliban government of Afghanistan and to wage war against Saddam Hussein's Iraq.

- ✪ Despite the unpopularity of the Iraq War—which had devolved into a long and bloody American occupation—President George W. Bush was re-elected to a second term, supported in large measure by the mostly white, mostly Christian, mostly conservative voters of the "red states."

- ✪ Acting aggressively to disseminate democracy to the Middle East, the Bush administration drew both praise and criticism at home and alienated many of the world's other leaders.

- ✪ Hurricane Katrina revealed the inability or unwillingness of government to protect all Americans.

Elections Have Consequences (2008-2018)

No war since Vietnam was more unpopular or divisive than the post-9/11 invasion of Iraq, and most political pundits believed that George W. Bush, having gained office by the margin of a few hundred disputed votes in Florida, a state governed by his brother Jeb, would be defeated for re-election.

They were mistaken. A slim majority stood behind the flawed incumbent rather than risk a change under Democratic challenger Massachusetts senator John Kerry, a Vietnam-era naval war hero and antiwar activist. But by three years into Bush's second term, it seemed that everyone, including those who had voted for him, was against the president.

Beyond Red State, Blue State

A self-described born-again Christian, George W. Bush achieved election and re-election with strong support from a socio-political bloc that had been growing since the Reagan years: the so-called Christian right. By the end of the twentieth century, this group was highly influential on the Republican agenda, which included federal funding (through tax credits) for educating children in parochial schools, support for a constitutional amendment banning abortion and for another, banning same-sex marriage. The Christian right also saw the Iraq War as a new crusade pitting Christianity against Islam.

Those who watched the 2004 election returns on television saw a new map of the United States emerge consisting of predominantly Republican-voting states (arbitrarily colored red by TV broadcasters) and predominantly Democratic-voting states (colored blue). The red states encompassed the entire South, most of the Midwest, and the western "heartland"; within this vast area, however, many large cities remained democratic enclaves—lone blue islands in red seas. The blue states included the Northeast, much of the upper Midwest, and the West Coast. The Republican red states were politically, culturally, and spiritually conservative, whereas Democratic blue states tended toward liberalism. Racially, red voters were overwhelmingly white, whereas blue voters were a more diverse group.

Bush in the Balance

A *New York Times*–CBS poll published on October 31, 2008, days before the general election, reported that 85 percent of respondents believed the country was "seriously on the wrong track," and 89 percent viewed the economy "negatively." George W. Bush was approaching the end of what most Americans considered a "failed presidency" and the Republican Party was tainted by it.

Even the Republican presidential candidate, Senator John McCain, behaved as if he were running against Bush as well as against Barack Obama, the Democratic candidate. Many saw a McCain presidency as a "third Bush term," a continuation of the status quo.

Revaluing Values

The 2008 election was a revaluation of the values that had sufficiently appealed to about half the electorate to have ushered Bush into office. He had run on a Reagan-style economic platform of cutting taxes, especially for upper-income Americans, and deregulating business. Although candidate Bush had rejected "nation building"—military and other interventions to promote the creation of democratic governments among emerging nations—he became a zealous nation builder after 9/11. The resulting war in Iraq was a drag on his presidency.

Then, in 2007-2008, the bottom fell out of the free market American economy. A worried electorate urgently demanded a solution.

Mortgaging the Future

Republicans traditionally presented themselves as the party of "fiscal responsibility" in contrast to the "tax and spend" Democrats. Yet during the Reagan administration, the national debt rose from $1 trillion to $4 trillion, and, after nearly eight years under George W. Bush, the national debt passed the $10 trillion mark.

Debt and Debacle

President Bush aggressively championed bold tax cuts and maintained the cuts even after the Iraq War got underway. As of 2008, operations in Iraq were consuming nearly $12 billion per month, and Bush proposed deep reductions or funding freezes in such domestic programs as grants for firefighters' assistance, low-income schools, family literacy, and rural housing and economic development. Still, thanks to heavy borrowing, the federal deficit for 2008 was projected at $482 billion in July. By the 2008 elections, predictions ran much higher.

Meltdown

In a climate of deregulation of the financial industry under Presidents Clinton and George W. Bush, credit became increasingly easy for businesses and individuals to obtain. Real estate values, especially the prices of private homes, had been rising since the early 1990s. By the beginning of the twenty-first century, the housing market was white hot. Deregulated lenders made mortgage and home equity loans requiring so little evidence of the borrower's ability to repay the loan that many people purchased homes priced far out of their budget range. While the real estate market soared, this was not a big problem. Strapped homeowners could quickly sell, and lenders could foreclose, resell, and recoup their investment. But even before the middle of the century's first decade, home values began to slip.

This was bad enough for homeowners, sellers, and mortgage lenders, but there was far worse to come. When the real estate market was *the* place to invest, big-name Wall Street investment houses and deregulated banks began to build many of their securities offerings on mortgages. They bought "bundled" mortgages—thousands of loans per bundle—and sold them as investments based on the assumption that home values would continue to rise. There was no way to evaluate the soundness of the individual mortgages that made up a given bundle, but investment rating agencies almost invariably gave the securities ratings of A or even higher.

In truth, many mortgage-backed securities were essentially fraudulent, the underlying mortgages the products of zealous mortgage brokers and starry-eyed home buyers.

As mortgage defaults began increasing in volume and tempo, the liquidity of the economy congealed. Banks stopped lending. When credit freezes, the economy seizes up. When America sneezes, an old saying goes, the world catches cold. The mortgage crisis quickly spread throughout Europe and Asia.

On August 9, 2007, the Federal Reserve ("the Fed") made massive securities purchases to inject $24 billion into the U.S. banking system and the next day tossed in another $38 billion.

The mortgage and credit crisis not only imperiled homeowners, banks, and the major private mortgage companies, but also Fannie Mae and Freddie Mac (the Federal National Mortgage Association and Federal Home Loan Mortgage Corporation), federally sponsored private investment companies that underwrite many mortgages made by banks and other lenders. By purchasing and securitizing mortgages, Fannie Mae and Freddie Mac enabled many middle-class families to own homes. The collapse of the housing market and the subprime mortgage meltdown that followed came as devastating body blows to the underwriters, and on July 13, 2008, the Fed and the U.S. Treasury Department announced a plan to bolster them. On July 23, the House appropriated $300 billion to provide more affordable mortgages to troubled homeowners. A week later, the Fed extended "emergency borrowing" to Wall Street. And on September 7, the Bush administration announced the outright federal takeover of Fannie Mae and Freddie Mac, effectively guaranteeing trillions of dollars in mortgages.

Amid government intervention in the "free" market on a scale unprecedented since the Great Depression, the venerable investment house of Lehman Brothers—weighed down by $60 billion in bad real estate holdings—filed for bankruptcy on September 14. The very next day, Bank of America announced its intention to acquire Merrill Lynch, another storied—and now faltering—financial titan. These two events sent Wall Street into a tailspin, the market losing 504.48 points on September 15, the worst point drop since the stock exchange reopened after the September 2001 terrorist attacks.

It was hardly over. On September 16, the government announced an $85 billion emergency loan to American International Group (AIG), claiming that the failure of this insurance giant would bring down already reeling financial markets. If the bailor was intended to bolster confidence on Wall Street, it had just the opposite effect, as the Dow Jones Industrial Average shed some 450 points on September 17.

With a new day came a new plan. On September 18, officials announced that the Fed—in concert with central banks in Europe, Canada, and Asia—was injecting some $180 billion into money markets to ensure that banks would be able to continue lending to each other.

On September 19, the government announced the most ambitious rescue plan yet. Secretary of the Treasury Henry Paulson proposed buying hundreds of billions of dollars of bad mortgages and so-called "toxic debt." Initial funding was pegged at $700 billion, and Paulson asked for absolute authority in disbursing the funds. The House of Representatives voted down the $700 billion emergency rescue plan on September 23. In response, the Dow plunged a staggering 780 points, the greatest single-day point drop ever.

A panic-stricken Senate "sweetened" the $700 billion bailout with a miscellany of tax breaks and pork barrel provisions, passed it, and then sent it to the House, which voted it up on October 3, 2008. Three days later, the Fed and other central banks from around the world slashed interest rates to stem the global economic meltdown.

Despite this, the Dow closed below the 10,000 mark for the first time since 2004. On October 13, 2008, however, the New York Stock Exchange staged the most spectacular single-day rise in history, with the Dow climbing 936 points. It would gyrate wildly over the next several weeks before the next economic bombshell hit. The CEOs of GM and Chrysler asked Congress for massive loans. Ford requested a smaller "credit line." These icons of American heavy industry needed quick cash to stave off imminent bankruptcy.

REMEMBER THIS

On October 8, 2008, the Fed agreed to provide the insurance giant AIG a loan of up to $37.8 billion on top of the $85 billion loan it made in September. The decision came even as lawmakers were investigating the AIG meltdown and were angrily grilling the company's top executives about $440,000 spent on a recent company retreat, which included luxury spa treatments, lavish banquets, and exclusive golf outings.

What Is the Government? Who Is the Government?

From the earliest rumblings of revolution in America, thoughtful people have been asking these questions in one form or another. In 2008, Americans began asking them with the greatest urgency.

The Republican contenders in the 2008 presidential primaries were familiar names, Rudy Giuliani, Mike Huckabee, Mitt Romney, and John McCain. Democrats in contention included two old hands, John Edwards and Hillary Rodham Clinton, and one newcomer, Barack Obama. The early expectation was that Republicans would select Rudy Giuliani (New York mayor in 9/11) to face Democrat Hillary Clinton (New York senator and wife of former president Bill Clinton).

Defying predictions, John McCain, a conservative with a reputation as a political maverick, won the Republican nomination by a wide margin.

The Democratic field offered two candidates of profound historic significance. Although she was very much part of the party's "establishment," Hillary Clinton was the first woman to be a serious contender for the presidential nod of a major party. As for Barack Obama, a first-term senator from Illinois, he was the first African American under serious consideration from a major party. In the end, Democratic primary voters were faced with a choice between two history-making candidates. They chose Obama, who presented himself as the greater agent of change.

Campaigns for Change

In a less extraordinary time, the campaign for the general election would have pitted McCain, the old hand, as a champion of the conservative Republican status quo against Obama, the upstart candidate for change.

Beyond party and politics, the differences between the two candidates were dramatic. McCain was white, the son and grandson of four-star admirals. An Annapolis graduate (standing 894 in a class of 899), he became a naval aviator. During the Vietnam War, he was shot down and became a prisoner of war. After his return to the United States, he resumed his naval career and then ran for a congressional seat from Arizona, earning a reputation for conservative "straight talk." He was sent to the Senate in 1987.

Born in 1961 in Hawaii, Barack Hussein Obama II was the son of a black father from Kenya, Africa, and a white mother from Wichita, Kansas. His parents met when both were attending the University of Hawaii at Manoa. They married and soon divorced. Ann

Dunham remarried, and the family moved to Indonesia in 1967, where Obama lived until the age of 10, when he returned to Honolulu and the home of his maternal grandparents. Dunham came back to Hawaii in 1972, remaining for a time until she again left for Indonesia to complete field work for her PhD dissertation in anthropology. Scholarships enabled Barack Obama to study at Occidental College in Los Angeles, Columbia University in New York, and, later, Harvard Law.

Obama, who worked as a community organizer in Chicago, went on to become an Illinois state senator and, in 2005, a U.S. senator. When Obama received the Democratic nomination, he tapped veteran Delaware senator Joe Biden as his running mate, a respected mainstream choice, whereas McCain chose Sarah Palin, the young, energetic governor of Alaska, who presented herself as a "hockey mom" sympathetic to the needs and desires of "Joe Six-Pack." She was also a cultural conservative, an evangelical Christian who opposed abortion under all circumstances, positions that appealed to the Republican base.

At first, Palin's presence gave McCain a significant boost, but a growing number of voters began questioning Palin's qualifications to be "a heartbeat away from the presidency," especially considering McCain's age (72 in 2008) and his history of melanoma. Exposure to the media revealed Palin as unable to articulate cogent policy positions and often scarcely able to speak in complete sentences.

First Tuesday

By 11 P.M. (EST), hours after most of the polls had closed, Americans learned that they had voted in record-shattering numbers for change, electing the nation's first African American president. They had also sent to Congress a solid Democratic majority.

VITAL STATISTICS

Barack Obama became the first African American U.S. president, winning 66,882,230 votes (53 percent) and defeating Republican John McCain, who polled 58,343,671 (46 percent). Obama took 365 electoral votes to McCain's 173.

Tribal Politics

A majority greeted the election of Barack Obama with hope and enthusiasm. But Republican Mitch McConnell of Kentucky, Senate minority leader, expressed the view of his party in 2010: "The single most important thing we want to achieve is for President Obama to be a one-term president." As many saw it, the Republican opposition became the "party of no." Many Americans gave Obama credit for averting a full-on depression in 2009 and pulling the economy back from the "Great Recession" of 2008. By the end of his first term, 11.3 million jobs had been created, and he was re-elected, albeit narrowly, over Republican Mitt Romney in 2012—having, however, lost Democratic majorities in both chambers of Congress.

His single most significant achievement was the Patient Protection and Affordable Care Act—popularly called "Obamacare"—which extended subsidized health insurance to millions who had been previously unable to afford coverage. Badly flawed in its execution, Obamacare proved controversial, and congressional Republicans repeatedly attempted to repeal it while also blocking other Obama initiatives.

What became increasingly clear during the Obama presidency was that American partisanship—the very danger George Washington had warned against in his farewell address of 1796—had hardened into "tribal politics," with Democrats and Republicans refusing to negotiate, let alone compromise, with one another.

President Trump

Many Americans were proud of having elected the first African American president and even spoke of having arrived at a "post-racial America." In the meantime, Republicans on what was considered the party's far-right fringe persisted in disseminating a rumor that Hawaii-born Barack Obama had really been born in Kenya, which meant that he was not a "natural born" American citizen and was therefore an illegal and illegitimate president. (Even had the rumors been true, U.S. law [8 U.S.C. §1401] defines as a citizen at birth a child born abroad of at least one U.S. citizen parent.) The bizarre position was called "birtherism," and it was espoused by (among others) Donald J. Trump beginning in 2011, long before he announced his candidacy for president in 2015.

The son of New York landlord and real estate entrepreneur Fred Trump, Donald Trump (born in Queens, New York in 1946) became a nationally famous real estate developer, who climbed to tenth place in a 1988 Gallup poll of the "most admired" Americans. Initially associated with spectacular Manhattan developments, he invested heavily in developing Atlantic City casinos beginning in the late 1970s—ventures that ended in bankruptcy. He recovered from that, and his name appears on major buildings and other projects worldwide.

Before entering politics, his life was colorful and a source of media gossip. He associated with celebrities and in 2003 became executive producer and host of NBC's wildly successful reality TV show, *The Apprentice,* with which he was associated until 2015, when he left it to begin his run for the presidency.

For most of his adult life, Trump was a liberal "New York" Democrat. During the Obama years, he became a conservative Republican and on June 16, 2015 announced his candidacy in a media event that began with his descent down the "golden" escalator of his Manhattan business headquarters, Trump Tower.

Trump ran on a "populist" platform, appealing frankly to a white working-class and middle-class electorate who felt left out by the "elite" Democratic Party of Barack Obama. At first, many considered his candidacy a joke, maybe even a publicity stunt intended to promote his businesses. But his populist, nationalistic, often unapologetically xenophobic message—driven by a campaign slogan emblazoned on a workingman's baseball cap, MAKE AMERICA GREAT AGAIN—carried him to victory over sixteen other Republican primary contenders, most of them mainstream names, including Jeb Bush.

The Democratic primaries were contested mainly between Hillary Clinton (who had served as President Obama's secretary of state) and Senator Bernie Sanders, an Independent from Vermont. Although Sanders's quasi-Socialist platform created a significant and passionate following, the Democratic establishment backed Clinton. In a dubious choice, she based her campaign on her political experience—even though 2016, like 2008, clearly promised to be a *change* election, in which voters wanted someone from outside the realm of traditional politics.

Still, few gave Trump a chance of defeating Clinton—especially after a campaign in which he called Mexican immigrants "rapists" and "drug dealers" ("and some, I assume, are good people"), called for a "total and complete shutdown of Muslims entering the United States," and made other extreme statements.

What many observers assumed was the final nail in the coffin of his campaign was driven on October 7, 2016, when *The Washington Post* released a 2005 video outtake from an episode of TV's *Access Hollywood*. It recorded Trump boasting to TV host Billy Bush that he kisses and gropes women at random. "I don't even wait. And when you're a star, they let you do it. You can do anything. Grab them by [their genitals]." The resulting scandal, dubbed "Pussygate" in echo of "Watergate," brought a chorus of appraisals that the Trump candidacy was dead.

It was not.

The scandal was soon overshadowed by the ongoing drama of the controversy over Hillary Clinton's unauthorized use of a private email server while she was secretary of state. On July 5, 2016, FBI director James Comey announced the bureau's recommendation that no charges be filed against her, but he nevertheless editorialized that "Clinton or her colleagues … were extremely careless in their handling of very sensitive, highly classified information." Then, on October 28, eleven days before the election, Comey informed Congress that the FBI was investigating some additional Clinton emails that had come to light as the result of an unrelated case.

By this time, Americans reconciled themselves to a contest between two unpopular candidates, one running as a seasoned political insider, the other offering the putative virtues of being an outsider.

Well before election day, news reports had emerged of Russian-based "interference" in the campaigns. The Russian activity included the hacking of Democratic National Committee computers and the theft of thousands of emails, which were published on WikiLeaks, the online vehicle for secret information. It also emerged that agents linked to the Kremlin and Russian President Vladimir Putin conducted an extensive social media campaign of disinformation aimed at promoting the candidacy of Donald Trump while damaging that of Hillary Clinton.

The upshot? The American electorate was faced with the prospect of an illegitimate election result, one that was even more disturbing than the tortured election of 2000.

Events quickly outrun books. This book was completed with the Trump presidency well into its second year. Media coverage has been relentless. The "establishment" Republican Party, which had fought Trump tooth and nail during the primaries, is now, with very few exceptions, solidly behind him. The Democratic minority has opposed the president's initiatives in Congress but has been consistently outvoted.

Yet, for a party in control of the White House and both chambers of Congress, Congress after nineteen months accomplished remarkably little—other than enacting massive tax cuts of benefit largely to the very wealthy and corporate America.

As this book was being readied for the press, the president was in the deliberate process of withdrawing the United States from its long post-World War II leadership of the "free world." He was challenging long-time allies—Britain, France, Germany, and Canada—imposing punitive trade tariffs on their imports. At the same time, he was making friendly overtures to Vladimir Putin and vehemently denying that Russia had played any significant role in influencing the 2016 election. Americans held their breath as the president engaged in talks with Kim Jong-un, "Supreme Leader" of North Korea, in an effort to persuade him to "denuclearize"—dismantle and renounce his nuclear and thermonuclear arsenal.

The Trump presidency is very much an open question as it approaches the end of its first two years. No one knows whether Trump will finish his first term, let alone run for re-election. Former FBI director Robert Mueller, appointed as Special Counsel for the U.S. Department of Justice, is in the midst of an investigation of Russian interference in the election and the possible collusion of the Trump campaign and even Donald Trump himself. Much of his presidency to date has been consumed with issues raised by the investigation.

It is a strange and anxious time to be writing American history. It is a time (to paraphrase Lincoln's Gettysburg Address of November 19, 1863) testing whether our nation, in the form long familiar to us, "can long endure."

The Least You Need to Know

- ⊗ In 2008, the national housing bubble resulted in a record number of mortgage defaults, which contributed to a worldwide financial "meltdown" as credit markets froze up, threatening a global recession … or worse.

- ⊗ The seemingly interminable Iraq War and the financial crisis prompted the presidential candidates of both parties to run against the Bush presidency, which was almost universally judged to have been a failure.

- ⊗ The 2008 election saw a woman run for the vice presidency on the Republican ticket and an African American for the presidency on the Democratic ticket, promising a historical landmark, regardless of result.

- ⊗ The campaign and election of 2016, pitting Donald Trump against Hillary Clinton, were unprecedented in their challenges to the traditions and norms of American government and of America itself.

Index